FRENCH WAR AIMS
AGAINST GERMANY
1914–1919

FRENCH WAR AIMS
AGAINST GERMANY
1914–1919

D. STEVENSON

CLARENDON PRESS · OXFORD

1982

Oxford University Press, Walton Street, Oxford OX2 6DP

London Glasgow New York Toronto
Delhi Bombay Calcutta Madras Karachi
Kuala Lumpur Singapore Hong Kong Tokyo
Nairobi Dar es Salaam Cape Town
Melbourne Auckland
and associate companies in
Beirut Berlin Ibadan Mexico City

Published in the United States
by Oxford University Press, New York

British Library Cataloguing in Publication Data
Stevenson, D
French war aims against Germany 1914–1919.
1. European War, 1914–1918 – Diplomatic history
2. France – Foreign relations – 1914–1940
I. Title
327.44   DC387
ISBN 0-19-822574-1

Library of Congress Catologing in Publication Data
Stevenson, D. (David), 1954–
French war aims against Germany, 1914–1919.
Bibliography: p.
Includes index.
1. World War, 1914–1918 – Diplomatic history.
2. France – Foreign relations – Germany.
3. Germany – Foreign relations ▪ France.
4. Treaty of Versailles (1919) I. Title.
D621.F8S75   940.3'2   82-1121
ISBN 0-19-822574-1   AACR2

Set by Syarikat Seng Teik Sdn. Bhd.
Printed in Great Britain
at the University Press, Oxford
by Eric Buckley
Printer to the University

Preface

For later generations, the First World War has seemed before all else to exemplify futility. The Governments and High Commands of Europe, it seemed in retrospect, had been caught up in a mechanism that had passed from their control, their gaze so focused on the means that the end had slipped outside their range of view. Yet policy was still determined by the statesmen and the military and diplomatic advisers who had been its arbiters in peacetime, and the war was prolonged by deliberate decision. It took the hideous course it did because not merely of a military stalemate but also of a diplomatic one. No Government was willing to jettison its war aims in the interests of a compromise peace, or to place itself at the enemy's mercy while a chance of victory remained.

Only recently have historians given these war aims the attention they deserve. Professor Fritz Fischer's pioneering work on Germany has been followed by V. H. Rothwell for Great Britain.[1] French aims have lacked a comparable work of synthesis, although many aspects of them have been illuminated in several recent studies of great thoroughness and perception.[2] It is as a first step to such a synthesis that the following pages are intended.

The term, 'war aims', raises problems of definition which will be examined in the Conclusion. I have tried to distinguish between private aspirations on the one hand and official policy on the other, although in reality the dividing line was never clear. By their nature, war aims are cast in the conditional tense, and should be seen as shifting, hypothetical options and orders of priority rather than as unalterable demands. Nor can war aims in their narrow sense, of objectives planned to be embodied in a peace treaty, be considered in isolation from foreign policy as a whole.

Official thinking is at the heart of what follows, because the Government was the centre of decision where internal and external influences on French policy converged. Unofficial opinion is discussed in accordance with its influence on that policy, although I have come to share Rothwell's conclusion from the British example that in general 'these pressures were less important than the preconceptions of the leaders and their response to the military situation and to the policies of their allies'.[3] To deal with unofficial opinion in its own right would require a second book, and a large one. Of the external variables, the diplomatic one was particularly influential, and due space has been given to France's relations with its allies, as well as to French policy towards the attempts made to end the war by a negotiated compromise.

As its title suggests, this book concentrates on policy towards Germany. The essential French objective was security against that country, and the wars with Germany's allies were fought largely as means towards this end. To discuss this properly, it has been necessary to consider French policy in Eastern as well as Western Europe, and economic as well as non-economic aims. French policy *outside* Europe – towards the German colonies and the Ottoman Empire – has been sketched in where it is relevant, but this forms a largely self-contained subject which other writers are treating in depth.[4] Finally, the geographical and historical background necessary to an understanding of the main territorial questions is provided in the Appendices.

There remains the pleasant task of recording the numerous obligations I have incurred over the past five years. My thanks go to my parents, for moral support; to the staff of the archives and libraries in which I have worked; to the Department of Education and Science, for awarding me a Major State Studentship in 1975–8; to the French Government, for a scholarship which I held in 1976–7; to the *École normale supérieure*, Paris, where I stayed in the same year; to Corpus Christi College, Cambridge, where I was a research student; to the Master and Fellows of Downing College, Cambridge, for electing me to the Research Fellowship which has made completion of this book possible; to M. Louis Cambon, Mme Arrizoli-Clémentel, Mme Louis Marin, M. Stanislas Mangin, and the *Société des amis d'André Tardieu*, for allowing me to consult the private papers of Paul Cambon, Étienne Clémentel, Louis Marin, Charles Mangin, and André Tardieu; to MM. Maurice Hamon and Jacques Portevin, of the *Compagnie de Saint-Gobain-Pont-*

à-Mousson; to the late MM. Jacques Millerand and Georges Wormser, who shared with me their reminiscences of the period; to Professor J.-B. Duroselle, who directed my research in Paris; to Mr I. Asquith of Oxford University Press; to Mrs G. Davies, for a highly efficient job of typing; to Professor A. S. Kanya-Forstner and Mrs Z. Steiner, both of whom read portions of the manuscript; and, finally, for his advice both as a Ph.D. supervisor and subsequently, to Dr C. M. Andrew. I am indebted to them all for their help and encouragement; for the many imperfections which remain in this book I take full responsibility.

Downing College, Cambridge
1981

Contents

Maps

Abbreviations

Details of the archival sources referred to here are given in the Bibliography.

AIAF	*Association de l'industrie et de l'agriculture française.*
AN	*Archives nationales*, Paris.
APD	*Archives départementales du Puy-de-Dôme*, Clermont-Ferrand.
BDIC	*Bibliothèque de documentation internationale et contemporaine*, Nanterre.
BIF	*Bibliothèque de l'Institut de France*, Paris.
BL	Manuscripts Room, British Museum, London.
BN	*Bibliothèque nationale*, Paris.
CAB	British Cabinet Papers.
CAEC	*Commission des affaires extérieures* of the French Chamber of Deputies.
CAEC:AC	*CAEC* hearings, April–May 1918, on *l'Affaire Czernin*, AN C 7491.
CGT	*Confédération générale du travail.*
CRD	Commission on the Reparation of Damage.
CTP	*Commission des traités de paix.*
EMA	*État-major de l'armée* (the French General Staff).
FO	Foreign Office Papers, Public Record Office, Kew.
FRUS	*Papers Relating to the Foreign Relations of the United States.*
FRUS, PPC	Ibid., *Paris Peace Conference, 1919.*
GQG	*Grand quartier général* (French GHQ).
H.C. DEB	*House of Commons: Parliamentary Debates.*
IARC	Inter-Allied Rhineland Commission.
IARHC	Inter-Allied Rhineland High Commission.
IOL	India Office Library, London.
JO (*Chambre/ Sénat*)	*Journal officiel de la République française. Débats parlementaires: Chambre des députés/Sénat. Compterendu in extenso.*

JO (*Chambre*)	*Comité secret* of 1 June 1917: Chamber of Deputies secret session of 1–4 June 1917, appended to *JO* (*Chambre*), 16 May 1925.
JO (*Chambre*)	*Comité secret* of 16 Oct. 1917: Chamber of Deputies secret session of 1–4 June 1917, appended to *JO* (*Chambre*), 2 April 1933.
LG Papers	Lloyd George Papers, House of Lords Record Office, London.
MAE	Archives of the *Ministère des affaires étrangères*, Paris.
ONCE	*Office national du commerce extérieur.*
PAM	Archives of the *Compagnie de Saint-Gobain-Pont-à-Mousson*, Blois.
SFIO	Archives of the *Société de géographie, Département des cartes et plans, Bibliothèque nationale*, Paris.
SHA	*Service historique de l'armée*, Château de Vincennes, Paris.
SPD	*Sozialdemokratische Partei Deutschlands* (the German Socialist Party).
USPD	*Unabhängige Sozialdemokratische Partei Deutschlands* (the German Independent Socialists).

Introduction

There is a streak of atavism in the rivalry of France with Germany, and Frenchmen in the First World War harked back to the Great Revolution and the two Napoleons, to Louis XIV and the *Ancien régime*, and even to the enmity of Gaul and Teuton in antiquity. Since medieval times French rulers had intervened in the Rhineland, first against the Dukes of Burgundy and then to create a zone of influence athwart the communications of the Habsburg Emperors between Italy and the Netherlands. The Franco-German problem in its modern form, however, was created by the dual political and economic revolution which spread across the Western world from the end of the eighteenth century. The Revolutionary and Napoleonic wars left a heritage which, if ambiguous, was decisive. In 1790 the French National Assembly had repudiated 'conquests' and territorial expansion; but three years later Danton and Carnot proclaimed that France's natural frontier was the Rhine, and for a while that frontier was established. In 1814 it was lost, and Prussia and Bavaria annexed the territory on the left bank of the river lying north of Alsace–Lorraine.

The intervening years had given birth in both France and Germany to mass patriotic feeling. For the next half-century Governments in Paris were under intermittent pressure from their subjects to regain the Revolutionary frontier, and some – most notably that of Napoleon III – tried to satisfy these aspirations through their diplomacy. This kept alive a tradition of xenophobia on the German side, which at times of crisis was inflamed. French nationalism, by contrast, was only mutedly of this reactive type until Bismarck's policies in the 1860s raised the first hint of a new Prussian danger. The shock caused by defeat in 1870–1, by the founding of the German Empire, and by the loss of Alsace–Lorraine, was therefore all the greater when it came.

It would be hard to exaggerate the repercussions of that shock on a generation of French statesmen, many of whom held high

office in 1914–18.[1] Defeat changed radically the tone of French
commentary on Germany, and a vast, cathartic literature after
1870 diffused the novel stereotypes of the brutal Prussian officer
and the disciplined, but mindless and subservient, masses at his
command. The ambitions of French foreign policy decreased,
with the older dreams of promoting national self-determination
across Europe taking second place to the immediate need for
safety against a renewed German attack. After the war came
twenty years of diplomatic isolation, during which Bismarck pro-
fited from French vulnerability to cause fresh tension in 1875
and again a decade later. All this left the leaders of the infant
Third Republic* determined never again to face a united Germany alone.

From 1887 to 1905 the danger of a Franco-German war receded.
French Governments were still theoretically revisionist, discon-
tented with the international status quo, and unwilling to renounce definitively their pretensions to Alsace–Lorraine. But
they were equally unwilling to make war for the lost provinces,
where by the 1890s an autonomist movement, professedly loyal
to the union with the German *Reich*, commanded an electoral
majority. At the turn of the century the sharpest tensions between the Powers arose from European expansion overseas,
which brought France into conflict with Italy and Great Britain
while allowing a limited *détente* between Paris and Berlin.

This overseas expansion contributed to a more general recovery of French power. Indeed, France acquired an empire second
only to Britain's in these years, although the country's influence
in world affairs still depended mainly on the home base. For all
the surface agitation of French politics, the Third Republic was
more broadly accepted than any other regime since 1789, and
had a solid record of administrative achievement. Its political
stability was aided by financial stability, shown in a steady balance-of-payments surplus and a currency whose value had been
constant for a century. Its army had been remodelled and re-
equipped after 1870, and more of the population was kept under

---

* The Third Republic came into being after the fall of Napoleon III in
1870, and survived until the second world war. It was France's first prolonged experience of representative government based on manhood suf-
frage.

arms than in any other Great Power. Finally, French diplomacy had a supple adjunct in its control of access to the Paris capital market, which only London surpassed as a source of international finance. These assets eventually permitted France to end its diplomatic isolation. The defensive alliance and military convention of 1892–4 with Tsarist Russia remained cornerstones of the Republic's policy down to 1917. In 1902 and 1904 two agreements liquidated most of France's colonial disputes with Italy and Britain. The first of these effectively annulled Italy's alliance obligations against France; the second, the celebrated *Entente cordiale*, was converted by the Moroccan crises of 1905 and 1911 into the beginning of joint Anglo-French strategic planning and habitual consultation over international affairs.

In spite of these successes, the Frenchmen of the early twentieth century were heirs to a long tradition of pessimistic speculation about national decline.[2] France unquestionably remained a Great Power, but it had been losing ground to its competitors for decades, and the disparities were widening. The war of 1870 was fought between two States of near-equality in material resources, and French explanations for the defeat had centred on intangibles, such as Prussian efficiency and morale. But after the 1890s French opinion grew aware that the balance in population and industrial production was moving heavily in Germany's favour.[3] At home, agitation mounted for legislation which would revive the stagnant birth rate; abroad, French consuls reported the superior efficiency and growth of German foreign trade in almost every section of the globe.

French industrialization had started earlier than in Germany, but fell behind in the quarter-century of economic difficulties which followed the Franco-Prussian War, and during the subsequent prosperity did little to reduce the gap. In 1914 France's income per head was still higher than was Germany's, but its strategic industries – its coal, steel, chemicals, and engineering – were far smaller, and were concentrated on the vulnerable northern and eastern frontiers. France grew rapidly more dependent on imported German coal – and especially metallurgical coke – in the decade before the war. So too did Germany on French iron ore, although the Ruhr firms partly compensated for this by buying ore concessions in Normandy and French

Lorraine. Indeed, German manufacturing proficiency was complemented by French financial strength and food and raw-materials production. Much of the business community on both sides desired closer co-operation, although such co-operation entailed the risk that the French economy's inferiority in military potential would grow still more pronounced.

The Third Republic had evolved its own conventions for formulating foreign policy.[4] In law, Presidents of the Republic had generous executive powers. Few used them, and Raymond Poincaré in 1913–14 was exceptional in his influence on foreign affairs. French ministries survived on average for nine months, and devoted much of their short existences to parliamentary management and domestic politics. The Council of Ministers, or Cabinet, generally left external questions to the Foreign Minister, who was sometimes assisted by the Colonial and Service Ministers and by the Premier.* Foreign Ministers, such as Théophile Delcassé (1898–1905) and Stephen Pichon (1906–11), had much longer average tenures than their colleagues and, although much turned on the strength of the competing personalities, their freedom from collective supervision by the remainder of the Government could be very great.

They were often more seriously challenged by their own administrative machine. Aristocratic sympathies lingered in the Quai d'Orsay,† and parliamentary supervision was resented, although the atmosphere of the Department was being altered by an influx of younger officials from the élite *École libre des sciences politiques*, who brought with them the Germanophobia of the pre-war Parisian student world. The Ministry had been restructured in 1907, with policy-making being concentrated in a huge *Direction des affaires politiques et commerciales*, whose head, the *Directeur*, was the highest of the Quai d'Orsay's permanent officials. The *Direction* was divided into four geographical *Sous-directions*, with the head of the European section acting as the *Directeur's* assistant. Other officials were seconded

* The President of the French Council of Ministers will normally be referred to as the 'Prime Minister' or the 'Premier'; the President of the Republic as the 'President'.
  † This shorthand for the French Ministry of Foreign Affairs is a convenient, if hackneyed, usage.

to the Minister's private office, the *Cabinet du Ministre*, which could make or break careers through its control of staffing, and might usurp the *Direction politique*'s responsibility for policy. Finally, many of the leading French Ambassadors were strong-willed and experienced men, who despised what they regarded as the careerism of the Paris-based officials and did not hesitate to place an independent interpretation on their instructions. The atmosphere within the Ministry was often thick with acrid personal jealousies, as officials not only vied with each other but also used devices such as press leaks to undermine Ministers and Ambassadors whom they deemed too cautious or indulgent towards foreign Powers.

External policy came under the surveillance of Parliament and the press. It rarely brought Governments down, although this possibility remained as an ultimate sanction. The Senate and the Chamber of Deputies exerted day-to-day control through interpellations and through their Commissions on Foreign Affairs. Even as sources of information, however, these were frequently ineffective, and the Paris newspapers, with their leaks and private contacts, were in some ways more formidable. Press censorship after 1914 was one of the sharpest differences between wartime conditions and those of peace.

Parliament and the press retained their importance in part because of the disaggregation of French society. Intermediary bodies such as pressure groups and political parties, able to mobilize sections of opinion in order to influence or win control of Government policy, were still much weaker than in Germany or Britain. In 1914 the German Socialist Party, the *SPD*, had ten times the membership and twice the proportion of the vote of the French *SFIO*, while one quarter of German wage earners belonged to trade unions, against nine per cent in France. Conversely, no French patriotic pressure group matched the numbers of the German Navy League or the vociferousness of the Pan-Germans, and French employer organizations lacked the control over their members and the degree of privileged access to government which German ones enjoyed. In 1914 Paris was still the only really big French city, and although France had pockets of large-scale urbanization and modern industry in the north and east much of it remained a decentralized society of prosperous small producers who felt no need to organize themselves in disciplined economic groupings or mass political parties with bargaining leverage on the national stage.

After 1905 French Governments and the informed sections of the public became aware that international relations had entered on a new and dangerous phase. Like its neighbours, France was an imperialist Power, and its attempts to present the Germans with *faits accomplis* in Morocco prompted the latter to respond with the Kaiser's speech at Tangier in 1905 and the sending of a gunboat to Agadir in 1911. Both the crises that resulted contributed to the mounting European tension, and helped confirm many French politicians and officials in their worst suspicions of the Berlin Government's designs. There were many signs that relations were unravelling as the war approached: new incidents in Alsace–Lorraine, obstacles placed by government to trading and financial co-operation, and, most menacing of all, the arms race that set in after Agadir.

French Governments were forced by these events to choose between conciliation, and standing firm in the hope that military and diplomatic preparedness was the best way to avert a war. For all the weight of inherited suspicion, a strong party favoured the first course. Jules Cambon, the Ambassador in Berlin from 1907–14, interpreted German actions in a reassuring light. The first Government of Georges Clemenceau negotiated a Moroccan compromise in 1909, and that of Joseph Caillaux reached a second, definitive agreement two years later. But the most delicate judgement, given the Germans' phobia of encirclement, was that required for managing the diplomatic alignment of which France formed the heart. Delcassé in 1901 and Poincaré in 1912–13 contributed to the Germans' unease by promising French funding for Russian strategic railways in the Polish marches. None the less, the Franco-Russian partnership was more fragile than it seemed, and French Governments were torn between their misgivings about Russian adventures in the Balkans and their nightmare of the traditional friendship between Tsar and Kaiser being renewed. The alliance was a marriage of convenience, qualified by French distaste for the Russian autocracy and by French doubts about the ultimate consequences if Russian ambitions were fulfilled. Relations with London were in many ways much closer, although the traditional colonial rivalry was not dead, and in the absence of a formal commitment Britain's dependability in crisis remained uncertain. Rumours in 1912 of a possible Anglo-German *rapprochement* steeled French determination to allow no opening to Berlin which would endanger the solidarity of the Triple Entente with London and St. Petersburg. Before the war and during it, the alliances themselves were among the highest stakes of European politics.

The international tension polarized French opinion between a Right committed to military preparedness and a Left which bitterly opposed such measures as the three-year military service law of 1913. The 'nationalist revival' of these years was most evident in Paris, among sections of the city's youth and of the French political leadership itself, but electorally it was weak and was balanced by the rapid growth of the *SFIO* and the main trade-union federation, the *CGT*. The French Left had apparently repudiated its Jacobin and patriotic past, for the *SFIO* was now committed to ill-defined international action against an imperialist war and the *CGT* was pledged to resist mobilization by an insurrectionary general strike. And in 1913 the Presidency of France's largest political party, the Radicals, went to Caillaux, who was no pacifist, but opposed the three-year law and hoped to halt the deterioration of relations with Germany. It was widely feared, not least in government, that French opinion lacked the cohesion needed to see it through a war. All the parties, however, including the *SFIO*, acknowledged the duty of armed resistance to aggression, and in the final years of peace even the *CGT* began to moderate its stand. Much would depend on the circumstances in which a war broke out.

In the crisis of July-August 1914 the French Government behaved more passively than that of any other Power, and when Germany declared war on 3 August the conflict appeared uniquely clearly in France as the outcome of aggression by the other side. The Socialist leaders accepted that the Government had sincerely tried to keep the peace; the *CGT*, after hesitating, also co-operated fully in the war effort. The French people heard the news of mobilization with resignation and anxiety, and if the soldiers finally marched away with more enthusiasm they did so in the expectation that the war would be victorious and, above all, short. They spoke little of revenge for 1870, still

less of Alsace–Lorraine, but felt simply that 'France had been
attacked, she had to be defended, and as this attack came from
a neighbour who had always given cause for grievance it was a
chance to settle the question once and for all'.[5] On this there
existed a consensus which, however badly flawed after 1917,
survived in its essentials to the Armistice.

The way in which the war broke out mattered also at the official level. The events of 1914, coming on top of the pre-war
crises and the memories of 1870, seemed evidence even to a
man as patient and imaginative as Jules Cambon that the German rulers were wedded irremediably to expanding their influence by the threat and use of force: that they might be over-
awed, but that peaceful coexistence was impossible. Much will
be said in later chapters about raw materials and strategic frontiers, but this should not obscure the less palpable, more altruistic, justifications of the war which figured in French politicians'
speeches and reflected, in part at least, their private thoughts.
The Germans were held guilty of premeditated aggression and
of a cynical disregard for international undertakings. Because
the enemy understood the language only of superior force any
compromise which left his military potential intact would be no
better than a truce. Finally, not only were the Germans ruthless
in their purpose; they were also callous in their methods. In a
France that was invaded, reports of enemy atrocities caused a
sense of outrage which perhaps even the revulsion felt in Britain
and America against U-boat warfare did not equal.[6] The Germans, it was considered, had outlawed themselves from international society, and if the Versailles terms seem harsh compared
with those inflicted on defeated Powers in the nineteenth century this context must be borne in mind.

I

The First Phase, August 1914–July 1916

1. *The Makers of Policy*

For the first few weeks it seemed that the war would indeed be of the kind that the European armies had prepared themselves to fight. The campaign in the west opened as a war of movement, whose swift reversals of fortune subjected both sides to alternating elation and dismay. French troops began by reaching deep into Alsace; within days they were forced into retreat while the German army overwhelmed the Belgians, occupied the coalfield of the Nord and the iron ore of French Lorraine, and menaced the capital itself. Then, on 6 September, the French counter-attacked on the Marne, the Germans in their turn pulled back, and Paris was saved. But at this point the fighting was transformed, and the Marne was followed not by a triumphant sweep across the Rhine but by the formation of an unbroken line of trenches from Switzerland to the North Sea. During 1915 the French Army's attempts to pierce this line gained negligible ground at a higher cost in lives than in any other year of the war. From start to finish the battle in the west was fought almost exclusively on French and Belgian soil.

Militarily, the first two years of war consisted of the phase of movement until November 1914 and that of stalemate thereafter. Politically, in France they saw the Premiership of René Viviani and, after October 1915, of Aristide Briand. For French war aims they were a period of gestation, in which fringe elements were clarified but the centre remained a vacuum. This chapter will consider the principles of wartime policy in whose context war aims were debated, the early ferment of ideas in government and in French society at large, and the first steps towards converting those ideas into the objectives of the State. But it will begin with the makers of policy themselves.

Viviani was ill-equipped to guide France through this crisis. An undogmatic socialist from Algiers, he had made his name in domestic politics as an orator and social reformer; in foreign affairs he was ignorant and inexperienced. He became Premier in June 1914 already suffering from the neurasthenia which eventually destroyed his sanity. His ministry was reconstructed on 26 August as a national coalition, many of whose members were more eminent and forceful than was he. Viviani's Council of Ministers met frequently, but still had only fitful control over the political veterans who headed the key Departments of State.

Nevertheless, the Council's meetings gave an opportunity to its habitual chairman, Raymond Poincaré. Moulded by his childhood in Lorraine, his memories of 1870, and his training in the law, Poincaré had led the politicians who tried before 1914 to prepare France diplomatically, materially, and psychologically for the impending conflict. In domestic affairs he was identified with moderate conservatism and fiscal orthodoxy; but it was on foreign policy that his undoubted abilities were concentrated. Incorruptible, well-informed, and conscientious he had a capacity for disciplined, if unimaginative thought, and an administrator's rather than a politician's cast of mind. Behind a cold and self-important façade, he combined an emotional patriotism with touchiness, timidity, and a mounting frustration with the limitations of his office.

Since his election in 1913 Poincaré had tried to use the powers of the Presidency to the full, but he was obliged to act only with the countersignature of the responsible Minister, and for this reason his influence fell sharply late in August 1914 when Théophile Delcassé replaced Gaston Doumergue at the Quai d'Orsay. Like Poincaré, Delcassé had been permanently marked by the defeat of 1870, although his vehement hostility to Germany owed more to the crises of the pre-war years. He felt that the events of 1914 vindicated his policies as Foreign Minister in 1898–1905, and was now committed to deepening the understanding with the Russians and to bringing yet further allies into the war. But he was well past the peak of his powers. His authoritarian habits, his secrecy and reserve, and his reputed willingness to sacrifice French interests to the Tsar's ended by exasperating his ministerial colleagues and much of the diplomatic corps as well.

The leading Quai d'Orsay officials in 1914 were the *Directeur politique*, Pierre de Margerie, and his assistant, the *Sousdirecteur d'Europe*, Philippe Berthelot. The Ministry's economic

expert, Fernand Pila, had an influence which was disproportionate to his lowly formal status. But in general Delcassé
ran his own ship, aided by his *Cabinet du Ministre*, and drafted
himself many of the Quai d'Orsay's statements of policy. Only
under his successor did the Ministry officials contribute as much
as did their counterparts in Britain.

Abroad, Delcassé was served by Camille Barrère, who had
been Ambassador in Rome since 1897, and Paul Cambon, who
had been in London since 1898. Both were censorious and opi-
nionated men who habitually took independent diplomatic initiatives. Maurice Paléologue, by contrast, had been at Petrograd* only since February 1914, but was a close friend of Poincaré. Often more perceptive than his colleagues, he was also
capable of serious indiscretions and lapses of judgement. Finally, Jules Jusserand, who had been at Washington since 1902,
again had behind him a career of distinction and did not hide
his frequent criticisms of departmental policy. But in 1914
American power was still underestimated in Paris, and American policy misunderstood. And even after Italy joined the
Allies, in May 1915, the Rome connection was never seen as
vital in the same way as were those with Petrograd and London,
especially as French relations with the Italians were clouded by
mutual suspicion and by veiled rivalry in the Eastern Mediterranean. For the first year of the war it is therefore on communications between Britain, France, and Russia that the greatest interest centres.

2. First Principles

War aims were never the exclusive domain of the President, the
Prime Minister, and the Quai d'Orsay. Other Ministers, such as
those for Colonies and Commerce, or Alexandre Ribot at Finance, co-operated in formulating extra-European and economic
aims. Nor did policy crystallize in isolation from unofficial currents of opinion. But it was ordinarily on a restricted circle of
no more than thirty politicians and officials that the burden of
decision rested. During the short-lived war of movement this
circle set the context in which war aims would subsequently
evolve. France, it was agreed, would make no peace separately

* The Russian capital was so renamed shortly after the outbreak of war.

from its allies, and would reject attempts at mediation by third parties; it would end the war only after a decisive military victory which would liberate Alsace–Lorraine.

The claim to Alsace–Lorraine was made known to France's allies within hours of the outbreak of war. On 5 August Doumergue, Viviani, and Poincaré agreed to support a Russian *démarche* in Rome only on condition that it was 'without prejudice to our national claims'.[1] This, Doumergue explained to the Russians and the British, meant Alsace–Lorraine, 'whose retrocession to France must in any event be assured'.[2] In speeches to the Chamber on 22 November 1914 and 18 February 1915 Viviani made the commitment public with his Ministers' full support.[3]

In the shock of the outbreak of war, a basic tenet of French policy had been reversed. Before 1914 Governments and the vast majority of the public had concurred that it would be wrong to start a war for the sake of Alsace–Lorraine. This had now given way to a commitment not to end the war until the lost provinces were regained. It was countered on the German side by a refusal in any circumstances to yield more than a few districts in Alsace.[4] France claimed Alsace–Lorraine initially for reasons of sentiment and history; it soon became clear that the provinces would also be a major increment to national power. But because this was the one territorial demand on which all shades of opinion could unite it was the one which could be publicly avowed; and that avowal made French Governments unable to accept a compromise without grievous loss of face.

On 5 September 1914 the British, French, and Russian Governments committed themselves to make no separate peace, and, 'when the time comes to offer terms', not to 'offer conditions of peace without previous agreement with each of the other Allies'.[5] This 'Pact of London' had begun as the result of a Russian initiative, which Doumergue and Delcassé took up enthusiastically, and the British embodied in a formula.[6] The Pact cast its shadow over the whole of subsequent French policy. For after the opening German offensive failed, the war became a test of will in which the Central Powers tried to sunder the Allied coalition by combining military pressure with diplomatic approaches to each of its members. Of the three main Allies it was the French who most firmly and consistently re-

sisted the temptation to seek an arrangement which would se-
cure their own objectives at the expense of Allied solidarity.
Preserving the coalition intact was as much a war aim as was
Alsace–Lorraine.

The implications of these two decisions – to claim the lost
provinces and to refuse a separate peace – were spelled out during the brief euphoria that followed the victory on the Marne.
Asked by the Russian High Command whether France would
now drive on 'into the heart of Germany to dictate peace', the
Council of Ministers replied that the French Army would 'continue its advance towards the Imperial [Russian] Army until the
Allied Governments can obtain for their nations every legitimate reparation and institute in Europe a state of affairs which
will guarantee for many years the peace of the world'.[7] Even as
this telegram was sent, French troops were settling in positions
which would alter little for the next three years. But Governments remained committed to decisive victory, and from 1914–
16 were determined to forestall mediation by third parties,
irrespective of the military position and irrespective of the quarter from which mediation was proffered. In November 1914
Delcassé considered a recent crop of such proposals to be evidence of German 'lassitude', and a reason for fighting on until
the enemy was reduced to 'impotence'. A year later, in spite of
the collapse of the Allies' position in the Balkans, Viviani telegraphed that neutral intercession must be resisted until Germany had been 'vanquished'. On 1 July 1916, as British troops
went over the top on the Somme, Briand and his Ministers
warned the London Government that any truck with mediation
would endanger Allied solidarity, and that compromise could
bring no 'lasting peace'.[8]

The greatest menace to this policy came from the United States.
Long before the Americans entered the conflict, trade with
them and the credit they extended were essential to the Allied
war effort. By 1916 thirty per cent of France's imports came
from America, and loans worth 3.4 milliard francs had been
raised to pay for them. Yet no neutral Government tried more
persistently than President Wilson's to intercede. As early as 4
and 5 August the American Ambassadors in Europe were instructed to offer their services, only to be rebuffed on the

French side by a message from Poincaré.[9] A month later Delcassé confirmed a warning given by Jusserand in Washington
that the prospects of success for such attempts were
'infinitesimal'.[10] Undeterred, early in 1915 Wilson sent his
closest confidant and adviser, Colonel House, to sound out the
European capitals. Assured by Delcassé that France would treat
only after Germany had been 'broken', House preferred not
even to allude to mediation, so rooted did he find the French
belief that Wilson's sympathies lay with the Central Powers.[11]

During the first half of the war the French were willing to pay
a heavy price to bring in Italy and the Balkan States, but they
wished only for benevolent neutrality from Washington, and
feared their interests would be damaged if America entered on
the Allied side.[12] They made this clear after Colonel House unexpectedly proposed such entry when he visited Europe again in
February 1916. In conversations in Paris, House held out the
prospect of an American intervention in the war designed to impose terms acceptable to Britain and France. His listeners responded not merely with (well-founded) scepticism about the
Colonel's ability to deliver; they also made clear that such an
initiative would be unwelcome. Neither the military position
(with the Allied offensives planned for the summer not yet
launched) nor the state of French public opinion made the moment opportune. Besides, France could agree to nothing without
consulting its allies; whereas House wished to deal only through
London and Paris, and did not conceal his suspicion of the Russians or his hopes for a post-war liberal alliance of the three
Atlantic Powers.[13]

House none the less left Paris believing an 'understanding'
had been reached, and hoping for a compromise whereby Germany would cede Alsace–Lorraine but be compensated in Africa or Asia Minor.[14] He was quickly disabused. The British
Ambassador noted that 'The French will not listen to buying
Alsace–Lorraine by the cession to Germany of some French
colonies'.[15] Grey, the British Foreign Secretary, perhaps not unwilling to throw the onus of rejection on the French, told House
that the British Government felt unable to raise the American
offer with them for fear of giving Briand the impression it would
not support him if he decided to fight on until decisive victory
had been won.[16] The French did not broach the matter at the

Allied diplomatic conference which met in Paris from 27–8 March, and House's initiative ran into the sand.[17] 'We feel', Briand commented in retrospect, 'that the conclusive defeat of Germany's militarism and ambition to dominate is a matter of life and death for France, and the sole guarantee of the future liberty of the world. Any peace proposal now can work only to Germany's advantage and be inspired by her interests.' Mediation would 'embarrass us, and cause harmful controversies in the [Allied] countries which the enemy would seek to exploit and to envenom'.[18]

Although the French persisted, as House lamented, in grotesquely misunderstanding his own and Wilson's motives, it is unlikely that an opportunity had been missed to bring about American intervention a year before it actually occurred. House appears to have pursued the semblance of agreement by exaggerating both to Wilson and the Allies their common ground; nor did he have any mandate from Congress or the American public. To count on House's project being realized, warned Jusserand, would be 'a grave imprudence'.[19] But the French reaction owed its vehemence to more than considerations of this kind. Briand's telegram shows the connection drawn instinctively in Paris between the diplomatic problem of parrying mediation and the domestic one of upholding civilian morale. The House proposal combined a possible threat to that morale with an incipient choice between Russian friendship and that of the United States. The French, as will be seen below, already knew the scope of the Russian war aims, and viewed them with no little trepidation. Yet, decaying and importunate though the Tsarist Government might be, the Russian alliance had been tested, and was holding down a third of the German army. Against this House could offer only a hypothetical liberal alignment which cut across all his country's traditions. In the remainder of this chapter these twin French objectives – of maintaining domestic unity and of preserving the alliances – will be examined in turn.

3. *Government and Society*

The war had broken out in circumstances which made possible a remarkable and unexpected national consensus. The reconstructed

Viviani Government of 26 August 1914 brought in representatives of the Socialists; the Briand Government which followed had a spokesman for the Catholic Right as well. The
French political truce was more complete than that in Germany,
and took longer to show strain. But the parties and pressure
groups which submitted to it had not renounced their longer-
term objectives. They had merely suspended them for the duration of a war which they expected to be short. The consensus
that France must be defended against invasion masked underlying differences over foreign policy and, especially, war aims.
And the war was not short. The French authorities grew pro-
gressively more anxious about the resilience of public morale in
the face of unprecedented national sacrifices which yielded little,
before the final months, but an unbroken string of pyrrhic victories and defeats.

The authorities were not without advantages. The war had begun with an enemy invasion and continued almost everywhere
on Allied territory; it naturally appeared as a defensive one.
Elections ceased, and political meetings were rare. The National
Assembly sat regularly after January 1915, but until November
1917 no Government was forced to resign by a defeat in the
Chamber. Finally, after initial dislocation, the French war economy settled down to high levels of activity combined at first with
only a moderate erosion of living standards and of the value of
the currency. The wartime Governments could benefit from all
this with the aid of an administration which had long experience
in monitoring – and indeed manipulating – public opinion. The
normal surveillance of suspect political organizations was supplemented by a ban on pacifist propaganda,[20] and the sporadic
evidence available suggests that, after the Marne, civilian
morale held steady for some time.[21] Among the instruments
used to keep it so was censorship of the press. Viviani's Government decided to forbid 'all publications suggesting or discussing
peace conditions',[22] and Briand, who came to power
'disposed . . . to consider "peace" a seditious word', repeated
these instructions to the censor even more emphatically.[23]

The authorities were aware that controversy over war aims
might detonate the political truce; but it was not enough simply
to stifle discussion of the subject, and in their public declarations they had to strike a delicate balance. Both the diplomatic

and military imponderables and the differences of outlook at home impelled Ministers towards caution, vagueness, and ambiguity. Yet if they said too little they would discourage those on the Right who hoped for large territorial gains, while feeding suspicions on the Left that France was fighting an imperialist war. A distinction therefore emerged between the tone of public statements and that of confidential policy. This distinction was not a contradiction – Governments were careful to avoid mendacity – but a contrast between precision and calculated ambiguity. Public declarations were shaped not only by confidential thinking but also by the official judgement of what was needed to sustain morale.

In time these declarations grew more ambitious and more categorical. At the outset Poincaré and Viviani portrayed the war as a defence of the status quo: 'the soil of the fatherland', and the 'independence' and 'security' given France by the Triple Entente.[24] But four months later, with his Ministers' approval, Viviani set out the kernel of a Western European programme. France, he said, would exact 'indemnities' to reconstruct the devastated areas, and it would not make peace until it had regained 'the provinces taken from it by conquest', restored Belgium's prosperity and independence, and 'broken Prussian militarism'.[25]

Two aspects of this programme were clarified during 1915. At the London Socialist Conference in February, Viviani's Minister of Public Works, Sembat, supported a resolution implying that the future of Alsace–Lorraine should be decided by a plebiscite. Faced with uproar among his Ministers and in Parliament, Viviani made explicit that the Government would fight on 'until the regaining of Alsace–Lorraine'. He also introduced the doctrine that the return of the two provinces would be not a 'conquest' but merely the 'restitution' of a population which had never reconciled itself to the unjust transfer of 1871. Hence, no plebiscite was called for.[26]

Still more important was Poincaré's elucidation of 'breaking Prussian militarism': that 'the only peace the Republic can accept is one which will guarantee European security . . . and effectively protect us against any renewed offensive by German ambition'.[27] The incoming Briand Government also called for 'guarantees of a lasting peace'. To reparations, Alsace–

Lorraine, and Belgian independence was added the more abstract concept of 'security', which should be 'guaranteed' by
some contrivance which would prevent the invasion of 1914
from ever happening again. At the same time Briand introduced
a second, more altruistic, notion: a Europe in which 'tyrannical
domination' would yield to 'the liberty of peoples enjoying t.ll
autonomy'.[28] This was to echo the great principle of national
self-determination, which earlier French regimes had supported
militarily, and which retained a residual appeal to French opinion. Yet Briand's utterances were still prudent and ambiguous.
He, Poincaré, and Viviani had set up a framework in which
French war aims could expand indefinitely or fall back on the
essentials of reparations, Belgium, and Alsace–Lorraine.

The problem of public opinion was twofold. There was opinion
in the mass: the amorphous citizenry whom the authorities tried
to influence through censorship and by judicious public statements. Until this opinion faltered in 1917 it left French Governments great freedom to decide what war aims to adopt. But
there was also organized opinion: the sections of society which
had combined in institutions independent of the State. In Germany a *Kriegszielbewegung* (war-aims movement) of right-wing
political parties, economic pressure groups, and extrapar-
liamentary leagues mounted a powerful agitation in favour of
far-reaching annexations and a peace which would destroy the
economic, military, and political independence of the Allies.[29]
In France controversy over war aims started later and was less
impassioned; the contending forces were also weaker relative to
government. But the alignment of these forces in France and
Germany was similar, and in both countries the division of opinion over foreign and over domestic policy tended to coincide.

The strongest challenge to the French Government's objectives came from within the pre-war Left, and the appearance of
national unanimity depended on the leaders of the *SFIO* and
the *CGT* being able to keep the rank and file of the working-
class movement under their control. For the first two years this
control was not in doubt. An opposition 'minority' spread out
from its base in the metalworkers' and schoolteachers' unions of
the *CGT* and the Haute-Vienne federation of the *SFIO*, but remained weak at national congresses and internally divided. The

minority Socialists did not question the principle of national defence, and continued to vote war credits. Unlike the *SFIO* leadership, they favoured contacts with the Socialists of the Central
Powers, but they were unwilling to press this at the risk of splitting the Party. The trade unionist 'minority' was more daring,
with two of its leaders, Merrheim and Bourderon, meeting
enemy Socialists at the Zimmerwald Conference in Switzerland
in September 1915. In the *Comité pour la reprise des relations
internationales*, set up in January 1916, Merrheim and Bourderon
rubbed shoulders with a far Left that challenged the principle
of national defence itself.[30]

The *SFIO* leaders defended their participation in the Government, and refused to be drawn into a peace agitation through
contacts with their German counterparts. But they were also
one of the first political groups to approve a programme for the
future peace and to try to commit the Government to it. The
party was the backbone of what became the French League-of-
Nations movement, committing itself in December 1915 to policies of disarmament, democratic control of foreign policy, and
compulsory international arbitration backed up by military and
economic sanctions. Its main parliamentary spokesman, Pierre
Renaudel, challenged Briand to deny that France desired
'annexations', and defended the party policy of holding a plebiscite after France had regained Alsace–Lorraine.[31]

No other party pressed its doctrines so insistently. Indeed,
French parties had set up national organizations only at the beginning of the century and could impose little uniformity on the
Deputies and the constituency electoral committees which nominally were affiliated to them. The Radicals were slow to determine their position in a national congress. The loose, oligarchic
groupings on the Right were represented through discreet lobbying by their leaders. Jacques Piou, President of the *Action
libérale*, believed France should have a military frontier on the
Rhine, and Louis Marin, of the *Fédération républicaine*, hoped
the left bank of the river would be annexed.[32] Marin and
another *Fédération* leader, Jules Méline, figured prominently in
the official and semi-official study-groups which, as will be seen,
generated a large body of ideas about the Franco-German frontier in 1915–16.

The Right had connections outside Parliament with the

patriotic leagues, the employers' associations, and the Catholic
Church. The Catholic hierarchy's loyalty to the anti-clerical Republic was not in doubt, despite Pope Benedict XV's official
neutrality and his appeals for a speedy return to peace. Indeed,
the Pope's position caused such tension that the Archbishop of
Paris, Cardinal Amette, feared the future of French Catholicism
was at risk.[33] In general, the clergy could be relied on to support a peace through victory, without greatly pressing the authorities in favour of any particular set of aims.

The French business community was represented by a number
of umbrella organizations, including the *Féderation des industriels et commerçants français*, the *Comité républicain du commerce, de l'industrie, et de l'agriculture*, and the *Association de
l'industrie et de l'agriculture française*. No one of these was
clearly dominant, and often more effective were the bodies representing individual industries, such as the *Union des industries
textiles*, the *Comité central des houillères de France* (coal), and
above all, the iron-and-steel masters' association, the *Comité des
forges de France*. Many members of these institutions had a profound lack of sympathy with politicians and officials, and desired
as little State interference in their affairs as possible. But the ad-
vent of modern warfare made French heavy industry a national
asset of immense strategic value. Its own future depended on
the solution adopted to the problem of the north-eastern frontier, a problem which 'haunted' the members of the *Comité des
forges* from soon after the outbreak of war.[34] Many French industrialists were placed in a dilemma by these events, their desires as patriotic citizens corresponding far from automatically
with their interests as producers.

The patriotic leagues were the most vocal portion of the
Right, if hardly the most influential. On the extreme fringe, the
royalist *Action française* called for German unity to be
destroyed.[35] The republican *Ligue des patriotes* launched an
agitation in March 1915 to coincide with a series of newspaper
articles in which its President, Maurice Barrès, argued that the
left bank of the Rhine must be annexed or become a buffer
State under French domination.[36] But both these organizations
were kept under police surveillance as potentially insurrectionary, and Barrès's press campaign was halted by the censor.
Neither the *Action française* nor the *Ligue des patriotes* had

politicians of influence among their leaders, and if any of their ideas penetrated official thinking it was in spite rather than because of their origin.

Far closer to government circles was the *Ligue française,* set up on the eve of war as an antidote to (though not mirror-image of) the notorious Pan-German League. Its *Comité d'honneur* included two ex-Premiers (Léon Bourgeois and Louis Barthou), a religious representation extending from Cardinal Amette to the Chief Rabbi, and a remarkable cross-section of the French parliamentary, business, and intellectual élites. Its local committees brought together Senators, mayors, and Chambers of Commerce across the country on a programme of victory, political unity, and the moral and economic regeneration of France. Like most patriotic groups, it was small, growing slowly from 2,000 members in 1914 to 40,000 in 1919, but its history shows how many of the most influential members of French government and society saw the war as an opportunity to curb the political disunity and moral decay which supposedly had sapped the country's strength before 1914. In any such revival the *Ligue* expected the gains registered in the Peace Treaty to play an important part, although it shared the Government's own delay in considering what those gains might be.[37]

How did this incipient controversy over war aims impinge on official policy? France, unlike Italy, entered the war with no ready-made territorial programme. Thereafter, as de Margerie lamented, 'our time being absolutely devoured by pressing and immediate business, nobody, except for professors and idealistic theoreticians, has the leisure to study these [post-war] questions. We catch a few glimpses of them in passing, just enough to convince us of their extreme complexity and of the risk we run of committing the most egregious errors. . . . '[38] In these circumstances, war aims were likely to be formulated only in response to urgent external or internal pressures. But on the domestic side there were few such pressures in 1915. Rather, the necessity of preserving a consensus militated against a precise commitment on the subject of war aims. The year 1915 was one not of decision but of a ferment of ideas from which policies could in time be drawn. The leading contribution to this debate, as will be seen, came from a number of official and semi-official bodies on the fringes of government, in which the spokesmen of private organizations had an important voice.

Even these bodies left undiscussed the central question of French security against Germany and how best it might be assured. For the moment, the Viviani and Briand Governments were content to pose this problem without defining solutions to it, and made no claim to territory in Europe beyond what had been lost in 1871. According to de Margerie, in February 1916 'France . . . had not yet envisaged what solution should be given to the problem of . . . the territorial changes which might result from the war'.[39] This did not prevent Berthelot, Delcassé, and probably de Margerie himself, from privately desiring much more than Alsace–Lorraine. But Ministers disagreed about the remedies for the German sickness, and even about how that sickness should be diagnosed. The Socialists officially placed much hope in representative government being implanted in a Germany whose unity must be respected;[40] most statesmen and officials trusted less in German intentions changing and more in a system of restraints on German power. Briand and his Commerce Minister, Clémentel, hoped none the less to exploit a peace movement within Germany based, respectively, on the *SPD* and on German business.[41] But for Poincaré, even attempts of this kind suffered from 'illusion'.[42]

Territorial claims were clarified partly in response to the movements of the Allied armies. In West Africa provisional agreements were reached with Britain to partition the conquered German colonies of Togoland, in August 1914, and the Cameroons, in March 1916. French colonial war aims were the outcome of a highly unusual process whereby diminutive pressure groups had penetrated Parliament and the bureaucracy so effectively as to include most of the responsible personnel. Even so, the timing of these aims responded more to diplomatic and military developments than to internal lobbying.[43] In Europe, Alsace–Lorraine was first claimed in the course of a joint diplomatic manœuvre with the Russians, and further decisions became necessary when, after the front had stabilized, the French found themselves occupying a region of some 100,000 souls in Upper Alsace. Although wary of gallicizing the district too quickly, they suppressed the tariff frontier along the Vosges and introduced French instruction into the schools.[44]

Longer-term planning for the lost provinces was entrusted to the *Conférence d'Alsace–Lorraine*, set up under the chairmanship of Louis Barthou in February 1915. Composed of lawyers, academics, parliamentarians, and officials, it prepared for a transition from German to French administrative practices that would not antagonize the local population.[45] However, the clauses for Alsace–Lorraine which the French Government presented to the Peace Conference drew on the advice not only of this body (which was moribund after 1916) but also of unofficial rivals to it. The *Groupe lorrain*, founded in April 1915, included Louis Marin and François de Wendel, a member of the Chamber of Deputies who headed a major iron-and-steel firm with interests on both sides of the pre-war frontier in Lorraine.[46] De Wendel also belonged to the *Comité Siegfried*, a much larger and more influential body than the *Groupe lorrain*, whose members included Barthou himself, Jules Méline of the *Fédération républicaine*, Jules Cambon and Frédéric-Albert Kammerer from the Quai d'Orsay, and leading representatives of the coal, iron-and-steel, and textile trades.[47]

The *Comité Siegfried* prompted planning in a further quarter. Its sub-commission on mines and metallurgy, which de Wendel chaired, quickly agreed that if France regained Alsace–Lorraine it must annex the Saar coalfield to the north; but on other points the coal and metallurgical representatives clashed.[48] Under pressure from de Wendel and Camille Cavallier, of the *Pont-à-Mousson* Company, the *Comité des forges* agreed to set up a Peace Treaty Commission in August 1915.[49] Over the next few months the *Comité* missed no chance to apprise the Government of its views.[50]

The Government, however, was formulating economic objectives of a much more general type. Above all, it hoped to profit from the Allied blockade in order to oust the Germans from the foreign markets they had captured before 1914. Accordingly, the *Office national du commerce extérieur* asked French Consuls and Chambers of Commerce across the world to report on the opportunities thus presented, and circulated the replies among over one thousand domestic firms.[51] This was followed by special efforts in the most promising markets. General Sarrail, who commanded the Allied troops in Salonika from the autumn of 1915, tried to build up trading contacts between France and

Greece as the basis of a more permanent enlargement of French influence in the Balkans.[52] Italy was another possible opening: in September 1915 Paul Claudel was sent by the Quai d'Orsay to gather information, and abortive plans were made to supplant the German holding in a leading Italian bank, the *Banca Commerciale*.[53] But the greatest opportunities seemed to lie in Russia, where prodigious French investments before 1914 had coexisted with disappointing progress for French commerce. Jules Méline chaired at the Quai d'Orsay a study-group composed of academics, civil servants, and spokesmen for French textiles, shipping, and iron and steel. Reporting in May 1915 on the prospects for improving trade, it then did little until it sent a delegation to be received by an unenthusiastic Russian Government a year later.[54]

All this activity produced few results. The authorities mostly confined themselves to generating advice and information. Some businessmen showed interest; but the majority of French industry, in the throes of adjustment to the armaments drive, with its capacity much reduced by the invasion, and labouring under shortages of every kind, was in no condition to seek out the markets that the enemy had forfeited. However, if this assault on German commerce was the main objective of the first eighteen months of war, attempts were also made to prepare the economic clauses of the peace. The claim to reparation for the devastated areas, for example, was articulated very early, even if the details remained to be worked out. Other economic war aims were studied by the Senate's Couyba Commission on postwar expansion and by the *Bureau d'études économiques*, set up in July 1915. Headed by Senator Jean Morel, and composed of a small number of parliamentarians and officials, the *Bureau* was asked to study 'the economic questions to be settled at the end of the war by international agreements'.[55] Later, the *Bureau*'s influence diminished, but it was briefly close to the heart of policy-making when economic war aims became a major government concern in the spring of 1916.

4. *France and its Allies:* (i) *an Over-Mighty Russia?*

For the first two years of war neither unofficial lobbying nor the movements of the Allied armies persuaded the French Government to define its full objectives against Germany itself. But in the meantime the Government accepted far-reaching undertakings against Germany's partners. This owed something to military events; something also to Delcassé's preoccupation with recruiting new members to the alliance and keeping the loyalty of old ones. The Allies promised sweeping annexations at Austria–Hungary's expense to Italy in April 1915, to Serbia in August 1915, and, after Delcassé had left office, to Romania in August 1916. Similar plans for the Turkish Empire began when Britain and France endorsed Russian claims to the Straits and Constantinople in March 1915. An interim Anglo-French agreement over the Turks' Arab territories was reached in the Sykes–Picot accord of January 1916, and was followed in April by a tripartite understanding with Russia over Anatolia. Finally, the fate of Germany's colonies was provisionally settled by the arrangements for Togoland and the Cameroons and, in February–March 1917, by Anglo-French promises of support for Japan's claims to the German North Pacific islands and in Shantung.[56]

Some of these commitments safeguarded France's own objectives, in West Africa or in Syria. Others were irrelevant or even contrary to French interests (as at the Straits) but were accepted as necessary to the higher imperative of defeating Germany. The upshot was that many of the essential goals of Powers such as Italy and Russia were defined and recognized while those of France remained obscure. So too did the plans of the alliance for Germany in Europe. This was in part, perhaps, because of the size and complexity of the issues at stake. But the root cause of the seeming paradox lay in the intricacies of Franco-Russian relations.

France was fighting in a coalition, as one corner of a delicate triangular relationship between partners of approximately equal strength. As a result of losing three-quarters of its coal output and nearly two-thirds of its steel in the first weeks of the war, France needed British coal and manufactures as well as the services of the Royal Navy, British shipping, and British Treasury loans. For French war aims within Europe, however, this leverage mattered little, as the Asquith Government was long reluctant to spell out its desires in more than vague and cautious terms. It did not, for example, commit itself in public on the subject of Alsace–Lorraine, although Sir Edward Grey was personally sympathetic to the French claim.[57] Delcassé did not object to conversations with the British: in January 1915 he gave his personal views in reply to an informal request from Grey, and by March was ready for a more sustained discussion.[58] But until the Battle of the Somme, in 1916, Russia was overwhelmingly more important to France as a land ally, and the supply of munitions and finance by the Western Powers did little to diminish the independence of Tsarist foreign policy. In contrast to the British, the Russians sounded out their partners in the autumn of 1914 with grandiose proposals for the European settlement. The appropriate response to these suggestions preoccupied the French authorities during the winter that followed.

In the east, the campaign of 1914 ended with the Russians occupying the Austrian part of Poland, Galicia, although they had failed to penetrate German territory and had lost the western fringes of their own possessions. The unanimity of the three eastern Empires over Poland was one of the first casualties of the war. On 15 August the Russians announced a scheme to unite all three areas of Polish settlement in an autonomous State under the sovereignty of the Tsar,[59] and a month later the Foreign Minister, Sazonov, informed the British and French Ambassadors of a thirteen-point plan in which this would be a leading element. Under Sazonov's dispensation, German power would be 'destroyed' by the loss of eastern Posen, southern Silesia, and the Niemen valley, as well as of Alsace–Lorraine and, if France desired, portions of the left bank of the Rhine.[60] Further Russian approaches in November culminated in a long audience given to Paléologue by the Tsar, in which Nicholas urged that the Allies should agree without delay on how they would respond if Germany should sue for peace.[61]

Delcassé's private intellectual evolution was bringing him close to the Russian viewpoint, as well as to the extreme of French opinion represented by the *Ligue des patriotes* and the *Action française*. Giving his personal ideas to the Russian Ambassador, Isvolski, in September, he suggested no French gains beyond Alsace–Lorraine, and instead put his faith in a Germany split into small, independent States, among which Prussia would lose its dominating position.[62] While not abandoning this aim, by the spring of 1915 he wished to combine it

with territorial changes of the sort Sazonov and the Tsar proposed, and by April he wanted France, Belgium, and possibly
Holland to annex the entire left bank of the Rhine.[63]

In his official capacity, however, the Foreign Minister was
more circumspect. Only after being warned by Paléologue that
Sazonov was growing impatient did Delcassé say that he had received the thirteen-point plan 'with as much interest as sympathy' and was ready to discuss it further.[64] But after the Tsar's
conversation with Paléologue Delcassé was content to send an
edited version of the audience to the British,[65] without indicating if he approved or disapproved of what had been said. Pressed
by Sazonov about the impression the audience had made in
Paris, Paléologue was forced to reply that he had no idea.[66]

At this point the focus of Russian interest shifted from Central Europe to the south. In March 1915 the Tsarist government
asked Britain and France to approve its claim to annex Constantinople and both shores of the Bosphorus. Grudgingly, and with
much subsequent recrimination, the western Allies acquiesced.
At the behest of Paléologue and his British counterpart, however, a final paragraph in this 'Straits Agreement' assured to
Britain and France from Russia 'the same sympathy for the
realization of the designs which they may form in other regions
of the Ottoman Empire *and elsewhere*'.[67] The significance of the
last two words is made clear by the Tsar's statement to Paléologue on 3 March (the day that he presented his claim to Constantinople) that he approved in advance 'everything that your
Government may desire. Take the left bank of the Rhine; take
Mainz; take Coblence; go even farther if you see fit.'[68] This conversation was carefully noted in the Quai d'Orsay, and interpreted as a blank cheque for rearranging the frontier with Germany, to be filled at the moment of France's choosing. Delcassé
was now eager for a conversation with Sazonov and Grey about
'the essential bases of the Peace Treaty'; but Sazonov could not
leave Russia and Delcassé was unwilling to delegate the task to
Paléologue.[69] As a result, after six months of contacts with the
Russians it was still unclear whether France endorsed the Tsar's
proposals for the *European* settlement, as opposed to the Russian ambitions at the Straits. Indeed the very generality of the
assurance the Russians had now given was a reason for continuing to avoid commitment.

Any closer discussion of Central Europe might have exposed profound disagreements between Petrograd and Paris, as well as inside the French Government itself. Even at the Straits, as Poincaré pointed out to Paléologue, French interests would be jeopardized if Russia dominated Turkey and became a Mediterranean naval Power.[70] Austria–Hungary was a second possible field of Franco-Russian conflict. In Sazonov's thinking, which Delcassé came to share, the Habsburg Monarchy would be reduced to little more than its Magyar and Germanic core, without the power to remain a counterbalance to Russia and to Germany in Eastern Europe.[71] But another party in the Government shared Paléologue's fear that this would open the way for the Austrian Germans to be annexed by Berlin while a 'Russian hegemony' was established to the east.[72] The question came to a head when Paléologue proposed to Sazonov that Austria–Hungary should be offered a separate peace on mild terms; Delcassé promptly carried in the Council of Ministers a resolution repudiating the Ambassador.[73] For the moment the Foreign Minister's doctrine prevailed: that Austria–Hungary was more useful as a bribe to keep Russia in the war and to bring in Italy than as a hypothetical future counterweight.

France was being schooled in the disadvantages of a coalition war. In Paris the defeat of Germany seemed overwhelmingly more important than that of the other Central Powers; in Petrograd, and later Rome, this was far from true. At the Straits and over Austria–Hungary the French had resigned themselves to potential dangers in the post-war European order for the sake of their immediate interest in victory over Germany. But the uneasy amalgam of conflict and co-operation which made up the peacetime diplomacy between the Allies continued after war broke out – and the stakes of that diplomacy were raised.

The spectre of an over-mighty Russia, and even the whole subject of war aims, was now made to seem irrelevant by the harsh intrusion of German power. Between March and October 1915 the Russians were expelled from Poland at a price, in casualties and prisoners, that approached two million men. Faced by this disaster, the Tsar ceased to press his allies for their views on the European settlement. Until the spring of 1916 the matter played little part in the relations of the three Powers. Instead their diplomacy concentrated on the intractable task of keeping the friendship, or at least not incurring the enmity, of the Balkan States. Delcassé, whose reputation was enhanced when Italy declared war on Austria–Hungary in May, tried to repeat his success by bringing in Bulgaria. But in October 1915 the Bulgars entered the war in alliance with the Central Powers, and the Allies could not prevent Serbia and Montenegro from being òverrun. The débâcle brought down Viviani's ministry, and on 29 October the Premiership passed to Aristide Briand.

5. *France and its Allies:* (ii) *Briand, Belgium, Poland, and the Paris Economic Conference of June 1916.*

The new Prime Minister was perhaps the most enigmatic and controversial politician of the Third Republic. In 1916 he posed as the uncompromising leader who would fight on until victory; within months of leaving office he became the most formidable French advocate of a negotiated peace. He pursued contrasting lines of action not merely at succeeding stages of his career but also simultaneously. He had made his name in pre-war politics as a conciliator, and it is unlikely that, at bottom, he ever found the role of wartime statesman congenial. Yet, baffled, his con-temporaries questioned whether he had underlying principles at all. For the German, von der Lancken, Briand was a man of fundamental coldness, 'for whom it is only in his fine speeches that emotion plays a role',[74] while Paul Cambon did not know 'where we are going . . . with this lizard of a Briand whom it is impossible to seize and at heart whose sole ambition is to shim-mer in the sun'.[75]

Briand was the product of a system in which Governments de-pended on precarious majorities in Parliament and in which rhet-orical persuasiveness counted for more than did administrative grasp. Unlike Viviani, he held the Premiership in tandem with the Quai d'Orsay: an unmanageable burden even for a man of more industrious habits.[76] As a result, he could do neither job effectively. Dogged by ill-health, and preoccupied with meetings of the Council of Ministers and an increasingly unruly Parlia-ment, he was sometimes absent from the Foreign Ministry for days at a stretch.

The incorrigible disorder of Briand's supervision left others free to influence – at times decisively – the making of policy. A phase of new power opened for the Quai d'Orsay officials, and especially for Briand's *Chef du Cabinet*, Philippe Berthelot. Although a diplomat all his life, Berthelot was distanced from his colleagues by his mildly left-wing sympathies, his unconventional artistic tastes, and his lack of experience abroad. He had formidable qualities of memory and hard work; but his judgement was less sure, he was relentlessly ambitious, and he had a knack of making enemies. None the less, he was indispensable to Briand, for whom he drafted the main outgoing instructions, with the Minister merely adding his initials or approving (if at all) by word of mouth.[77]

Berthelot soon came into conflict with de Margerie. He also clashed with Jules Cambon, who on Briand's accession was given the Secretary-Generalship at the Ministry, a new supervisory post with indeterminate powers. A veteran diplomat and the pre-war Ambassador in Berlin, Cambon was a complex and mercurial man, who lacked the natural authority of his brother in London. By January 1917 he was complaining that 'his, Berthelot's, and de Margerie's offices are three separate compartments without any intercommunication, where the same business is transacted without it being realized . . . .'[78] Briand's ministry drew towards its close in a shambles of faction-fighting and parallel policies. This incoherence in turn enabled its representatives abroad to indulge their taste for independent action, with disconcerting results.

Briand began, however, with the intention of profiting from the setbacks of 1915 in order to strengthen, under French leadership, the military, diplomatic, and economic unity of the coalition. At the Chantilly Conference in December 1915 plans were laid for a simultaneous offensive in the New Year, for which the Allies' military advisers had the highest hopes. It was a false dawn. At Verdun on 21 February the Germans initiated a battle which would continue with little abatement until July. Verdun became the supreme test of endurance for the French army, a purgatory through which three-quarters of that army eventually passed and which persuaded Frenchmen as did nothing else that the experience of the Western Front must never be repeated.[79]

Against this background, French policy towards Belgium, towards Poland, and for the post-war economic order began to

crystallize. After the Germany armies had swept through Luxemburg and Belgium in August 1914 it had been clear that no
French security arrangements would be complete if they left out
the northern flank. France was as deeply committed as was Britain to preventing Belgium from becoming a German satellite.
But the Belgian Government (now in exile at Le Havre) maintained a prickly independence from its allies and also, very early, drew up territorial demands of its own. Most of these were
directed not against Germany but against two neutral States:
Luxemburg and the Netherlands.

Such pretensions caused embarrassment in Paris. Poincaré
and Delcassé assured the Belgians that France would not obstruct their claim to Luxemburg, but de Margerie had reservations, and Berthelot wished to bring Belgium and the Grand
Duchy into France's own 'orbit'.[80] Alarmed by this debate, the
Belgians tried to force the issue by proposing a joint Allied declaration of support for their country which would refer to its
'just claims'. Briand had 'every reservation' on this point,[81] and
the eventual Declaration of Sainte-Adresse on 14 February 1916
went little beyond France's existing unilateral commitments. Britain, France, and Russia undertook to restore Belgium's full
political and economic independence and to aid financially its
recovery;[82] but this was no more than the restoration of a status
quo which neither Paris nor Le Havre any longer considered
satisfactory.

At the same time as Luxemburg soured relations with the
Belgians, a much more serious dispute began with Russia over
Poland. It originated with the project for an Allied diplomatic conference to be held in Paris on 27–8 March 1916. With the Eastern Front now stable, Russian interest in discussing war aims
had revived, and Sazonov proposed that at Paris Britain and
France should give Russia a free hand to settle the eastern frontiers of Germany and Austria–Hungary in return for its supporting whatever they decided for Germany in the west.[83] Briand
peremptorily refused, alleging that the enemy would interpret
any such discussion at Paris as a sign of Allied 'weariness'.[84]

One question, however, Briand was eager to discuss. The
conquest of Poland by the Central Powers had opened a bidding
match between the two sides for Polish favours. There was a

tradition of French sympathy with Polish aspirations, but Briand
was driven to act in March 1916 by fear for the balance of power. This was in part a short-term fear: that the Poles would grow
so exasperated with Russian dilatoriness that they would enlist
in droves in the enemy armies. But it was also a long-term fear:
that the Poles would come to demand not mere autonomy, but
independence.[85] Even de Margerie, the Poles' leading supporter
at the Quai d'Orsay, regarded them as 'unstable', and feared
that if they had independent control of their foreign policy they
would gravitate into the German camp.[86]

France and Russia therefore came into dispute neither over
Poland's international status nor its frontiers, for de Margerie,
at least, regarded the greatest possible extension of Poland to
the west as an essential means of reducing Prussian power.[87] Instead, controversy arose over Briand's desire to reassure the
Poles by issuing a public Franco-British endorsement of the
Tsar's promise of autonomy: a proposal the Russians rejected
absolutely, and considered an interference in their domestic
affairs. The French broached the subject in mid-March, at the
Paris Conference at the end of the month, and again in the middle of April, at which point Sazonov warned that the alliance
might be at risk.[88] Finally, Viviani, now Deputy-Premier, and
Albert Thomas, the Under-Secretary for Armaments, brought
Poland up again when visiting Petrograd in May.[89] Each time
the French backed off in the face of Russian objections, and after May Briand let the subject rest until November, when it was
revived by the action of the Central Powers.

To raise the Polish question was to play with fire. Partly because of Sazonov's readiness to make concessions to the Poles
he was replaced by the Germanophile Sturmer in July. Yet to
do nothing seemed equally dangerous, and hence Briand persisted in the face of Russian warnings. Still wary lest the solidarity of the Allies should be imperilled by premature discussion of
their aims, the French brought up such subjects with their partners only when, as over Poland, action was made imperative by
the pressure of events.

By the end of 1915 similar pressure was building up in another
sphere. When Briand came to power post-war economic co-
operation with the Allies had been under public discussion in

France for some months.[90] Economic war aims took their origins in part from the years before the war, from resentment of the Germans' success and suspicion of the methods by which that success had been achieved. But on this were superimposed the multiple crises caused by the war itself. France's fiscal system was less adaptable than Britain's, and a sharp inflation, with no precedent for a century, eventually began to undermine the early social concord. With so much of their heavy industry occupied, the French faced unusual handicaps in adjusting to a war economy, and by the end of 1915 both the Government budget and the balance of payments were heavily in deficit.[91]

These problems could not be considered in isolation. The Dresden Conference of November 1915 seemed the first step towards a *Mitteleuropa*, or customs union of the Central Powers,[92] and it was feared in the French Commerce Ministry that the world was drifting into a pattern of autarkic blocs in which the Allies would need an association of their own. More immediately, the early post-war years were likely to be critical. The Ministry forecast for them acute world shortages of food and raw materials, worsened for France because the devastation of the north and east would hinder it in earning foreign exchange. The Ministry therefore hoped that France's allies would both grant preferential access to their own commodity production, and endorse the French claim to reparations from the Germans. Finally, both the French and British Governments believed the Germans were planning a post-war 'economic offensive': that they were stockpiling raw materials and manufactures in order to flood the Allies' home markets directly the fighting ended.[93]

The prominence of the Ministry of Commerce under Briand owed something to its new incumbent. Étienne Clémentel had a background as a notary in the Auvergne and as a financial expert in the Chamber. He now began a tenure of over four years at the Ministry, during which his energy and imagination made him the leading influence on economic war aims until his schemes collapsed at the Peace Conference. His career is the best example of what could be achieved by a Minister who concerned himself with war aims, if also of the limits to such influence.[94] On Clémentel's suggestion Briand proposed an Allied economic conference to discuss co-operation in post-war reconstruction, the ending of all economic dependence on the enemy, and customs agreements which would create 'an economic bloc' in opposition to that being formed by the Central Powers.[95]

Most of the Allies agreed to the principle of the conference with little difficulty. The main obstacle was Britain, whose commercial policy had traditionally rested on quite different lines from those Clémentel proposed. But on 4 February 1916 Clémentel reached a private understanding with Runciman, the President of the Board of Trade, at Chat Hill in Northumberland. He agreed that protective tariffs, which were a sensitive subject in British politics, should be dropped. Other means would be selected to reserve the Allies' 'natural resources' in the first instance to their own needs, and to stimulate their production of all goods for which they had previously depended on enemy supplies.[96]

The Ministry of Commerce draftsmen now prepared the agenda for the conference, working in liaison with the *Bureau d'études économiques* and the Quai d'Orsay. They introduced many new provisions into the Chat Hill agreement, including 'coercive measures' to prevent an enemy 'economic offensive', and a joint Allied commitment to seek ways of making good the losses of the devastated regions. They also divided the post-war measures into those which would apply only for a 'transitional period', and those intended to be permanent. The 'transitional period', whose length Clémentel estimated privately at twenty to twenty-five years, was a device intended to mollify liberal opinion in Britain and keep open the possibility of the German business community putting pressure on its Government to compromise. In this form the agenda was approved by the Council of Ministers by mid-April, and was ready to serve as the Government's position in negotiations with France's partners.[97]

After a preliminary round of visits by Clémentel to the Allied capitals the Economic Conference met in Paris from 14 to 17 June 1916. At first sight, Clémentel and Briand had good reason to be satisfied with its outcome. Not only was the Conference due to French initiative, but the great majority of a French-inspired agenda was adopted. The Allies declared their 'solidarity' with the devastated regions, and their intention to seek methods of joint action in reconstructing them. They also undertook to conserve their raw materials primarily for themselves, to take common sanctions against post-war dumping by the enemy, and to seek a more general economic independence from the Central Powers.[98] There remained, however, an unbridgeable gap between intention and fulfilment. The Paris resolutions were valueless without more detailed follow-up agreements, but even with Belgium negotiations for such an agreement failed,[99] and both Russia and Italy feared losing valuable agricultural exports to Germany and Austria without gaining equivalent outlets elsewhere. At the Conference they were able to attenuate a Franco-British proposal to refuse the Central Powers most-favoured-nation status for five years after the war. Subsequently, although Britain and France soon ratified the resolutions, Italy and Russia never followed suit. And in the United States, where the Allies were already unpopular because of controversies arising from the blockade, public opinion responded to the Conference with violent indignation. The sweeping declarations of June 1916 were condemned to remain unrealized.

The failure of the Paris Economic Conference, like much else in the first two years of war, underlined the restrictions imposed on French freedom of action by the Russian alliance. Without the alliance, decisive victory over Germany was unlikely. To preserve it French blood and treasure were committed to objectives – such as Russian annexation of the Straits and the dismemberment of Austria–Hungary – which many of France's leaders thought against the national interest. It was partly for the alliance that the French Government approved the murderous offensives of September 1915 on the Western Front; also partly for the alliance that it resisted the blandishments of Colonel House. In return it had the general promise of Russian support for its objectives given in March 1915. But when Briand tried to commit Russia more specifically – in Poland and the economic sphere – he failed. In spite of this, he felt unable to be so quiescent as Viviani. The initiatives taken in the spring of 1916 were the first of a succession of French *démarches* designed to win Allied support for different portions of their claims on Germany. The next of these *démarches*, however, would concern not Poland or economics but the central French desire for security on the Rhine. How and why this came to be so will be considered in the next chapter.

II

The Emergence of a Grand Design, July 1916–March 1917

1. *The Briand Government and Security, July–November 1916*

1916 was the year in which the warring Powers put forth their greatest efforts. They never fully recovered. The conflict was now demanding sacrifices which in 1914 had not been dreamt of, and such unprecedented slaughter seemed justifiable only if it could yield unprecedented results. Growing numbers of Europeans desired from the war not merely security but absolute security: the assurance that no such tragedy could ever happen again. But they disagreed about how absolute security could be attained. On the Left ideas of a conciliatory peace, making possible disarmament and international arbitration, continued to gain ground. The need for victory itself was increasingly questioned. European Governments, by contrast, still adhered to a peace *through* victory, to dictated terms which would cripple the enemy's independent power.

In France, as elsewhere, both unofficial groups and the authorities proclaimed 'guaranteed' security as their objective.[1] In the first two years of war French leaders had pondered means to that objective without giving any particular set of guarantees the sanction of collective policy. This was now to change. French war aims remained contingent on a victory which might be incomplete, if it came at all. But in the winter of 1916–17 the phase of discussion gave way to a phase of provisional conclusions, and a programme was adopted which would influence French Governments far into the future. The timing of this transformation owed something to unofficial lobbying: more to changes in the authorities' assessment of the military position and of the policies of their allies. The process of decision was obscured, however, by a singular administrative incoherence, due to Briand being unwilling or unable to keep all the threads of French diplomacy in his own hands.

By the third year of war French national unity was weakening. Criticism of the authorities' political and strategic competence had been set in motion by the disappointments of 1915, and was intensified by Verdun. In its first secret session, in June 1916, the Chamber of Deputies vented its feelings against the High Command. The days of automatic parliamentary solidarity were over, and henceforward Briand was hampered by persistent discontent among a large minority extending well outside the Socialist ranks. Within the *SFIO* itself, the *minoritaires* were now a serious challenge to the leadership, able to command one third of the votes when the Party's National Council met in April and in August. Even more sinister were signs of disaffection among the troops, which began in June 1916, and became more frequent from November. Finally, the French war economy was coming under strain, with living standards falling and the remarkable tranquillity of labour relations being ended by the first big strikes, in January 1917. French opinion, if more solid than opinion elsewhere, did not escape the growing European malaise.

Not only the Left was becoming more articulate. In September and October 1916 the press was briefly allowed to air its views on war aims, and it gave publicity to designs for changing the status of the Saarland and the left bank of the Rhine, as well as for ending German unity.[2] Meanwhile, the employers' organizations were 'preoccupied with the economic conditions of peace'.[3] The *Fédération des industriels et des commerçants français* adopted recommendations in September 1916; the *Association de l'industrie et de l'agriculture française* in the following January.[4] And in February 1917 a new patriotic pressure group appeared, the *Comité de la rive gauche du Rhin*. The *Comité* agitated for German sovereignty over the left bank to be ended, and the German troops there to be removed; by leaving the region's fate otherwise imprecise it was able to mobilize a spectrum of opinion ranging from Barrès to Radicals such as Édouard Herriot and the *Comité*'s President, J.L. Bonnet.[5]

As in 1915, this broadening public debate was reflected within the Government. The existing forums for discussion were joined early in 1916 by Léon Bourgeois's *Comité national d'études politiques et sociales*, which included trade unionists as well as politicians, businessmen, and academics, and had a stronger left-wing representation than did most bodies of this kind.[6] Bourgeois himself, a former Premier, and now Minister without Portfolio under Briand, had represented France at the Hague Peace Conference in 1907, and was to become the most eminent French champion of the League of Nations. In August, the members of the *Fédération républicaine* on the *Comité national* warned Briand and Poincaré that the latter was about to pass a mild resolution favouring international arbitration and opposing a long post-war occupation of the Rhineland. The resolution was speedily abandoned, and Bourgeois himself hardened in favour of an occupation after he had discussed the subject with the Premier.[7]

His colleagues' growing interest in war aims was therefore forcing Briand to give a stronger lead. Well before this incident, however, he had embarked on soundings of his own, directed notably towards the iron-and-steel producers. This choice was not fortuitous. With Alsace–Lorraine now settled, public and governmental interest was shifting towards more general measures for safeguarding France's future prosperity and security, which might necessitate infringements on far more territory than had been lost in 1871. This shift was probably inevitable, so closely did the lost provinces' economy and those of the regions of heavy industry to the north and east cohere. But the links were especially apparent to the *Comité des forges*, whose members were preparing a collective opinion which they could impress on the authorities in confidence. The industry was far from monolithic, and the first report of the *Comité*'s Peace Treaty Commission, presented in June 1916, caused such dissension that it was finally accepted only in revised form at a General Assembly in the following February.[8] None the less, the *Comité* now not only officially supported German coal deliveries and the annexation of Alsace–Lorraine and the Saar, but also approved the principle of any territorial extension beyond that.

The industry's strategic importance had been made clearer than ever by the voracious demands of war. As the memorandum of the *Comité des forges* remarked, France's future economic growth and military capacity would alike depend on the fortunes of its iron-and-steel manufacturers. Increasingly, this doctrine won governmental acceptance. In May 1916 the staff of

Marshal Joffre, the French Commander-in-Chief, argued that the Saarland should be annexed because its coal was indispensable to the future prosperity of France's eastern industries.[9] In July a memorandum by Paul Claudel reached the same conclusion from the premiss that to correct the disproportion in 'economic forces' between France and Germany was the fundamental precondition of a lasting peace.[10] At a higher level, both Berthelot and Briand himself were kept informed about the disputes in the *Comité des forges*. The Prime Minister met Pinot, and corresponded with Henri Darcy, a dissenting voice who was also President of the *Comité central des houillères de France*.[11] By the autumn of 1916 the authorities were fully cognizant of the steel industry's views.

Certain aspects of those views, however, must be borne in mind. Both Pinot's testimony[12] and, later, the report by the Peace Treaty Commission of the *Comité des forges* show that the industrialists were well able to distinguish their desires as patriotic Frenchmen from their interests as manufacturers. It was primarily for the first motive that they wanted the frontiers pushed forward. They took for granted the return of Alsace–Lorraine, both for sentimental reasons and because it would gravely weaken Germany's military power by depriving the enemy's heavy industry of most of its domestic iron ore. Given this, the Saar must be annexed as well, in order to prevent France's coal deficit from worsening. But the Saar could not relieve the French industry's special shortage of coking coal, and, if coupled with Alsace–Lorraine, would double the capacity of French metallurgy and plunge it into a crisis of overproduction. Pinot and the Peace Treaty Commission therefore desired Alsace–Lorraine and the Saar in spite and not because of their private commercial needs, and it was only further annexation beyond this point that they deemed unambiguously in the industry's interest. Indeed, while the patriotic arguments for annexing the Saar united the *Comité des forges* (except for Darcy), it was the narrower concern of how to avoid a production surplus that divided it between de Wendel and the metallurgists on the one hand and Schneider and the metal-using industries on the other.[13] The *Comité* helped to enlighten Ministers and officials about complicated questions of which many of them were ignorant, but it was more influential as a peculiar version of a patriotic

pressure group than as an expert witness on the requirements
of French capitalism. And, as a patriotic pressure group, its
views resembled those which politicians and their advisers had
already been formulating. Finally, the *timing* of the moment
when Government policy was clarified cannot adequately be explained by reference to domestic pressures of this kind.

Between the summer of 1916 and the spring of 1917 the external
influences on the French leaders fluctuated violently. In July the
pressure on Verdun relaxed, and the Allies briefly held the initiative. The Anglo-French offensive on the Somme followed
that of the Russian General Brusilov in the east. By the autumn, with the Somme a failure, Romania overwhelmed within
months of entering on the Allied side, and rumours that the
Tsar might make a separate peace, the picture was more sombre. Nevertheless, the Allies made plans for another concerted
attack in the new year, and in March 1917 Prince Sixte de Bourbon emerged from conversations with the highest members of
the Briand Government believing that 'everyone in France is
absolutely decided to pursue the war against Germany with the
utmost energy until the latter is decisively and definitively
beaten . . . .'[14] In 1916 the number of French effectives under
arms was at a peak from which the High Command expected it
to fall. It could still be argued, however, that France had taken
a larger share of the burden of the war on land than had any
other Ally, and it was thought that this would be important in
determining the conditions of peace.

In March 1916 Briand had refused a general discussion of war
aims with the Russians, and his Ministers approved a similar declaration to the British on 1 July.[15] During the next two months
this official wisdom began to alter. Several of the French leaders
turned their minds to war aims; in part from concern with the
domestic debate, in part from misplaced optimism about the
military position, and in part because they expected a new
attempt at mediation by America. But these disparate initiatives
merged into a more formal and collective discussion because of
evidence that France could not delay further before consulting
the governments in Petrograd and London.

In June and July the domestic debate came to the Premier's
attention through Bourgeois's activities and the *Comité des*

forges. Meanwhile, the early successes of the Brusilov offensive revived anxieties about the equilibrium of Central Europe which since 1915 had seemed redundant. Jules Cambon feared that if the Habsburgs were defeated the Russians would rest on their laurels while the Austrian Germans were united with Berlin.[16] A dramatic telegram from Paléologue warned that in the light of Russia's recent gains, with Sazonov now replaced by Sturmer, a Russo-German separate peace could materialize by the winter. This could perhaps be stopped, he suggested, by Allied undertakings to fight for peace conditions 'which would confirm irrevocably the divorce between Russia and Germany', and in particular trade the award of Alsace–Lorraine to France against that of Prussian Poland to the Tsar.[17]

Briand's response was that such conversations would still be premature.[18] But if the Premier, characteristically, was drawn into considering the subject more by domestic than by external pressures, for Poincaré it was the reverse. The President believed renewed intercession from Washington was impending,[19] and was also impressed by the forebodings of Cambon and of Paléologue. At first hesitant about following the Ambassador's advice, by 12 August Poincaré considered Austria's collapse so near that he asked Joffre to draw up the conditions of an armistice with the Central Powers. The General promptly went beyond his mandate, authorizing his staff to report not only on an armistice but also on a peace treaty.[20] Finally, by 24 August Poincaré and Bourgeois were agreed that 'it is time to demand commitments from our allies to our war aims'.[21]

Pressure was now applied from a new direction. In London, too, partly because it feared being outpaced by the French, the Government was attempting a closer definition of its aims.[22] On 24 August Paul Cambon broached the subject with Sir Edward Grey, acting – as was his habit – unofficially and without instructions. Cambon's chief preoccupation was to forestall a Russo-German accommodation over Poland; Grey's to handle the expected American mediation in a way that would not redound to Germany's advantage. But both, reported Cambon, agreed on 'the necessity for an immediate conversation between the Great Powers'.[23]

By 19 September the French Government's deliberations had gone far enough for Briand to tell the British Ambassador,

Bertie, that France would claim not just Alsace–Lorraine but also 'a rectification of the frontier to secure France against attack'.[24] But the Premier initially refused Grey's offer of inter-Allied conversations, possibly because he was reluctant to raise the left bank of the Rhine with the British until he had a firmer assurance of Russian support.[25] He remained unconvinced by Paléologue's warnings that the Russians might defect,[26] and only a new shock from outside at last pushed the French leaders into urgent debate.

The shock was a letter from Jean Doulcet, an official at the French Embassy in Petrograd. Doulcet, too, dwelt on the danger of a separate peace in the absence of an agreement which promised gains to the Tsar in Prussian Poland.[27] When Poincaré read out the letter in the Council of Ministers, his audience was 'very disturbed', and foresaw the war concluding in 'a sort of disaster'.[28] Discussion followed in informal conclaves of politicians and officials, and subsequently in the Council itself.[29] At the Élysée Palace on 7 October Poincaré and Briand conferred with Bourgeois, with Charles de Freycinet (another ex-Premier, who was now a Minister without Portfolio), and with the Presidents of the two Chambers, Deschanel and Dubost. A compromise formula was agreed: France would demand from the Allies full discretion to settle the future of the left bank. The Government's views about the fate of Germany and Austria–Hungary, Briand suggested, should be made known to the Russians by a special representative.[30] By the beginning of October, therefore, the ministry had lighted on the solutions which it would adopt officially early in the following year.

Two more detailed sketches of a possible security programme were now coming into being. After Poincaré's approach to Joffre, the General Staff drew up a first set of peace proposals in August, and a note in October on 'The Status of Germany'. Second, by 6 November the Cambon brothers had prepared a long dispatch for Paul to use in further conversations with Grey. It is uncertain how far the Cambons were influenced by the military recommendations, although it is clear that the Army leaders could not dictate to the civilian authorities as could their counterparts in Berlin. Rather, their opinion carried weight in the measure that it shared in the consensus of civilian thinking and was able to clarify that thinking through specific proposals backed by a professional strategic judgement.

This was demonstrated by the fate of the General Staff memoranda of August and October 1916.[31] The second of these took the extreme position earlier favoured by Delcassé, and advocated that Germany should be divided into nine independent States. This notion was not taken up by the Cambons, and did not reappear in official thinking until after the war had been won. The August memorandum, however, dealt more modestly with the frontiers of France and France's northern neighbours, and its similarity to the Cambons' programme makes it highly probable that they knew of it, even if they felt free to ignore certain of its ideas. In this memorandum the General Staff took economic considerations explicitly into account when they recommended annexing not just Alsace–Lorraine but also the entire Saar coalfield. They also insisted that to protect Western Europe against aggression in the future German sovereignty over the left bank of the Rhine should cease. Instead, the region would be occupied for thirty years while Germany paid off an indemnity, and would be split into small, autonomous States in perpetual customs union with France. During the occupation, these would differ little from French protectorates. This was the first of many attempts to reconcile French strategic interests in the Rhineland with lip-service to national self-determination. It was accompanied by the recognition that Rhineland security arrangements would be valueless without some solution to the problem of the northern flank. Luxemburg, the General Staff considered, if it did not opt for union with France or Belgium, should be permanently occupied, while Belgium itself should be linked to France in a perpetual alliance, with full military and customs union. In short, in the interests of security France would gain means of expanding its influence in the Rhineland and the north to the point where it might eventually be able to make large annexations in both.

The recommendations of the Cambons were more moderate in their content; more temperate and urbane in tone.[32] While clothing their assumptions in altruistic language, the brothers took for granted that there existed an identity between the solutions dictated by abstract justice and those which were in conformity with French interests. The 'lasting peace' which they aspired to would rest on the disarmament of the Central Powers, on 'territorial guarantees' awarded to Germany's neighbours, and on a more general European reorganization in which both 'the independence of nationalities' and the balance of power would be respected. The Cambons accepted that the German nation-State would survive, and relied on arms limitation and territorial changes to keep it in check. Economic constraints, apart from the general principle of reparation, interested them only in so far as they were linked with more tangible frontier alterations.

Such a link led them to claim 'at least' the frontier of 1790 for Alsace–Lorraine, as possession of the Saar was 'essential for our industry'. Annexing the remainder of the left bank was rejected not on principle – on the contrary, it would be a 'glorious advantage' – but because it might create 'great difficulties', and the alternative of two neutral and autonomous buffer States under Allied protection and temporary occupation was therefore preferred. At all events, France must have the 'preponderant voice . . . in the solution of this grave question'. To the north, the Cambons were more indulgent than the military towards Belgium; less so towards Luxemburg, which they believed could not remain independent and must be annexed by Paris or by Brussels. Finally, in the east a Poland under Russian sovereignty would do much to weaken Germany by gaining Posen, the coalfield of Upper Silesia, and a sea outlet along the lower Vistula. On this adventurous note the brothers' main proposals ended.

Before the Cambons' memorandum could be accepted, the process set in motion in the summer got bogged down. Paul Cambon complained when no instructions arrived to guide him in further talks with Grey;[33] Paléologue urged repeatedly a precise agreement which would commit the Russians irreversibly against Germany.[34] But the plan for a mission to Russia had been postponed, and there may have been disagreement about whether Petrograd or London should be approached first.[35] The Cambons' memorandum apparently caused violent controversy in the Council of Ministers, for some of whom it went too far and for others of whom nothing short of annexation of the left bank should be stipulated. In these circumstances Briand, who himself was in agreement with the memorandum, continued to postpone decision.[36]

2. *The German and American Peace Notes and the Allied Replies, December 1916–January 1917*

During 1916 the Allies' relations with the American President worsened, as a result of House's failure in the spring, of American hostility to the Paris Economic Conference, and of disputes arising from the Allied blockade of the Central Powers. Less visible was the drift towards confrontation between Washington and Berlin. By the end of the year the German military and naval leaders were pressing for an unrestricted submarine campaign which was expected to paralyse the Allies so quickly that even if the Americans took it as a *casus belli* their intervention would come too late to be effective. The note published by the Central Powers on 12 December, in which they declared their willingness to negotiate but did not specify their terms, was intended to clear the ground for this. The Germans hoped to impress on their own and American opinion that the Allies were chiefly responsible for the war being prolonged, as well as to draw the Allied public into a peace negotiation which could bring the Germans closer to their objective of splitting the opposing coalition. Finally, the note was intended to forestall the mediation planned by Wilson as a last attempt to end the war before he was sucked into it over the U-boat question.[37] Undeterred, however, the American President published a note of his own on 20 December, in which instead of offering mediation he called on both sides to state in detail the peace conditions they would accept. For when stated, as up to now, in general terms, he observed, those conditions seemed 'the same on both sides'.[38]

When the German and American notes arrived French war aims were still undefined. There was no possibility of them being clarified in the interests of a negotiation with the Central Powers, whose note de Margerie judged to be a means of softening up German and neutral opinion in preparation for a war '*à outrance*'.[39] Briand denounced it in the Chamber as a 'crude snare' designed to 'poison' Allied morale, and the Government's position became that the Allies should send an absolute rejection which would exclude all further contact.[40]

Wilson's note required far more delicate handling; and seemed initially to face the Allies with one of their most difficult decisions since the outbreak of war. Its timing suggested to de Margerie that it had been 'concerted with Germany', and led Briand into anxious enquiries about how far France depended on American food and munitions.[41] The Federal Reserve Board in Washington had taken action in November to restrain American lending to the Allies,[42] whose war effort was now in danger of collapsing through shortage of foreign exchange. Wilson's note also menaced Allied domestic solidarity. Briand's speech in the Chamber on the German note was well received by all shades of French opinion, but the *SFIO* and the *CGT* voted in their National Congresses for a detailed reply to Wilson of the sort the President had requested. The leaders of the two organizations now began a shift to the Left which eventually would bring the *Union sacrée*, or political truce of 1914, to an end.[43]

By agreement with the British, the Quai d'Orsay took the lead in drafting the Allies' replies to the Central Powers and to Wilson. The first draft, which was largely the work of Jules Cambon, dwelt on the German leaders' insincerity and bad faith, while expressing the Allies' own objectives in the usual elusive generalities, in order to leave no scope for the conversation to continue.[44] But the second draft, that in reply to Wilson, referred him to the first as an adequate synopsis of the Allied terms.[45] It therefore side-stepped the essence of the American request. This policy, of which Berthelot was the leading architect, was based on a calculated risk. Although conflicting signals were coming out of Washington, it soon became apparent that Wilson's note had *not* been concerted with the Germans and that the Americans feared a conflict with the latter to be imminent. Berthelot concluded that at bottom Wilson was well-disposed towards the Allies and a munitions embargo was unlikely. And if the Allies refused to disclose their peace conditions to Germany, they could not let themselves be drawn into negotiation by the USA; what mattered most was still to break off the exchanges as decisively as possible.[46]

There was one crumb of comfort for the President in the second French draft reply: a warm adherence to the 'creation of a League of Nations to assure peace and justice across the world'. The war had everywhere strengthened agitation for a mechanism of this kind, and Wilson had come out in support of the principle in May 1916. In France the idea won favour which spread beyond the Socialist enthusiasts for arbitration, and it was approved at the November Congress of the prestigious *Ligue des droits de l'homme*.[47] At the level of government, Briand and Asquith discussed 'international sanctions' in September 'as a gesture to the Socialists and the Labour Party'.[48] The attitude of the leading French officials was similarly opportunist. In August 1916 Léon Bourgeois's *Chef-adjoint du Cabinet*, Jarousse de Sillac, was sent to the USA to research into a future system of 'international arbitration'.[49] He returned to find both Jules Cambon and de Margerie highly sceptical about the idea of supranational organization, and expecting at most (in Cambon's case) 'a sort of confederation between the Western European Powers and the United States'. Of the men de Sillac interviewed, only Bourgeois accepted that Germany should be included in the League.[50]

The Quai d'Orsay's drafts were considered on 26 December at a Franco–British Conference in London. Despite British misgivings about the imprecision and invective of the proposed reply to Germany, the French view prevailed and on 30 December the document was published substantially as Jules Cambon had written it. Berthelot, speaking for an ailing Briand, argued that the second reply should be even less detailed, for fear that Wilson should use it to try to open a conversation between the two sides. The British disagreed, and the document was reconsidered by a joint commission. As approved on the following day (and published, after additional changes, on 10 January 1917) the reply kept much of its original French wording, but included a final paragraph which set out the Allies' aims more concretely and comprehensively than had any previous statement.[51]

This paragraph was sufficiently elastic to be compatible with the French territorial programme which was being elaborated in the same weeks. It alluded unmistakably to Alsace–Lorraine, and even to 'appropriate international arrangements to guarantee land and sea frontiers against unjustified attacks'. This was far more explicit than the Germans' reply to Wilson, and the paradoxical consequence was a major Allied diplomatic victory which opened the way for American war entry in the following spring. Although drawn out reluctantly and under British pressure, the French could benefit from this success without being seriously restricted in their negotiating freedom. At the same time, by paying formal homage to the League of Nations, they were better able to maintain the solidity of their home front in the difficult times that lay ahead.

3. *The Grand Design Accepted: the Cambon Letter and the Northern Flank, January 1917*

Even the emergency caused by Wilson's note had been surmounted without the Briand Government resolving its dissensions over war aims. The French representatives had gone to London without clear terms of reference on the subject, and collective policy remained confined to public declarations and the secret agreements reached thus far with France's allies. But early in the new year, when Briand, Berthelot, and the one remaining Socialist in the Government, Albert Thomas, were absent at a conference in Rome, Jules Cambon raised his and his brother's memorandum with Poincaré. Viviani introduced the document into the Council of Ministers, which approved it without discussion. When Briand returned he accepted the decision and sent out the memorandum as instructions to Paul Cambon on 12 January 1917.[52] In this way the Government had at last equipped itself with a programme of war aims.

How had the earlier deadlock been broken? The French representatives at the London Conference were impressed by the coolness of the new Lloyd George ministry to their claims in Alsace–Lorraine, and by its desire to subject them to a plebiscite. This may have helped persuade Ministers of the need to consult the Allies without delay.[53] But the document they accepted in January, and forwarded to Paul Cambon, had been revised, in part by Berthelot, so as to become a more sober, less ambitious programme than that of the previous November.[54] A new paragraph approved the principle of the League of Nations. Austria–Hungary was no longer to be broken up, as originally envisaged. Polish sea access was suppressed. Nearer home, the demand was now for the Alsace–Lorraine frontier of 1790, with the earlier 'at least' omitted. A new formula for the left bank spoke no longer of buffer States, but of 'neutrality' and 'provisional occupation'; it demanded definitely only that the region must no longer be under German sovereignty. Everything else was left to inter-Allied negotiations, in which France would keep the 'preponderant voice'. This was the policy of the free hand, acceptable, according to Ribot, even to the Socialists, while making possible, in the opinion of other members of the Government, a system of buffer States which could lead on to annexation.[55]

The dispatch of the Cambon letter did not mean that the French nation was committed to fight on until the letter's provisions had been integrally fulfilled. The document was intended for discussion with the British, and had been sanctioned by the heads of the executive. To send it was therefore a serious step. But it remained confidential. It could be repudiated without public loss of face. It deliberately left the crucial question of the Rhineland vague, and it is doubtful whether it would otherwise have won the Government's approval. There were now the outlines of an official doctrine for assuring French security in the future, where previously there had been the aspirations of isolated institutions and individuals. That doctrine was the outgrowth of a consensus, even if within and still more outside the Government that consensus continued to be challenged. It was still a far more limited consensus than that which existed over Alsace–Lorraine. Consultation of the French Army and the steel industry had ceased well before the moment of decision, and Ministers had been subjected to irresistible pressure neither from here nor from any other quarter in French domestic politics. Sanction by the legislature and the political parties was not sought: one branch of government had accepted a programme of aims as a basis of consultation with one ally. Subsequently the men who had caused the programme to be adopted were able much to expand its applications. But nothing irreversible had yet taken place.

Briand may have planned to formulate war aims in a more comprehensive way. Early in 1917 he appears to have set up three commissions to study aspects of the question of the left bank.[56] In January he assembled a body of historians and geographers in the *Comité d'études*, which held sessions from 28 February onwards under the chairmanship of Ernest Lavisse, the Director of the *École normale supérieure*, who was an Honorary President of the *Ligue française*. But the *Comité*'s brief limited it to gathering information; lacking an important contingent of officials it found itself working in detachment from the

Quai d'Orsay, and it seems that of those in high office only Poincaré read conscientiously what it produced.[57]

A sequel to the sending of the Cambon letter demonstrated the Government's continuing reluctance to assume commitments. The question at issue was that of France's northern flank. In public the French were pledged to restore Belgian independence; in private they wished to ensure that this independence would not be exercised against their interests. Friction also continued over Luxemburg, whose population, according to the information reaching Paris, preferred French to Belgian sovereignty if the pre-war status quo were to be revised.[58] In May 1916 the Belgians formally presented their own claim to annex Luxemburg if the Grand Duchy ceased to be self-governing, only to be met in Paris with a resounding silence.[59]

Later in the summer it was France's turn to take the initiative, with Clémentel, backed by Poincaré and Briand, proposing a customs union to the Belgians.[60] Clémentel's own concern may have been primarily economic, forming part of a vaster plan for a Western European free-trade area that would take in Italy and possibly Britain. Yet he acted with little support and much criticism from French industry, where the Government's intention was widely supposed to be the political one of strengthening French influence at Brussels after the war.[61] Because of this possibility, as well as doubts about the commercial advantages of the scheme, in October the Belgians rejected Clémentel's advances.[62] Two months later the Government in Le Havre again demonstrated the potential dangers of its independence, by insisting on sending its own replies to the German and American peace notes. In Paris and London it was feared that this insistence masked Belgian aspirations towards a separate peace.[63]

Fears of this kind had led the French General Staff in August 1916, as well as Berthelot at the Quai d'Orsay, to advocate military and economic links which would align future Belgian policy firmly with that of France.[64] But the Cambon letter, as approved by the Council of Ministers, recommended that Belgium should incorporate Luxemburg, and did not specify any *quid pro quo*. In the version sent to Paul Cambon, however, all reference to the Grand Duchy was removed. This was

Briand's decision, taken without his Ministers or Jules Cambon being consulted, and based on advice from Berthelot. The latter had argued for some time that France itself should annex Luxemburg, and now cited the Grand Duchy's strategic value, its iron ore, and the supposed francophilia of its people as reasons for avoiding a commitment to the Belgians about its fate.[65]

A week later Paul Cambon complained that the dispatch of 12 January gave him no guidance over Luxemburg.[66] The cat was now out of the bag. Jules Cambon discovered Berthelot's minute in the relevant dossier, and presented Briand with a 'Note in Reply' rebutting it.[67] It might be possible, thought Cambon, to take the south-western corner of the Grand Duchy, where the iron ore was located, but to annex the whole of Luxemburg would be a 'dirty trick' that would imperil the more important goal of close military and diplomatic co-operation with Belgium, and perhaps even prevent the Anglo-French alliance from continuing after the war. He therefore wished to liquidate the Luxemburg asset now rather than to hold it in reserve. He also feared that a plebiscite in Luxemburg would set a precedent for holding one in Alsace–Lorraine, and he doubted whether France could win either. But his protests were of no avail. Briand telegraphed to Paul Cambon that the wording of 12 January should stand.[68] For the time being the French Government refused to foreclose on its options in the north.

4. *The Application of the Grand Design*: (i) *Poland, Russia, and the Doumergue Agreement, November 1916–March 1917*

After his experiences in the spring Briand allowed the Polish question to lie dormant in his dealings with the Russians, and the subject was reopened by the declaration of the Central Powers on 5 November 1916 that the Polish areas they occupied would become an independent kingdom at the end of the war. The mass Polish recruitment which the German High Command had hoped for did not result, but once again the British and French Governments feared that the Allies would be outbid in the competition for Polish sympathy. Briand thought the Russian counter-declaration too reserved,[69] but when he was invited to associate himself with it he seized his chance. On 16 November he and Asquith announced their 'entire solidarity' with the

Russian promises of 'restored unity' to the Poles:[70] a first step towards the 'internationalization' of the question which the Tsar had hitherto resisted. Conflict resumed over the reply to President Wilson's peace note,[71] but the French Government eventually contented itself with an allusion in the reply to a declaration made by the Tsar to the Poles on Christmas Day 1916.

Behind this new boldness lay the Quai d'Orsay's conviction that the strategic import of the matter went far beyond the danger of Polish recruitment by the Central Powers. For de Margerie, satisfying Polish aspirations was the only way to prevent the enemy from 'realizing their fatal project of a *Mitteleuropa* dominating Europe and the Orient'.[72] And, even in its milder, revised form, the Cambon letter spoke of 'expanding the Polish provinces of Russia . . . . Berlin would thereby be militarily completely exposed . . . .' In turn, the change in boundaries would make the question 'international', and enable France and Britain to have their say.

Poland now took its part in a general discussion of war aims between Petrograd and Paris, of the sort one side or the other had repeatedly postponed since the outbreak of war. After Balfour replaced Grey as Foreign Secretary in December 1916 pressure from London for conversations was relaxed, and Paul Cambon allowed the dispatch of 12 January to rest unused until July. Instead, the plan to send a special representative to Petrograd was revived. The choice fell on the Minister of Colonies, Gaston Doumergue, who was to do his business on the sidelines of a military conference held in the Russian capital in February 1917.

Doumergue was a right-wing Radical and former Premier, who was among the harsher of Briand's Ministers in his views on the subject of security. His Department was one of the few which had been forced to make decisions about its post-war objectives. He left for Russia with a copy of the Cambon letter but without written instructions,[73] and arrived uncertain of his mandate. He told the Senate in June 1917 that the original purpose of the mission had been to secure Russian support, in a written convention, for the French claim to Alsace–Lorraine.[74] Although Paléologue's warnings were among the stimuli which prompted his superiors to act, however, the Government's conceptions differed from the Ambassador's. Paléologue and Doulcet had wanted to combine an agreement on Germany's western frontiers with one of its eastern frontiers which would rule out all possibility of compromise between Petrograd and Berlin. But Briand imagined he was merely dotting the i's on the Russian promise of support given in March 1915, and was taken aback when the Prusso-Polish frontier was brought into the discussion.

Doumergue received insufficient guidance on a second point. The Council of Ministers had endorsed the Cambon letter only after it had been given an imprecise, compromise wording. But Doumergue, inadequately instructed from Paris, felt free to conclude a highly specific – and in some ways more ambitious – convention. Only after this did Briand try to substitute a looser formula, more likely to win his Government's approval, but in this he did not succeed.

There was one final element in the confusion. Some members of the Government, and Poincaré in particular, apparently supposed that France needed Russian backing before it could negotiate safely with the British.[75] Doumergue seems initially to have thought that London would be informed of his convention,[76] and, indeed, if this had been no more than a vague Russian undertaking to support France's claims in the west it might have been possible to reveal it to the British without exposing any differences of view. But in the event Britain was told nothing until the German Chancellor made the Doumergue Agreement public in July 1917, and the affair left a legacy of distrust.[77]

Feeling a need for closer guidance than the Cambon letter, Doumergue telegraphed to Paris on 1 February, summarizing what he intended to tell the Russian Emperor. France, he proposed, would regain Alsace–Lorraine with 'at the very least' the frontier of 1790, including the whole of the Saarland. The rest of the left bank would be divided into self-governing States politically and economically independent of Germany, with no armed forces of their own. They would be occupied by France until the Peace Treaty had been executed in full: a process which might last a generation.[78] Doumergue had therefore gone considerably beyond what the Ministers had approved in January, but had received no confirmation or rejection of his ideas before, on 3 February, he won Russian approval for them in a long audience with the Tsar.[79] On the 8th Paléologue asked for authority to confirm this by exchanging letters with Pokrovski, the new Russian Foreign Minister.[80]

At this point Doumergue's independent-mindedness in Petrograd was reinforced by Berthelot's in Paris. Paléologue was informed that 'I see nothing but advantages in confirming by a written agreement the conversation between M. Doumergue and the Tsar on the lines indicated in your telegram. . . .'[81] This reply was both drafted and initialled by Berthelot; there is no evidence that it was seen by Briand, and Ribot later hinted to the Senate that it was not.[82] Nor was the Council of Ministers consulted, although Paléologue had not sent even the exact text that he proposed to sign. None the less, letters were exchanged on 14 February, confirming the stipulations for Alsace–Lorraine and the left bank which Doumergue had set out in his telegram of 1 February and in his conversation with Nicholas II.[83] But on 13 February a note presented in Paris by Isvolski altered the whole context of the question. Reviving its initiative of March 1916, the Tsarist Government announced that in return for supporting whatever settlement Britain and France favoured for Germany's western frontiers it would expect their backing for its own plans for the frontiers between Russia and the Central Powers.[84]

Berthelot's first assumption was that Paléologue had tried to draw his superiors into an agreement about the borders of Poland, and that the Ambassador must be disavowed: France should stand on the agreement of March 1915 and refuse a *quid pro quo*.[85] Briand himself now saw the mission as a mistake, but attempted to salvage what he could be changing course in the middle of negotiations. On the 16th he unveiled in the Council of Ministers a new formula, whereby France and Russia would each support whatever alterations the other might desire to its frontier with Germany.[86] This wording, even more general than the Cambon letter's, would replace the embarrassing explicitness of the documents Paléologue and Pokrovski had exchanged. But it also marked Briand's conversion to a design of the sort his representatives in Petrograd had recommended: one that would bind the Russians to claims against Germany which would make a separate peace impossible.

The Premier was at last attempting to bring the negotiations under his personal control. In a telegram to Paléologue on 16

February he retrospectively accepted responsibility for the authorization to exchange letters which had been sent on the 9th. But at the same time he considered that France must comply with the new Russian request, even though that request might rule out all possibility of an Austro–Hungarian separate peace, and even though France had 'already paid' for the Domergue Agreement when it acquiesced in Russia's demands at the Straits. Whatever its disadvantages, the 'maximum Russian programme' in Central Europe was the one most conducive to 'the necessary enfeeblement of Germany', and France's interest was for Russia to absorb Prussian Poland and to establish a frontier on the Carpathians. Briand therefore proposed that France and Russia should promise to support each other in seeking frontiers with the Central Powers which would give them 'militarily and industrially every guarantee of the security and economic development of the two nations'.[87] Even more emphatically than Delcassé, it seemed, Briand was abandoning hope of separating Austria–Hungary from Germany, and resigning himself to the maximum extension of Russian power in the east.

From here on the negotiations were handled by Briand and Isvolski in Paris.[88] On 8 March Poincaré and Doumergue objected to the Russian demands, in an ill-tempered session of the Council of Ministers.[89] But two days later a note from Briand to the Russian Ambassador recognized Russia's 'complete liberty to fix its western frontiers', and justified this as *completing* rather than supplementing the agreement of March 1915.[90] The bargaining had become extremely confused and, as within a few days both Briand and the Tsar fell from power, the loose ends were never tied up.

This was shown in the following May when the Russian Provisional Government raised the Doumergue Agreement with the French special representative in Petrograd, Albert Thomas. Thomas had been a Minister under Briand, but had been kept very ill-informed, for until now he had supposed that France had merely received a free hand for the settlement in the west.[91] Questioned about the episode, Briand commented that the Paléologue–Pokrovski letters had never been discussed by the Council of Ministers, and had lost their validity. Instead, he implied that his text of 16 February had been accepted by the

Russians, and it was this impression he had allowed Thomas to receive.[92] But when Briand's successor, Ribot, examined the dossier, it did not support this view, and he was obliged to inform Thomas that the Government did indeed consider itself bound by the Pokrovski–Paléologue exchange.[93] Thus, only two months after Briand's departure, the Quai d'Orsay itself could not reconstruct exactly what had happened. Nothing could better illustrate the chaos from which the policy had emerged.

5. *The Application of the Grand Design*: (ii) *the Austrian Counterweight and the Mediation of Prince Sixte de Bourbon, November 1916–March 1917*

Even in the first years of the war soundings between the opposing coalitions had not entirely ceased, and hopes lingered in both camps of splitting the enemy's diplomatic unity. By the end of 1916 most of the belligerents had strained their military capacity to the utmost, and the conflict passed into a new phase, lasting until March 1918, of more sustained attempts at mediation by third parties and at direct contacts between the two sides. Hope of decisive victory was not abandoned, but the balance between force on the one hand and diplomatic inducements and propaganda on the other shifted in favour of the latter. Governments were driven to seek orders of priority among their war aims, and to consider which might be jettisoned in the interests of bringing an opposing Power to terms. On the Allied side this heightened the frictions between the members of the coalition; in Germany it sharpened the rivalry between the expansionist pressure groups in Berlin. An extra desperation was added to these conflicts by the growing fear that the longer the war went on the more likely it was to end in economic collapse and revolutionary upheaval: a foreboding that would be vindicated by events.

Thus far, Briand has appeared as an intransigent fighter to the finish, a man who spurned both neutral mediation and the enemy's public and private approaches. In October 1916, when the Belgians reported Germany's supposed willingness to restore both Belgium and annexed Lorraine, Briand replied that all such offers had 'as their object to dissociate the Allies, and they must not be listened to'.[94] But by temperament and background the Prime Minister was a man of compromise, who liked to keep his options open,[95] and he did not rule out contact with the Germans if the time and place were of his choosing. Of the exchanges between its agents and French politicians, journalists, and businessmen which periodically excited the German Legation in Switzerland during 1915 and 1916, one stands out. In January 1916 the Quai d'Orsay set up an agency at Berne to gather intelligence from the enemy press, placing at its head Haguenin, a well-connected French academic who had been employed before 1914 at the University of Berlin. Haguenin made known to the Germans that he had authority from Poincaré, Viviani, and Briand to conduct soundings, and even held out the possibility of a Franco-German separate peace, on the absolute condition of France regaining Alsace–Lorraine.[96] The German leaders were not prepared to pay this price, and they allowed the episode to remain at the level of private conversations. It was unclear how far Haguenin spoke even for Briand, and by the end of the year he conceded that among those in high office in Paris the Premier alone was willing to contemplate a compromise.[97] But Briand alone could not have overcome the conviction of most French Ministers and officials that decisive victory over Germany was the only acceptable outcome to the war. On this essential principle individual statesmen wavered in the phase of peace contacts that was opening, but the course of collective policy did not deviate.

Briand's similar concern to keep a free hand in dealing with the Austrians led him into bizarre contortions of policy. Although France had no claims of its own against the Habsburgs, it was committed to support the aspirations of Italy, of Serbia, of Romania, and of Russia. Briand in February 1917, it appeared, like Delcassé in January 1915, was unwilling to court Vienna if it would endanger the alliance with the Tsar. One action taken on the Government's own initiative seemed to tie its hands still more firmly. In the first week of 1917, primarily on Berthelot's initiative, the draft of the Allies' reply to President Wilson was altered in order to include 'the liberation of the . . . Czecho–Slovaks from foreign domination'.[98] If France's existing undertakings were fulfilled a diminished Austria–Hungary could still survive. But if in addition the Czechs and Slovaks won their independence the Monarchy would be reduced to its German and Magyar heartland, the former part of which would be tempted by union with its northern neighbour. The Quai d'Orsay had been in contact with the Czech nationalist leaders, Masaryk and Beneš, since the spring of 1916, and Berthelot had decided to make a gesture in their direction.[99] In so doing he appeared to write off Austria–Hungary if the Allies won the war.

Yet by 1916 little survived in Paris of the historic animosity against Vienna. Before the war hopes had occasionally arisen that the Habsburgs could be extricated from the German sphere of influence and turned into a counterbalance to Berlin. Even after 1914 some Frenchmen, such as Paléologue, Jules Cambon, and Poincaré, remained loyal to such hopes; others, probably including Berthelot, believed Austria–Hungary could never be other than a vehicle by which Germany could dominate south-eastern Europe. But the terms of this debate were altered when the Emperor Franz Josef died in November 1916 and reports arrived within weeks that his successor, Charles, was ready to consider a separate peace.[100]

Some of the Quai d'Orsay officials were already in contact with a possible intermediary, in the shape of Charles's brother-in-law, Prince Sixte de Bourbon, who was serving with the Belgian Army in Flanders. The exchanges which followed between Charles and the Allies through Sixte shed new light on French policy for containing Germany in Western and Central Europe. The handling of the affair in Paris suffered from the usual confusion of the Briand ministry's declining months. Sixte first met William Martin, the Director of Protocol at the Quai d'Orsay; he was introduced in November 1916 to Jules Cambon and subsequently to Poincaré.[101] Only on 8 March did Poincaré tell Briand, who had meanwhile opened his own channel to the Viennese Court via the Duchesse d'Uzès.[102] Taking the Cambon letter as their authority, and acting before they had informed the Premier, Poincaré and Jules Cambon made clear to Sixte that France would desire Alsace–Lorraine with the frontier of 1814, and held out the possibility that Austria might gain from Germany Silesia or even Bavaria.[103] Before leaving Paris for discussions which he held with Charles on 23–4 March the Prince was told that France would also require 'reparations, indemnities, and guarantees on the left bank of the Rhine'.[104] He passed on these indications, including the reference to Silesia, to the Emperor, and returned with a letter of support from Charles for France's claims to Alsace–Lorraine and the Saar.[105]

Only now did the French inform Britain of the opening to Vienna. A new phase in the conversations began, during which they were dominated and eventually ruptured by the question of Italian war aims. Even without this obstacle the hopes invested in Sixte's mediation would probably have been disappointed, for the impression he gave that the Austrians were ready for a *separate* peace was misleading. Like the Doumergue negotiation, the affair shows how weak was the Council of Ministers' control over the diplomatic initiatives taken under Briand, and the disproportionate power given to the statesmen and officials most immediately concerned by the vacuum and confusion at the heart of French government. It also shows how the security policy adopted by the ministry when it approved the Cambon letter was continuing to expand. The Government was provisionally committed to a security programme based neither on breaking Germany up nor on a peace of reconciliation, but on disarming the *Reich* and containing it by a ring of as yet ill-defined territorial 'guarantees'. In the west these would include annexing Alsace–Lorraine and the Saar, while the remainder of the left bank of the Rhine would be (according to the Cambon letter) separated from Germany and (according to the harsher language of the Doumergue Agreement) recomposed as buffer States under French occupation until the Peace Treaty had been executed in full. In the east the leading 'guarantee' would be the enlargement at Germany's expense of a Poland under Russian sovereignty. At the same time, if the resolutions of the Paris Economic Conference were implemented, all forms of Allied economic dependence on the enemy would end, and the pre-war industrial imbalance between France and Germany would begin to be redressed. Finally, while in public the French moved closer to advocating Austria–Hungary's destruction, in private they had made known to the Habsburg Emperor a plan to preserve, and even strengthen at the expense of Southern Germany, a Danube Monarchy which would become France's natural ally in Central Europe. In the west French objectives were crystallizing; in the east several, potentially conflicting, options were kept open. The Briand ministry's grand design was a set of preferences rather than of hardened and irrevocable commitments, and much of its detail remained to be worked out. Its fulfilment was contingent on the outcome of the war and on the goodwill of France's allies. And it was adopted at a moment when the configuration of international power favoured France more strongly than it ever would again. The ink on the Doumergue Agreement was barely dry when the French found themselves at the great watershed of the war.

III

The Watershed, March–November 1917

1. *The Crisis of 1917*

In the months now opening, the certainties which had shaped a generation of public affairs were swept away. Until the spring of 1917 the established political balance within the European States and the pre-existing distribution of international power had withstood the strains of total war with astonishing resilience. For both, those strains were now unbearable. In March Tsar Nicholas II abdicated, unleashing forces which within a year reduced Russia to anarchy and foreign domination. In April the Germans' unrestricted submarine offensive brought the United States into the conflict. These developments were matched by almost equally dramatic events inside France, where the tragic failure of the Nivelle offensive provoked mutiny in the Army and a collapse of civilian morale which briefly threatened to lead to insurrection. Until the implications of these changes became clear French statesmen had to reckon with such imponderables that their war aims were thrown into confusion. When the fog began to lift the programme of the spring of 1917 had not been explicitly abandoned, but it no longer figured even in confidential statements of policy, and in some of those statements was contradicted. The outlines of a successor were emerging, better tailored to the new international circumstances and the changed susceptibilities of French domestic opinion. In short, these were months of adjustment to a sharp decline in France's relative, and even absolute, power.

The French crisis of 1917 was diplomatic, military, and political. The diplomatic element was a weakening of the country's bargaining strength within the Allied coalition. The Tsar had never objected to France's territorial claims on Germany, although he had exacted a high price for supporting them. But the Governments which succeeded him in Petrograd pressed insistently for Allied war aims to be diminished, and France's strongest partners were now not Russia, but Britain and the United States. Yet neither Anglo-Saxon Power had hitherto been willing to assume long-term peacetime obligations of the kind embodied in the Franco-Russian alliance. And both Washington and London regarded even the French pretensions to Alsace–Lorraine, let alone to other parts of Germany, with scepticism verging on hostility. Finally, the progressive enfeeblement of France's war effort was changing the Government's relationship with its leading allies from near parity into dependence.

The military crisis opened with General Nivelle's ill-fated offensive on the Chemin des Dames in April 1917. Nivelle had replaced Joffre in the previous December, and his confident assertions that the German lines could be broken did something to bolster the French Army's flagging morale. The blow was all the heavier when, after much heart-searching, the French civilian authorities agreed to the offensive and it yielded only the same small gains and long casualty lists as its predecessors. Outbreaks of indiscipline began in April and gathered in frequency during May before reaching a climax in the first week of June. From then on they rapidly subsided, although it was February 1918 before the Army's convalescence was complete. Most of the mutinies were refusals to move up for the attack rather than refusals to defend the line. They were protests less against the war itself than against the way in which it had been fought, and they were not direct assaults upon the State. But they were an anxious moment for the Government, and reinforced Nivelle's successor, Pétain, in his conviction that for the rest of 1917 only attacks with limited objectives were possible and all prospect of a decisive breakthrough must be ruled out. It was not only to restore morale that Pétain wished to keep casualties to a minimum. The Army's losses had been so great that it was suffering from a 'crisis of effectives', and it seemed essential to conserve manpower if France were to have its say in the eventual terms of peace.[1]

Nivelle's failure also struck at civilian confidence. This, like that of the troops, had been sustained by repeated promises that victory was near and the next offensive would be the last. In April 1917 such promises were discredited once too often, and privations which had hitherto been patiently endured became intolerable. By 1917 the real income of Parisian wage-earners had fallen by a tenth since the war began, and for the first time for decades there was a crisis in the national food supply.[2] The first strike wave in January was followed by a bigger one in May and June, at the very moment when the mutinies reached their height and the Government faced one of its sternest parliamentary tests.

Like the mutineers, the strikers used pacifist and revolutionary slogans; but also like them they had goals that were generally limited and concrete, and could be satisfied short of political upheaval and a peace of capitulation. More disturbing was the pessimism registered in the surveys – which the authorities now multiplied – of civilian morale. In May–June and in November 1917 depths of depression were reached which spread to all social classes and regions of the country.[3] And the effects of the Nivelle offensive, of events in Russia, and of falling living-standards were barely offset by the entry on the Allied side of the United States. It was far from clear at first that the Americans could compensate for the eclipse of the Russian alliance, the main pillar of French security in Europe for the twenty-five preceding years. There is evidence that by 1917 much of French opinion would have been content to end the war with no change in the status of Alsace–Lorraine, let alone the left bank of the Rhine.[4]

In the end the French Government, unlike the Russian, did not lose the power to decide between peace and war. But the political nation responded to the shifts in the broader public mood, and there was a partial breakdown in the national unity established three years earlier. The Socialist leaders moved to the Left, and favour for a compromise peace grew even in the non-Socialist ranks. This was especially true of the Radicals, whose President, Caillaux, did little to discourage the opinion that he would be willing to head a Government committed to liquidating the conflict by negotiation. War-weariness in France therefore had no such cataclysmic political consequences as in Russia, but showed itself in the growing unruliness of Parliament and in the appearance of a large minority in the Assembly and in the country which pressed for war aims to be revised. Between 26 August 1914 and 12 December 1916 there were two ministries, with an average life of fourteen months. From 12 December 1916 to 13 November 1917 there were three, with an average life of less than four months. In the same period the

Chamber met five times in secret sessions of up to a week in length. Governments returned to their peacetime preoccupation with their majorities, and Painlevé, in November 1917, was the first wartime Premier to resign as a result of being defeated in the legislature. Between May and November 1917 parliamentary debates over war aims grew frequent and acrimonious: war aims became, as had long been feared, one of the obstacles over which the political truce broke down.

To these other sources of uncertainty was added obscurity about the intentions of France's enemies. 1917 was a year of peace initiatives, launched either through third parties such as the European Socialist movement and the Pope, or as direct approaches to the Allies from the Central Powers. War-weariness was evident in Austria–Hungary and in Germany itself, where there was industrial unrest and a movement to revise war aims which, numerically at least, was stronger than in France. The *Reichstag* resolution of 19 July, by apparently repudiating peace terms which included annexations and 'violent' economic and financial impositions, placed the Allies in a quandary: should they court the German opposition or ignore it?

French policy in these troubled months was shaped principally by Alexandre Ribot and Paul Painlevé. Ribot held the Premiership in conjunction with the Foreign Ministry from 20 March to 7 September. Painlevé held the Ministry of War before taking on the Premiership as well from 13 September to 13 November, with Ribot, for the first six weeks of this short-lived ministry, staying at the Quai d'Orsay. Widely differing in character and outlook, the two men shared in the misfortune of facing some of the most complex and harrowing decisions of the war.

2. The Russian Revolution and the Suspension of the Grand Design, March–September 1917

During his first Premiership, in 1892–5, Ribot had presided over the formation of the Russian alliance. He returned to see his handiwork undone. To the Right of Briand in domestic politics, he had been a competent Minister of Finance since 1914, and brought to his office both experience in handling Parliament and administrative expertise. He also had a knowledge of and respect for British and American institutions; he spoke good English and had an American wife. His private character was less attractive: his deviousness and the self-satisfaction of which his diaries reek undermined the confidence of his colleagues and helped to bring about his fall.

Ribot gave closer personal attention to foreign policy than had Briand, and was better able to contain the rivalries in the Quai d'Orsay. Jules Cambon became the most influential permanent official; Berthelot was replaced as *Chef du Cabinet* and suffered a period of eclipse. But conflicts between the Quai d'Orsay and other Ministries increased. Albert Thomas, at Armaments, hoped to reorientate French policy to the Left, and benefited from his private network of informers in Russia and in Northern Europe. Painlevé, at War, pursued in August 1917 a parallel diplomacy of his own. Poincaré, by contrast, lost influence, although he remained a source of moral support to the harassed and sometimes indecisive Premier.

Ribot's private inclinations in foreign policy were not illiberal: he had found the Doumergue Agreement 'all bad' even when it was signed, and had 'reservations' about occupying the left bank, both because of the expense and because of the 'danger of creating another Alsace–Lorraine' in what he recognized was an irreversibly Germanized region.[5] In Parliament on 21 March he denied that France was fighting a war of 'conquest', having overridden objections from Poincaré beforehand that this would needlessly prejudge the question of territorial guarantees beyond Alsace–Lorraine.[6] But Ribot also took care to provide in his statement for 'guarantees of a lasting peace', which should be 'material' as well as 'moral', and his Government initially remained loyal to the expanded war aims of Briand's last weeks in office. On 12 April an unrepentant Poincaré told Sixte de Bourbon in Ribot's presence that France would require the Alsace–Lorraine of 1814 and clauses neutralizing the left bank of the Rhine; on the same day Jules Cambon again held out to the Prince the prospect of Silesia.[7] And a month later Ribot himself confirmed that his Government felt bound by the letters exchanged between Paléologue and Pokrovski in February.[8] His altered presentation in Parliament – which included a gesture towards the 'great ideal' of the League of Nations – was largely a rhetorical sleight of hand.

The February agreement, however, was being undermined by forces outside the Government's control. At first, much French comment supposed that the Russian Revolution*[9] was a new 1792, which by removing an oppressive, incompetent, and Germanophile regime would enable the awakened Russian giant to concentrate its energies on the war. In fact, the Revolution ruled out Russian participation in the Allied offensives projected for the spring. Authority devolved upon a Provisional Government, composed of Deputies from the Tsarist Parliament, in uneasy rivalry with the Petrograd Soviet of workers' and soldiers' representatives. Almost immediately the two clashed over war aims. The new Foreign Minister, Miliukov, exchanged private assurances with the Allies that the pre-Revolutionary secret treaties would remain intact,[10] while the Soviet resolved, in a celebrated formula, to press for 'a general peace without annexations or indemnities, on the basis of the free national development of all peoples'.[11]

Ribot's response to these events was complicated when his representatives in Petrograd took up radically opposed points of view. Paléologue soon concluded that anarchy was inevitable and that all that could be done was to delay the process by a few months, essential though even that might be for the outcome of the war.[12] But on 22 April Albert Thomas arrived on a special mission, bearing a letter by which the Ambassador was recalled.[13] Thomas was one of the most intelligent and energetic, as well as uncompromisingly patriotic, of the French Socialist leaders: he was an effective Minister of Armaments and won notoriety by haranguing the munitions workers at Le Creusot from the summit of an enormous pile of shells. Seeing his main purpose in Russia as being to secure a new offensive, he was swayed by his conversations with the Petrograd militants and concluded that the Allies must 'jettison ballast' if they hoped for an upsurge of 'revolutionary patriotism' like that of 1792.[14] But Paléologue demurred, advising Ribot to accept the rupture of the alliance rather than to renegotiate France's war aims.[15]

The question was therefore whether France should limit its

* The conventional usage will be followed of referring to the revolution of 17 Mar. 1917 (when Russia became a Republic) as the February Revolution; that of 6–7 Nov. 1917 (when the Bolsheviks took control of Petrograd) as the October Revolution.

objectives in the hope that a revivified Russian war effort – so far elusive – would result. Ribot had not abandoned all such hope, but he came down firmly on Paléologue's side by telegraphing that he would oppose any inter-Allied conference intended to revise the coalition's aims.[16] This decision, like the contemporaneous German one to allow Lenin to return to Petrograd, was a response to immediate exigencies in which the longer-term destiny of the Russian Revolution had a low priority. But war aims were now among the stakes of the domestic Russian struggle for power. When on 3 May the Provisional Government forwarded to its allies a manifesto repudiating annexations, Miliukov qualified the effect by sending a more belligerent covering note.[17] The note caused riots in Petrograd, Miliukov's fall from office, and the restructuring of the Government with a stronger representation from the Soviet.

Miliukov's fate was a warning that the war-aims question now endangered such domestic stability as Russia still possessed. It was also undermining the political truce in France itself. The leaders of the *SFIO* had already shifted their ground in response to President Wilson's speeches during the winter, and the French Left, like the Left all over Europe, was galvanized by the news from Petrograd. On 21 May Pierre Renaudel attempted to bring matters to a head by informing Ribot that the Socialists could support a claim to Alsace–Lorraine only within the frontiers of 1870 rather than those of 1790.[18] The diplomatic problem of fending off the Russians and the domestic one of preserving the *Union sacreé* were becoming inextricably confused.

Ribot responded to this convergence of internal and external pressure with tactics that would become habitual. On the one hand, the Council of Ministers unanimously reaffirmed the claim to the 1790 frontier.[19] On the other, in the Chamber on 22 May, he preserved the essentials of his position by combining a smoke-screen of democratic rhetoric with a prudent silence over the Saarland and the left bank that the Socialists did not challenge.[20] And an evasive reply to the Russian manifesto renewed Ribot's earlier distinction between 'conquests' – which were disavowed – and 'indispensable guarantees'.[21] For the time being this holding operation was sufficient to protect the war aims that the Government had inherited.

Within a week, however, Ribot and the Socialists were brought
into public confrontation in far more serious circumstances. On
22 April the Bureau of the Socialist International, quiescent
since its débâcle in 1914, invited the member-parties to a conference in Stockholm. Despite the protests of the *minoritaires*, the
SFIO executive decided to refuse, while the Council of Ministers agreed that if passports to Stockholm were requested they
should be withheld.[22] But the aspect of the question was altered
when the Russian Socialists subsequently launched a parallel
appeal of their own. And on 27 May two *SFIO* Deputies, Mar-
cel Cachin and Marius Moutet, returned to Paris from a trip to
Petrograd which Ribot had permitted in the hope that they
would urge on their Russian colleagues a 'war *à outrance*'.[23] Instead, they imported into France a whiff of revolutionary fervour, together with knowledge of the confidential Straits and
Doumergue Agreements. Under their entreaties, the *SFIO*'s
National Council resolved on the 28th to accept the Stockholm
invitation unconditionally, with Renaudel and the leadership
bowing to the consensus of the meeting. It was a historic decision, from which the *Union sacrée* never recovered. It came as
the mutinies and the strike wave reached their culmination and as
civilian morale, especially in the great cities and in the southern
half of France, fell to the lowest level of the war.[24] The decisions
of the next few days were taken with the Government under
pressure to deploy troops on the streets of Paris and with a sharp
fear of revolution in the air.[25]

Ribot learned of the Socialist resolution while he was conferring in London with the British. Unlike Lloyd George, who
favoured granting passports for the Stockholm Conference,
Ribot was sceptical, although the news from Paris caused him
temporarily to hesitate.[26] But he returned to find his Ministers
loyal to the policy of refusing contact with the enemy and therefore hostile to passports being given.[27] All the more did this
seem necessary once the Socialists, now informed about the
Straits and Doumergue Agreements, sent a delegation to ask for
both to be annulled.[28] The decisive event, however, was Pétain's
warning on the 31st, in the sub-committee of Ministers known
as the *Comité de guerre*, that if the Socialists went to Stockholm
he could not answer for discipline in the Army.[29] By comparison
with this, even the release of German troops made possible if

the Russians stayed on the defensive, in protest against the French decision, would be a lesser evil. Accordingly, prompted by two of the largest non-Socialist parliamentary groupings, the *Gauche radicale* and the *Fédération républicaine*, and with his Ministers' unanimous support, Ribot told the Chamber on 1 June that the passports would be refused.[30]

The issue was partly one of form – whether French citizens should meet enemy nationals in wartime – but also one of substance, for in the circumstances of 1917 a refusal to discuss war aims was also a refusal to reduce them. Until this point most decisions on foreign policy had been taken by the Ministers and officials immediately responsible, with limits on their freedom being set by the policies of France's allies and, less immediately, by the need to conciliate the political groups which made up the Government and its parliamentary support. In May 1917 not only diplomatic considerations – co-operation with the British and earning Russian goodwill – but also the domestic one of retaining Socialist support suggested that the *SFIO* should be allowed to go to Stockholm. Other Governments, in London and Berlin, felt the benefits outweighed the risks, and Ribot himself wavered in the matter. But for once the constraints placed on the Government by its supporters were exposed, and on the insistence of Pétain and of his own ministerial and parliamentary following Ribot responded to the challenge not with concessions but with resistance. At the same time, disagreement over foreign policy reopened the old domestic fissure between Left and Right.

This became clear when, after Ribot made his announcement, the Chamber went into secret session and conducted its most sustained debate on foreign policy of the entire war. Ribot eventually disclosed much more than he had intended, and read out portions both of the Cambon letter and of those exchanged between Pokrovski and Paléologue. But the even more compromising arrangement of 10 March for Russia's frontiers did not come to light. Both Briand and the Premier made long contributions. For Briand, France's duty was to claim the maximum from its allies now in order to bargain from strength in the peace negotiations.[31] Ribot was less forthright, giving the impression of disapproving of the secret treaties even if he did not disavow them. Indeed, he said, he would be willing to abandon the Doumergue Agreement if the Russians would forgo their gains under the Straits Agreement at the same time. Yet he insisted on the need for 'guarantees' – at least in the absence of a revolution which would bring down the military autocracy in Germany – and he was careful not to criticize the Cambon letter as he did the 'rigidity' of the Doumergue Agreement, or to suggest that the letter might cease to be official policy.[32] With this crux negotiated, Ribot's task was simple, and in the small hours of 5 June the Deputies passed by 467 to 52 a resolution proposed by Charles Dumont and accepted by the Government. The opposition was overwhelmingly Socialist, although Renaudel and nearly half his party voted with the Ministers.

The Chamber now expected from the war 'the liberation of the invaded territories, the return of Alsace–Lorraine . . . and the just reparation of damages. Far removed from any thought of conquering and subjugating foreign populations, it trusts that the efforts of the armies of the Republic and the Allied armies will permit, once Prussian militarism has been overthrown, lasting guarantees of peace and independence to be obtained for both large and small nations in an organization, to be prepared for at once, of the League of Nations.'[33] Harmony was apparently restored: yet the Dumont resolution was as ambiguous as the *Reichstag* resolution which followed it. 'Alsace–Lorraine' was, as usual, undefined. It was unclear whether the League of Nations alone was a sufficient 'guarantee', or not. And although 'conquest' was rejected, Ribot himself had said that the Doumergue Agreement provided not for conquests but for guarantees. Finally, did the overthrow of 'Prussian militarism' mean no more than victory, or did it also imply democratizing Germany's institutions?

Some of these uncertainties were resolved when the Senate in its turn went into secret session on 6 June. Here, with no left-wing critics to contend with, Ribot affirmed that his Government still aspired to the Alsace–Lorraine of 1790, and that a neutral and autonomous buffer State between France and Germany 'cannot be considered a conquest; it is a protective measure'.[34] His audience's patriotic enthusiasm spilled over into their final resolution for 'war until the restitution of Alsace–Lorraine, the punishment of crimes, the reparation of damages, the obtaining of guarantees against a renewed offensive by German militarism'.[35] The League of Nations, which Ribot wanted to be mentioned, was excluded through the efforts of Georges Clemenceau.[36] Yet even the tone of the Premier's own remarks, dispelling the Dumont resolution's equivocations, showed how for the Socialists that resolution had been a hollow victory from the moment of its achievement.

The secret session failed to still the ferment in the French Left, and for the remainder of the summer the war aims adopted in the spring of 1917 continued to figure both in France's relations with its allies and in domestic debate. On 13 June the Russian Provisional Government formally proposed an Allied conference to 'revise the definitive aims of the war'.[37] This met with a stony silence in the western capitals until Miliukov's successor, Tereshchenko, unexpectedly withdrew his own suggestion.[38] By the time a conference was mooted again, in September, few in France believed any longer that a tide of 'revolutionary patriotism' in Russia was possible.

In Parliament, however, the Socialists' resentment about the Stockholm passports continued to simmer. On 28 July the new German Chancellor, Michaelis, dealt a theatrical stroke by making public a substantially accurate account of Ribot's and Briand's statements to the secret session, presumably on the basis of information from a French Deputy.[39] In the Chamber on 31 July and 2 August Ribot held wearily to the established line. Pressed point-blank by Cachin to disavow the Paléologue–Pokrovski letters, he replied: 'I will not do here what you request. When I say that we repudiate all annexations . . . does that not suffice?'[40] Tereshchenko, too, was trying to ascertain Ribot's precise attitude towards the letters, and offered to publish them if the French Government desired. With characteristic tortuousness, Ribot consented only on condition that the Straits Agreement was published simultaneously, and Tereshchenko, afraid of complications with his own public opinion, promptly backed away.[41]

As late, therefore, as the middle of August, and even into September, Ribot successfully parried the efforts of the French and Russian Socialists to tie him down over the February arrangements for the left bank of the Rhine. Those arrangements were never formally abandoned between the summer of

1917 and the adoption of very similar claims by the Clemenceau ministry at the end of the war. Yet after August 1917 it grows harder to trace them as a continuing element in official policy; and certain statements of that policy contradict them. The plans for the Rhineland and the Saar were not rejected, but the directors of French diplomacy turned their attention to other concerns. In July the Russians launched their long-awaited offensive. It failed; and the breakdown of all authority in the former Tsarist Empire accelerated. The Provisional Government's bargaining power was destroyed, and it was no longer necessary to humour it over the Stockholm Conference or over other projects to revise the Allies' aims. But Tsarist Russia had been alone among France's partners in endorsing Briand's plans for the Saar and the left bank, and for the moment those plans were made irrelevant by the collapse of Russian power.

3. *Painlevé, the General Staff, and the Austrian Option, July–August 1917*

Since the sixteenth-century friendship between Francis I and the Turks French rulers had sought out eastern counterbalances to their Central European rivals. As the scale of the Russian disaster became apparent the authorities scrutinized the wide horizons of Eastern Europe in quest of a successor to the Tsar. In both the Foreign Ministry and the General Staff there were those who argued that in Austria such a successor could be discovered. But by June 1917 the Sixte initiative had foundered, and that contacts were reopened through another channel owed much to the exceptional position within the Government enjoyed by Painlevé. The War Minister was a former Professor of mathematics at the *École polytechnique*, and an intelligent administrator, if an indifferent performer in Parliament. A full generation younger than Ribot, and some way to the Left of him in domestic questions, he was tipped as one of his most probable successors.

The fragmentary evidence available strongly suggests that Painlevé favoured a compromise peace. Through his mistress, and her Austrian brother and sister, the German agents in Switzerland received a stream of reports on his intentions. In March 1917 it appeared that if he became Prime Minister Painlevé would accept a 'reasonable understanding' with Germany; in July that he was ready to make peace without waiting for the Americans, by exchanging colonial and commercial concessions for Alsace–Lorraine.[42] More remarkable was the sympathy with such ideas that existed among Painlevé's subordinates. The Second Bureau of the General Staff, under Colonel Goubet, was the centre of a foreign intelligence network second only to the Quai d'Orsay's; and during 1917 it passed on from analysis to policy recommendations and eventually to diplomacy on its own account.

Military thinking under Painlevé combined Anglophobia with a curious mixture of pessimism and over-ambition. A memorandum by the Third Bureau of the General Staff on 12 July argued that Germany was likely to remain a Great Power after the war, and that France's true interest lay in an alliance with Berlin. But it posed conditions which would make such a *rapprochement* impossible: not just Alsace–Lorraine, but also a protective glacis, provided at the least by a defensible frontier north of that of 1814 and ideally by France, Belgium, and Holland annexing the entire left bank of the Rhine.[43] Painlevé's *Sous-Chef du Cabinet*, Commandant Herscher, offered a possible solution to this dilemma. He agreed that France had no interest in an 'excessive abasement' of Germany, for the latter was needed as a balance to the Royal Navy if France's colonies and foreign trade were not to be at Britain's mercy. However, he saw the key to French security in the future not as the Rhine frontier, but as a restructured Austria–Hungary incorporating a reunited Poland. With this achieved, the restoration of Alsace–Lorraine would allow a lasting reconciliation with the Germans as well as being 'the best antidote to revolution' in France itself.[44]

If both Herscher and the Third Bureau suffered from wishful thinking about enemy intentions, this was in part caused by their revulsion against the course that Government policy was taking. France, they feared, was locked into an interminable conflict with Berlin which would ruin the country's social cohesion and military strength to the principal advantage of the Anglo-Saxon Powers. Even Ferdinand Foch, the fiery new Chief of the General Staff, shared the pessimism of Pétain and of Painlevé himself about the immediate prospects on the Western

Front, and believed it was time to concentrate on bringing Austria to terms.[45] In June 1917 a chance to act upon these musings was presented when Count Revertera, a highly placed member of the Austrian court, made known to one of Goubet's informants that he desired a conversation with Count Armand of the Second Bureau. Armand was a mysterious figure who appears to have stayed in contact with the Germans after the outbreak of war. His strange behaviour in the following weeks may have a sinister, if still obscure, explanation.[46]

The Second Bureau's imagination was fired by the possibility of an Austrian separate peace which would smash for good the German plans for a *Mitteleuropa*, or close political, military, and economic association with the Habsburg Empire after the war.[47] Foch, Pétain, and subsequently Lloyd George approved the principle of a conversation.[48] Ribot, however, agreed only on condition that Armand listened to Revertera without trying to open a negotiation.[49] Unperturbed, Painlevé authorized Armand to speak generally of the influence a reformed Austria might enjoy over 'a restored Poland and even the German lands where she was formerly pre-eminent'.[50] And Armand, exceeding his authority in turn, told Revertera categorically when they met in Switzerland on 7 August that Austria could expect Bavaria, Silesia, and a Poland restored to its frontiers of 1772.[51]

The conversation was therefore bedevilled by acts of insubordination on the French side as well as by a basic misunderstanding; for it was clearly with a general, not a separate, peace in mind that Revertera responded by offering to forward to Berlin the Allies' conditions for an agreement with Germany. Yet, in spite of Painlevé's feeling that Armand had been 'too absolute',[52] he sent him back for a second meeting with Revertera on 22 August at which the Frenchman produced a set of 'terms' for Germany as well. Armand asked for the Alsace–Lorraine of 1814 and for arrangements to prevent military preparations on the left bank of the Rhine, although indicating that Indochina or Madagascar could be ceded in return. About Silesia and Bavaria he remained silent, for a general peace with the Central Powers was not to be granted on the same conditions as a separate one with Vienna.[53] It appeared that Armand was holding out for *both* the guarantees envisaged by Herscher and the Third Bureau; but a strengthened Austrian counterweight detached from Germany was the preferred solution, with protection on the Rhine forming part only of a more remote multilateral compromise. Either way all the aspirations towards *rapprochement* had resulted in proposals which still cut right across the Germans' aims.

For whom did Armand speak? Certainly, at least in the first conversation, for the Second Bureau; but not for the Council of Ministers, or even for Ribot and the Quai d'Orsay, to whom the dossier on the episode was never forwarded.[54] A question mark remains over Painlevé himself. The War Minister was pessimistic and willing to sound the enemy out, although he was never prepared to abandon Alsace–Lorraine, and he hoped to gain much more if victory permitted it. Most probably he was badly served by Armand, like Briand by Doumergue, and his vague statements of intent were converted into something more categorical. Again like Briand, Painlevé maintained a channel to the enemy to keep his options open; he did not speak for the Government as a whole, and the affair was treated much less seriously in Paris than in Vienna and Berlin. Finally, it was to Austria rather than to Germany that Painlevé directed his most serious efforts, and at the end of August he told Ribot that Vienna was unready for a separate peace and the contact had therefore been suspended.[55] The War Minister and his subordinates asked more searching questions about French policy than did the officials of the Quai d'Orsay, and more pitilessly juxtaposed the cost of the war against its likely gains. But they, too, were unable to renounce France's fundamental goals of security against Germany and the reconquest of Alsace–Lorraine.

4. *Britain, America, and the Readjustment of French War Aims, March–November 1917*

Throughout the spring and summer months French policy was being adapted to the most brutal displacement of the international system since 1870. Against the enfeeblement of Russia and of France itself was set the entry into the war of the United States; but the new Power's military capacity and its thrust of policy were unknown quantities. In the final weeks of crisis between Washington and Berlin the French authorities showed the same circumspection as hitherto. Briand cautiously welcomed

American intervention,[56] but Berthelot regarded the new allies as 'necessary undesirables',[57] and one official feared that their arrival would 'advance perhaps by many decades the era when they will intervene in the affairs of Europe as in those of a contemptible little continent which they will crush with the weight of their mass'.[58] Even before Wilson's 'Peace without Victory' speech in January 1918 it had been apparent that American diplomacy was of a kind unfamiliar in Europe, and Ribot himself foresaw 'that before Germany has been thoroughly beaten she may propose terms which President Wilson may consider acceptable, but which would not be acceptable at all to France and England, and that Wilson may put pressure on the Entente Allies to accept them'.[59]

Until the spring of 1917 the relationship between Britain, France, and Tsarist Russia had been one of rough equality; from then on the United States, although always more of a *primus inter pares* than was Germany on the opposing side, advanced towards the status of a dominant partner. In March 1917 the French Government hoped that Washington would send only a small force of volunteers, whose political leverage would be slight, but after the upheavals of the summer a mass American conscript army became essential to French strategy.[60] Without the US Treasury loans – likened by French statesmen to the *'Pactole'*, the fabled river of gold – without American shipping, wheat, and oil, without above all the prospect of near-limitless reinforcement in armaments and men at the very moment of the French Army mutinies and of Russia's withdrawal from the fighting, it is doubtful if the Allies could have won the war. Yet at first the American contribution was disappointing, relieving an Allied financial situation that was growing desperate, but doing little to solve the mounting shortages of shipping, food, and manpower. American aid remained less tangible than psychological, and its psychological effect was double-edged, for Wilson intended his pronouncements to encourage the left-wing opposition not only in the Central Powers but also in the Western European Allies.* This added one more complication to the task of preserving political harmony in France.

* Unless qualified, 'the Allies' will be taken as including the Americans after April 1917, although strictly the USA entered the war as an 'associated Power'.

Like the Russian Revolution, American entry was a challenge to which traditional diplomacy seemed inadequate. Jusserand was able and experienced, but had not established a close relationship with Wilson, and often put a more favourable gloss than his superiors on the President's oracular remarks. On 15 April André Tardieu, officer, Deputy, leader-writer for the most prestigious Paris daily, *Le Temps*, and one of the most dazzling stars in the French political firmament, was appointed High Commissioner in the United States.[61] Confined by his brief to technical co-operation, he soon encroached on political affairs as well. At the end of the month, Viviani, now Ribot's Minister of Justice, arrived in Washington to discuss, among other subjects, war aims. Although Balfour disclosed many of the Allies' secret treaties to the American leaders during a simultaneous visit of his own, neither now nor later did the French apprise Wilson of the Cambon letter and their understanding with the Tsar.

Viviani did, however, give the Americans partial satisfaction in another respect. The treatment meted out to Germany, he hinted, might be milder if 'Prussian militarism' were ended and the country equipped with democratic institutions as an earnest of its good intentions.[62] Ribot himself, unlike earlier French leaders, had suggested that the best 'guarantee' of a lasting peace would be for the German people to destroy the 'military despotism' and 'armed autocracy' in Berlin.[63] Appeals of this kind were in part an olive branch to the Socialists and to Wilson, and might sharpen the dissensions on the German home front. Yet in the security debate of the preceding winter the value of a German revolution had hardly been discussed and it is unlikely that all the leading French officials agreed with the course now being adopted.[64] Ribot was the only French wartime statesman to suggest that German democratization was a possible *alternative* rather than a supplement to more concrete guarantees, and the Clemenceau Government eventually claimed against the fledgling Weimar Republic securities similar to those desired by Briand against the Kaiser two years earlier. Establishing liberal democracy in Russia and in Germany was never so important for the French leaders as it was for Wilson and for House.

The United States entered the conflict uncommitted to any of the war aims that successive French Governments had elaborated, and suspicious of such of them as it knew. On 6 August a confidential note from Wilson urged his allies to accept the Russian invitation to a conference to revise their aims, and there to abandon both territorial 'aggrandizement' and 'exclusive and aggressive economic arrangements'.[65] Ribot's habitual caution was therefore more than usually evident in his first attempts to harness American power in support of French objectives. He began by authorizing Jusserand to propose a successor to the Paris Economic Conference of June 1916, which this time would implicate Washington in its decisions.[66] After a month of taking soundings, Jusserand warned that the Americans' 'instinctive fear . . . of committing themselves' might make them refuse a conference altogether, or at best only limit rather than extend the existing resolutions.[67]

Similarly, when Ribot raised the League of Nations, he found that Wilson thought discussion of it 'premature'.[68] Wilson may have disapproved of Ribot's speeches to the Chamber, in which the Premier had envisaged not a universal body but an association of liberal democracies not so very different from a prolongation of the wartime alliance.[69] As usual with his gestures towards the League, however, Ribot had in mind not only Wilson but also the growing internationalist movement in France itself, and especially the need to dampen Socialist agitation in Parliament.[70] For this reason, on 22 July he set up a commission to study the League, headed by Léon Bourgeois and compósed largely of academics and Foreign Ministry officials.[71] The commission quickly showed a preference for a markedly stronger type of organization than was favoured in Britain and the USA.

Changes in French opinion also made pressing the third of the subjects over which Ribot approached Wilson in these weeks: Alsace–Lorraine. At the end of June the Government learned that the *SFIO*'s National Council favoured settling the provinces' fate by a plebiscite, and that Thomas had said the same on his return from Russia.[72] At a banquet on 4 July Ribot, with his Ministers' approval, expressly ruled this out, and the hapless Thomas was forced on the same occasion publicly to acquiesce.[73] In the same month Daniel Blumenthal, a former mayor of Colmar in Alsace, was sent to help Tardieu orchestrate a propaganda campaign designed to win over to the French claim an initially sceptical American public.[74] But when

Blumenthal was introduced to Wilson, the President was visibly perturbed by the arguments that he deployed against a plebiscite.[75] Then, on 20 July, Poincaré found Ribot 'very preoccupied' after learning from Paul Cambon that Lloyd George was evading all commitment on the subject of the two provinces.[76] Indeed, both Cambon and his brother shared doubts that were probably widespread in official circles about whether in a plebiscite Alsace–Lorraine would opt for reunion with France.[77] With the Italian Foreign Minister, Sonnino, also keeping quiet,[78] it appeared as if the claim even to the first of the territories on which France had designs had been thrown back into the balance. For the next few months French Governments were repeatedly alarmed by the attitude of their Allies towards Alsace–Lorraine.

At the end of three years of war France had to start again virtually from scratch, for it had elicited hardly more British than American support for its European aims. The resolutions of the Paris Economic Conference and the reply to Wilson of 10 January 1917 were under attack in the British Cabinet as mistakes, which had needlessly stimulated popular resistance in the Central Powers.[79] Paul Cambon chose this inauspicious moment to read out to Balfour the letter which had been pigeonholed since 12 January. The Foreign Secretary noted the main points, including the 'rather wild project' of a buffer State, which he 'said nothing to encourage'.[80] But the conversation had no sequel, and Cambon did not mention the Doumergue Agreement at all before it became public knowledge at the end of July: a glaring example of the lack of confidence between the two countries.

This lack of confidence was the more serious because Britain's relative power within the coalition had reached its height. British shipping and economic and financial aid remained indispensable to France; and the French Army, until now the main weight in the other half of the scales, was obliged in the summer and autumn of 1917 to leave the initiative on the Western Front to Sir Douglas Haig. In the diplomatic sphere, Britain was needed both as a potential counter to the Americans and as a post-war guarantor. Yet London had traditionally stood aloof from continental rivalries, and Anglo-French relations were still riddled with suspicion and misunderstanding. The French emerged from the rubble of the Russian alliance into a new and harsher world.

The coalition's diplomatic unity was now tested by an attempt at mediation from the Vatican. In essence, Benedict XV proposed a return to the status quo ante, with disputes such as that between France and Germany being settled by negotiations in which 'the aspirations of the population' would be taken into account.[81] The French authorities supposed the note had been conceived in association with the Central Powers;[82] it had certainly followed papal soundings in Vienna and Berlin. And it came after repeated rumours that Germany was ready to compromise over Alsace–Lorraine.[83]

There was, therefore, reason to believe that the note was a cover for more concrete enemy proposals. Nevertheless, when put to the test most of the French Catholic press and hierarchy criticized the initiative and did not want it to be pursued.[84] The Council of Ministers condemned the note, and Ribot told his allies that in his view nothing more was called for than a simple acknowledgement of receipt.[85] Telegraphing subsequently to Jusserand, he summed up his policy in the same way as had his predecessors on such occasions. To speak of peace as imminent would be 'to enter into Germany's game . . . . Until the United States has made the decisive effort it is preparing we shall not be in a favourable position to negotiate.'[86]

Neither Britain nor America were willing to dismiss the note so curtly. The British prepared a reply for transmission by de Salis, their representative at the Vatican, and Ribot, who had not seen the relevant telegram and supposed the communication would be oral only, associated himself with the *démarche*.[87] When de Salis overstepped his instructions and handed the telegram over, France seemed to have endorsed a document which, by inviting enemy assurances over Belgian independence, was conceived very much from the British point of view. Barrère reported in alarm that the telegram might entangle the Allies in a 'mechanism' from which they could not extricate themselves without grave damage to their diplomatic solidarity and civilian morale.[88] Ribot promptly telegraphed to London and was able to stop the British contacts with the Papacy from going further,[89] but his position was endangered from another quarter when on 27 August Wilson unilaterally published his own reply to Benedict XV.

Ribot had wanted no reply; or at least that France should be consulted first.[90] Yet as alarming as the circumstances of Wilson's message was its content, for the President stated more forcefully than ever his thesis of the two Germanies: the autocracy, and the masses, to whom, if their genuine representatives came to power, might be granted a more lenient peace. Wilson also made ill-concealed criticisms of his allies' plans for 'punitive damages, the dismemberment of empires, the establishment of selfish and exclusive economic leagues . . . .'[91]

By seizing the initiative in this way the American President had placed his partners in the dilemma of accepting him as their spokesman or of breaking the public unity of the coalition. Ribot's first reaction was that France and Britain must assert their independence, and he forwarded to London a proposed communiqué which would implicitly dissociate the two Governments from Wilson's reply.[92] Balfour dissented, arguing that by saying merely that they would make no addition to Wilson's statement they could conciliate the President while not explicitly supporting his more contentious remarks. In concurring in this judgement, Ribot registered his failure both to prevent his Allies from answering the Pope and to assert France's diplomatic freedom.[93]

The episode gave the French Government a foretaste of the more spectacular way in which its hand was forced in the Armistice negotiations fourteen months later. Ribot had decided to refuse conversations with the Central Powers and to gamble on victory being possible with American assistance: a gamble whose outcome was still far from certain. Time was perhaps on France's side in the war with Germany; but time was also altering its status in the coalition from partnership to inferiority. After the summer of 1917 the war aims given prominence in French diplomacy were those it seemed likely that the Anglo-Saxons would accept; but Wilson's reply to the Pope was the clearest evidence yet of how narrow was the common ground. In addition, the British had shown that if forced to a decision they valued good relations with America more highly than they valued them with France. Wilson, Jusserand observed, had thus been able by default to assume the leadership of the alliance.

The more France grew dependent on American assistance of all kinds, he feared, the more 'a Head of State assuredly well disposed to us, but . . . who naturally cannot attach the same importance to our peace terms as we do ourselves, will be free to choose the hour and the circumstances of the ending of the conflict'.[94]

For the remainder of the Ribot Ministry, and its successor under Painlevé, France practised the diplomacy of renunciation. This was clearest outside Europe, where French aims were challenged not only by the strictures of Wilson and the Russians against *all* imperialism but also by the efforts of Britain and Italy to expand their shares of the dying Ottoman Empire at France's expense. By the end of 1917 a largely British force had conquered much of Palestine, and Lloyd George's Government had won Zionist approval for a British administration of the territory. Against this combination of force with a version of national self-determination the French colonialists' enthusiasm for the Holy Land counted for little.[95]

Within Europe, however, the initiatives launched by Ribot in July grew into lobbying of a more systematic kind. French diplomacy in London and in Washington followed a new but far less grand design, which was to remain the centrepiece of policy until the following year. In Western Europe it was concentrated on Alsace–Lorraine, in economic life on the control of raw materials, and in Eastern Europe on a resurrected Poland.

The Western European problem was partly the Franco-German frontier itself; partly the anchor for that frontier to the north. Clémentel continued to pursue a closer economic association with the Belgians, but was unable to reach agreement with them either on co-operation against Germany or over bilateral commercial ties, and after June 1917 conversations ceased.[96] In the same month, however, Ribot clarified and limited French intentions towards Luxemburg. In a discussion with the Belgian Minister, de Gaiffier, embodied afterwards in an exchange of notes, he specified that 'the annexation of Luxemburg . . . did not figure in France's war aims', and undertook to discourage any annexationist agitation.[97] Jules Cambon privately went further, and indicated to the Belgians that France would positively support their claim.[98] In contrast to their predecessors, therefore, Ribot and Cambon appeared to be writing off both France's own interest in the Grand Duchy and any chance of winning a Belgian *quid pro quo*.

Further south, French ambitions in the spring of 1917 had reached out to the Saarland and the Rhine; but by the autumn Allied support was uncertain over even the Alsace–Lorraine of 1870. According to an intercepted Belgian telegram, Wilson doubted whether the inhabitants of southern and central France were committed to rejoining the lost provinces, and himself considered their recovery might not be a *sine qua non* of peace. Ribot asked Jusserand to make plain that 'there can be no lasting peace without reparation of the violence done to France in 1871':[99] of the claim he had earlier upheld to the frontier of 1790 he made no mention. Although the Ambassador was able to extract more definite assurances of sympathy from House and from Lansing (the American Secretary of State),[100] Wilson still held back from a public declaration, and confusion over the question of a plebiscite remained.

French pressure on the British also had only incomplete success. When Painlevé became Prime Minister, he hoped to use his friendship with Lloyd George to extract from him a public promise of support for the restoration of Alsace–Lorraine without a plebiscite.[101] In a meeting at Boulogne on 25 September he reduced the British Premier's misgivings by insisting that this was something over which France itself would never compromise.[102] But it took a further trip by Painlevé to London before Lloyd George declared, in typically cloudy language, that 'however long this war may last, this country intends to stand by . . . France until she redeems her oppressed children from the degradation of a foreign yoke'.[103]

These new concerns of French diplomacy were paralleled by a reorientation of French strategy. Under Joffre that strategy had been moulded by the needs of co-operation with the Russians and the British, and had shown a Clausewitzian concern to pierce the German front and roll back the enemy to the Rhine. A *stratégie des gages* – winning territory as a bargaining counter for negotiation – was explicitly denied.[104] But collaboration with the British broke down after Nivelle's offensive, and the French High Command interpreted Haig's ill-starred campaign in Flanders as an attempt to gain control of the Belgian ports for precisely such a political design. A decisive memorandum by the Third Bureau of Pétain's staff was subsequently approved by the Commander-in-Chief. France, it argued, would be best positioned in the peace negotiations if it could conserve its manpower but at the same time take a prominent part in the next assault on Germany by attacking in Alsace.[105] There, in contrast to the northern battlegrounds of 1915 and 1916, could be won such 'valuable pawns' in enemy territory as the Nönnenbruch potash basin and the textiles and engineering of Mulhouse.[106] In the event, the hour of a *stratégie des gages* was postponed by the German offensives of March–July 1918, but the acceptance of the Alsace plan reveals much about the French authorities' state of mind in the preceding autumn. The plan did not exclude the complete defeat of Germany, but it might also enable France to salvage something in a compromise peace. There is no direct evidence that Painlevé's interest in such a compromise was connected with the change in strategy, but it seems highly probable.[107]

In the sphere of economic war aims American entry presented Clémentel and Ribot with both a threat and an unprecedented opportunity. On the one hand, Jusserand reported on 30 August that there was no possibility of Wilson agreeing to a second conference like that of June 1916.[108] On the other, all the leading world exporters of food and raw materials, except the Argentine, were now on the Allied side. Moreover, since November 1916 the Allies had successfully controlled the international wheat trade through a Wheat Executive, with which the Americans co-operated. Clémentel was impressed by this, and by the alarm that the prospect of a post-war economic boycott caused the German Government and public. Finally, the grain shortage of 1917, following the coal shortage of 1916, underlined the handicap which France would suffer if it had to compete for raw materials in the free market before its industries had been reconstructed.

Clémentel set out his reflections on these events when he visited London in August 1917.[109] He did not abandon the resolutions of the Paris Economic Conference, but he singled out one of them as decisive and left the rest to gather dust. If similar controls to those on wheat were extended to a dozen key commodities, he argued, the Allies would have a *'gage'* to set against the territory held by the enemy, and even if they stayed on the defensive the mere threat of a post-war blockade could bring the Central Powers to terms. Clémentel's new suggestion was not only narrower than its predecessor; it was also a means towards a victory on the cheap, a pawn analogous to that envisaged by Pétain, which could be relatively painlessly acquired and yet would strengthen France's hand in a negotiated compromise. The plan had important post-war implications, for such controls on world trade in commodities would supposedly be more efficient than armed force in compelling delinquent Governments to accept arbitration in international disputes. They would also assure France itself of sufficient 'means of livelihood' during the difficult transition to a peacetime economy.

Clémentel's ideas were now endorsed by the Ministry as a whole. At La Fère-Champenoise on 6 September Ribot made his most direct appeal yet to the German people to safeguard the peace of the world by overthrowing 'the baleful tyranny of a military despotism'. But should the German people not respond, it was its 'economic interests' which would suffer most from Allied counter-measures.[110] A month later Poincaré, Painlevé, and Ribot 'warmly approved' an unofficial letter from Clémentel to Wilson.[111] In it, the Commerce Minister depicted his proposals both as certain to make the German people force peace upon its rulers and as 'the most efficient sanction' of a future League of Nations.[112]

The Clémentel plan was intended as a golden bridge whereby the maritime powers could be drawn into commitments on the ever more pressing problem of France's post-war economic security. It was also associated with an attempt to foster revolution in Germany. This attempt was adopted with reluctance and was quickly abandoned. Revolution was seized on less as a means of reforming Germany's behaviour in the future than as an instrument which might help win the war when few other instruments remained at hand. But the plan needed British and American co-operation, and Clémentel's letter to Wilson remained without reply. Revisiting London in October, the Commerce Minister urged that for his scheme to see the light of day Britain and France must give the President 'the impression that we are united'.[113] This he was unable to obtain, and he left

London with little more than personal sympathy from Stanley, the President of the Board of Trade. When the Painlevé Ministry fell the raw materials plan was left suspended, neither the direct approach to Wilson nor the attempt at combination with the British having clarified the views of France's partners.

Few questions with which the French leaders were concerned were liable to disturb the European balance more profoundly than was that of Poland. Before the Tsar fell the French pressed intermittently for greater autonomy to be given to the Poles, but they feared that an *independent* Poland, deprived of Russian backing, would become a German satellite.[114] The February Revolution seemed at first to offer a way out of this dilemma. The Provisional Government intimated to its Allies that it meant to grant independence to a reunified Poland, while remaining in a 'military union' with it.[115] It even invited them to associate themselves with these pledges. Although Ribot wished to confine himself to promising independence, and feared a public undertaking to reunify the country as well, the French Government duly joined those in London and in Rome in declaring its solidarity with Russia 'in the intention of reviving Poland with its territorial integrity . . . .'[116] Ribot conquered his misgivings and came privately to favour a Poland reconstituted in the historic boundaries of 1772,[117] while a Presidential decree of 4 June set up an autonomous Polish army on the Western Front in the hope that this would be a vehicle for French influence in the infant State.[118]

It became less and less apparent how these promises to the Poles could be fulfilled. With the Russian army crippled, the Central Powers' grip could be relaxed only by a decisive victory on the Western Front: a contingency which after April seemed remote. While France remained officially committed to an independent Poland, Painlevé's officials in the General Staff inclined towards attempting to divide the Central Powers at Russia's expense, and in August Armand offered sovereignty over a reunited Poland to Vienna. There remained the possibility, however, of an independent Poland strong enough to resist subjection to Germany even without Russian support. But for this the Western Allies would have to do more than countersign Russian undertakings to the Poles and themselves assume responsibility for creating an independent and reunited State. Staking national prestige on this was a desperate expedient in late 1917, and yet the bankruptcy of the Russian and the Austrian options drove the French, at a moment of retreat elsewhere, into paradoxical boldness in the east.

The decision involved a fateful choice between Russian and Polish aspirations; but the altered balance in Eastern Europe gave the French new reason to prefer the latter. In August the Polish expatriates set up a Polish National Committee to represent their cause in Rome, Paris, Washington, and London. To recognize the Committee could be construed as favouring the territorial gains from Russia which its President, Dmowski, desired.[119] None the less, on 20 September Ribot acknowledged it as the 'official Polish organization' in France, and declared his sympathy with its objective of the 'reconstitution' of an 'independent and sovereign Polish State'.[120] The Premier acted without consulting his still hesitant Allies, and afterwards urged them to follow suit, arguing that because the Committee would be established only in the western capitals the Russian objections to it could be ignored.[121].

Recognition of the Committee was a major victory for de Margerie and the Polish party in the Quai d'Orsay. De Margerie now hoped to win over his superiors and then the Allies as a whole to a proclamation that 'the reconstitution of a united, independent Poland with its own maritime coast and the mouth of the Vistula is . . . a peace condition on a par with restoring Belgium or Serbia'.[122] By late October Ribot's successor as Foreign Minister, Barthou, saw 'no disadvantage' in such an announcement;[123] Painlevé, however, warned that 'the present *military* circumstances' precluded any promise of other than 'a very general character', and in particular that it would be 'premature' to give an undertaking about access to the Baltic.[124]

For a moment, it seemed that Painlevé and the Foreign Ministry would come into head-on conflict over Eastern Europe: indeed, it was surprising there had not been such a conflict long before. But at this point reports came in that the Central Powers had agreed on an 'Austrian solution' to the Polish question: that the provinces formerly under Austrian and Russian rule would be united in a new kingdom linked by a personal union with the Habsburg monarchy. Unless the Allies could match this with a counter-offer, the General Staff believed, the enemy was likely to seduce the Poles.[125] Painlevé therefore took the view that at the forthcoming Allied conference in Paris it would be necessary 'to oppose clearly . . . the Allies' solution to that which the Central Powers suggest or declare'.[126] There was now unanimity within the Government that it was through an independent Poland that security in Eastern Europe must be found.

5. War and Peace under the Painlevé Ministry, September–November 1917

Under Painlevé the French home front entered its most dangerous phase of weakness since June. Civilian morale had recovered only feebly, and in November it was shaken by a combination of food shortages with bad news from abroad, especially Russia.[127] When Painlevé took over he prevailed on a reluctant and exhausted Ribot to continue at the Quai d'Orsay; Thomas, exasperated by Ribot's conduct in the successive crises since March, left office in protest.[128] The *Union sacrée* had run its course, and although the Socialists refrained from outright opposition the inexperienced Painlevé had even greater trouble in handling Parliament than did Ribot earlier. In September the Chamber was prey to 'an extraordinary pessimism and malaise'; by November the Ministers agreed that 'one third of the Deputies . . . desire peace, without daring to admit it'.[129] In public Painlevé and Ribot reaffirmed their loyalty to the ambiguous formulas of the Dumont resolution, including that of 'guarantees'.[130] The Premier made a new concession to the Socialists, however, by declaring that France's aims were 'independent of the outcome of battles', and would not expand if victory came.[131] And in private the Ministry's discussions of the military situation were sombre,[132] with its pessimism being shown by its attraction to Pétain's *stratégie des gages* and the Clémentel plan.

In these bleak conditions Painlevé was called upon to judge the most important diplomatic contact established with the Germans during the war. In April 1917 the Baron von der Lancken, head of the Political Department of the German occupation administration in Brussels, secured authority from the Berlin leaders to use his Belgian contacts to sound out French politicians and officials and to offer token cessions in Alsace and Lorraine.[133] Von der Lancken had been Counsellor at the German Embassy in Paris before 1914, and his attention soon concentrated on Briand, as the only man with the authority and the rhetorical power to win the French public over to a compromise.[134]

As usual in such First World War negotiations, the intermediaries muddied the waters by exaggerating to each side the goodwill of the other. In June 1917 Briand was approached by the Countess de Mérode, who implied that the Germans were ready to compromise over the lost provinces.[135] Briand reported the episode to Poincaré, who apparently warned him to take affairs no further; Ribot, by his own account, was not informed.[136] Undeterred, Briand agreed in principle to meet von der Lancken in Switzerland,[137] although only at the end of August did the contacts enter their decisive stage. Briand was now given fresh assurances by new intermediaries, the Baron Coppée and his son, and by the Belgian Premier, de Broqueville. According to the latter, the approach was in good faith and the Germans might be willing to return Alsace–Lorraine if equal treatment for their post-war commerce were guaranteed.[138]

Once Painlevé's Ministry had been formed, an enthusiastic Briand proceeded to consult its members. He found the new Prime Minister eager to approve the interview.[139] Indeed, Painlevé believed that peace negotiations might be imminent, and that though the Allies' present position on the Western Front was favourable for bargaining, it must deteriorate if the war of attrition continued.[140] Unlike Ribot, therefore, Painlevé set little store by the contribution of the Americans, and believed the time to negotiate was now. Poincaré, too, although probably for different reasons, seems at first to have favoured the meeting Briand proposed.[141] Ribot felt the German approach was almost certainly a 'snare', but acquiesced when on the 18th Painlevé told Briand that he would approve a first conversation if the Allies were agreed.[142] Two days later Briand gave Ribot a letter to be used as a basis for consulting them. With this the affair reached the end of its first, Franco-Belgian, stage.

Briand was probably sincere in his affirmations that a peace was possible which would satisfy French honour over Alsace–Lorraine. But he appears to have been misled by de Broqueville

and the Coppées, and in turn to have made their statements
more definite when he consulted the members of the Government. The evidence from the German side neither confirms
Briand's assertions about Alsace–Lorraine nor vindicates
Ribot's fear that the whole manœuvre was intended to be
publicized.[143] But instead of being judged simply on such
grounds the affair was complicated by acts of bad faith on the
part of the two men. Briand's letter of 20 September set out a
list of prior conditions for a meeting with von der Lancken,
without clarifying whether the Germans had accepted these or
not. It failed to specify Briand's grounds for believing that his
informers were accurate and that the German could be trusted.
Finally, although it excluded a separate peace by France, the
conditions that it listed made no mention of the claims of any
other Ally.[144] In approaching France's partners, Ribot and Jules
Cambon were therefore placed in some embarrassment, which
they overcame by forwarding neither the letter itself nor a summary of its contents. Instead, they sent a telegram to the leading
French Ambassadors in which they carefully marked their distance from Briand and gave the impression that he had wished
to proceed without the Allies being consulted.[145]

Given this wording, the chorus of disapproval which filtered
back from the Allied Chancelleries was predictable.[146] Painlevé
himself told Lloyd George on 25 September that his Ministers
wanted to avoid all conversations 'until the German military
power was broken'.[147] This was certainly the view of the half-
dozen Ministers whose opinion he had sought,[148] and it is likely
that in the light of their objections he had changed his mind.
But unlike Ribot, Painlevé did not see the German offer as a
'snare'; on the contrary, he told Lloyd George that he doubted
'whether France would continue fighting if it were offered both
nine-tenths of Alsace–Lorraine and the whole of Belgium'.[149]
Painlevé and Ribot might differ in their estimates of von der
Lancken's sincerity, but they were united in their fear that
French morale had sunk so low that the conversation would lead
on to a separate peace. On the 23rd Briand was therefore told
he could not go to Switzerland, although he secretly remained in
contact with the Belgian intermediaries until January 1918[150]
and his simmering resentment of Ribot's action now caused a
first-class parliamentary storm.

After von der Lancken left the intended rendezvous frustrated, a Franco-German compromise grew more remote than ever. On 9 October the German Foreign Minister told the *Reichstag* that his Government would never make the smallest concession over Alsace–Lorraine.[151] In the Chamber three days later Ribot reiterated the French Government's determination not to waive its claim. At the same time he let slip an aside about German approaches to a 'high political personality', in which Alsace–Lorraine had been promised in return for a separate peace.[152] Briand retaliated by reading out in the Chamber corridors his letter of 20 September, and the Government accepted a debate in secret session for the 16th. It took the form of a personal duel between Ribot and Briand, in which the latter was able to shift the controversy to the propriety of his personal conduct, and to obscure the questions of substance. Painlevé, playing the same equivocal part as he had since the beginning, denied that his Government had refused an 'honourable peace', but did nothing to defend his colleague. The Socialist who had prompted the debate, Mayéras, concluded that Ribot had sabotaged a promising opening, and, although the Chamber voted by 313 to none to pass on to the order of the day without further comment, there were 187 abstentions.[153]

Painlevé was now determined to replace Ribot. On 22 October he reconstructed his Ministry, contemplating readmitting Thomas and even Briand himself, but eventually merely replacing Ribot by Louis Barthou.[154] This meant that the success of the Government's critics in the Chamber was as hollow as in June, for Barthou was the author of the Three-Year Law of 1913, just as great a *bête noire* to the Socialists as was his predecessor, and no man to favour a compromise peace. Instead, while at the Quai d'Orsay he took a bolder stand than Painlevé over Polish access to the sea and over the left bank of the Rhine. In the Chamber on 25 October he set himself against the Premier's assertion that France's war aims would not vary with the military situation. On the contrary, he said, 'it is the conditions . . . of victory which will fix . . . the conditions of peace', and he did not exclude 'the neutralization of certain territories' from these conditions.[155]

Barthou's tenure of the Quai d'Orsay was too brief for him to influence permanently the course of policy. But that he, and not a man disposed to compromise, was Ribot's heir is important. By October 1917 the creeping paralysis of French morale was advancing towards the heart of government. Ministers doubted the firmness both of Parliament and of the population as a whole. Painlevé's advisers in the Ministry of War were pessimistic about the military prospects and anxious for a negotiated settlement if one could be found. The Prime Minister himself was eager to accept the von der Lancken invitation and later to remove the Minister who more than any other blocked experiments of this kind. But Painlevé – who for all his intelligence and open-mindedness had little force of character – gave way over von der Lancken and could replace Ribot only by Barthou. On the fundamental question of war and peace, a majority of Ministers held out against pursuing either the opening offered by Benedict XV or direct contact with Berlin. They wagered that American assistance would enable France to impose its terms, despite the evidence that Wilson viewed those terms with embarrassment and distaste.

The war-aims programme of the Cambon letter and the Doumergue Agreement had been adopted in response both to internal and external pressures, but the final stimulus had been less domestic than a change in the Government's assessment of its Allies. In 1917 Ribot and Painlevé were exposed both externally and at home to pressures for the revision of that programme more powerful than anything experienced before. All the onslaughts of their parliamentary critics, however, obliged them to do no more than change the presentation of their ideas, and they gave no public undertaking which contradicted the programme of the spring. Among both Ministers and Deputies the majority in favour of pursuing security and Alsace–Lorraine was eroded, but it survived.

Externally, however, in 1917 the French came face to face with dilemmas which would harass them for more than twenty years. As their bargaining position weakened so the choices that confronted them became more cruel. The Tsar's was the only foreign Government to endorse the Cambon letter; but after the removal of Miliukov the Russians added to the pressure to diminish Allied war aims at the same time as their own power dwindled. There was little chance of Italy being a substitute, not only because it was more internally divided and militarily enfeebled than was France, but also because of the continuing rivalry that prevented any confidence and frankness from developing between Paris and Rome. After the war, it was suspected, Italy would revert to its former German sympathies,[156] and, with neither Russia nor Austria–Hungary available, Britain and America would remain alone among the Great Powers both as long-term guarantors of France and as short-term sources of indispensable economic support.

It was because France could not in the long term equal Germany that among the fundamental obstacles to peace in 1917 remained the alliances themselves. The schemes for compromise that the General Staff and Briand pondered all depended on German gains from France's allies and, more explicitly, from Russia.[157] But whatever France might win from such a peace, it would remain overshadowed by Germany and in a far worse international isolation than had followed 1871. While the French leaders stood out against abandoning their allies no movement could occur. In 1917 it was possible to take the decision that was taken: to go on. The alternative, if alternative it was, was to stop the massacre by submitting to the Germans' terms, and from this even Briand and Painlevé recoiled. But there was no middle way.

IV

The Clemenceau Ministry and the Allies,
November 1917–October 1918

1. The New Ministry

Clemenceau's Government came to power at one of the darkest moments of the war, and the concerns of its diplomacy were forced on it by the circumstances of its birth. On 7 November 1917 the Bolsheviks seized control of Petrograd, opening the way towards a Russian separate peace. In the ominous winter that followed, the Germans gained numerical superiority in the west for the first time since 1914, and Clemenceau saw his task as that of sustaining French resistance through the impending storm until the American war effort could be brought decisively to bear.[1] In this sense his ministry's priorities were simple and heroic, shorn of the imponderables and complexities that had tormented his predecessors. Yet the American effort remained frustratingly small. In February 1918 there was still only one United States division in the line, and the burden of resisting the German offensives of March–July fell almost exclusively on the battle-weary French and British Armies. Partly because of the depredations of the German U-boats, American commodities and manufactures, too, were slow in coming, and in November 1917 France was desperately short of the food and raw materials it needed to keep its economy functioning.

In the twelve months before the Armistice neither the military position nor the attitude of France's allies permitted Clemenceau to claim in Western Europe more than the Alsace–Lorraine of 1870. But in the east he tried to bind the coalition to new arrangements which would compensate for Russia's eclipse. Finally, he hoped for guarantees that France would be protected in the economic crisis that was expected to accompany the return of peace. The period of confidential soundings and public declarations that had begun in December 1916 with the German and American peace notes continued until February 1918. But in March the Treaty of Brest-Litovsk in the east and the opening German offensive in the west brought the months of expectancy to an end. On both sides interest in negotiation waned. Yet even in the worst military emergencies the French continued to draw up their plans for Eastern Europe and the future economic order. And in the final phase, ushered in by the reversal of military fortunes in July, their preparations were accelerated. By the time the guns fell silent Clemenceau's ministry was elaborating European war aims as far-reaching as those of the spring of 1917.

In foreign policy the new Prime Minister therefore moved at first along the lines set out by Ribot and by Painlevé. Until the last weeks of the fighting he saw his primary duty as being 'to carry on the war', and rarely gave his full attention to the terms of peace.[2] 'My war aim', he told the Chamber, 'is to win.'[3] This emphasis concorded with his private character. A man of action, habitually domineering, brutal, and impetuous, he yet was capable of an oratory whose staccato grandeur had astonishing power to inspire. 'Clemenceau', wrote Léon Blum, 'is the supreme example of that class of temperament for which a hatred, often contemptuous, of the remainder of mankind, makes it impossible to believe in the utility of any action whatsoever, and yet which nothing can prevent from action, because without action it cannot live.'[4]

Clemenceau's long and chequered past had given him a status in French politics that was unique. Since the 1890s he had been outbid on his Left by an internationalist and revolutionary socialism which he despised. But he had inherited from his radical and journalistic origins an inveterate suspicion of the French Establishment, be it the Army or the diplomatic corps, and this suspicion left its mark on his methods of rule. He had a stark and ruthless, if occasionally impulsive, intelligence, but little taste for detail, and he rarely set his thinking down on paper. Bypassing the normal bureaucratic machinery, he surrounded himself with able men, often a generation younger, whose power far outweighed what their formal positions might suggest. On censorship and civilian morale he was advised by his civil *Chef du Cabinet*, Georges Mandel; on military affairs by Mandel's counterpart at the Ministry of War, General Mordacq. He took decisions rapidly, alone or with his circle; his Council of Ministers met only once a week, was told of little, and was left to register a succession of *faits accomplis*. With most of the politicians who had ruled France for the first three years of war now out of office, Clemenceau's pre-eminence in his Government and in politics more generally became the outstanding feature of French public life.

Like Painlevé, Clemenceau held the Premiership in conjunction with the Ministry of War; the Quai d'Orsay he entrusted to Stephen Pichon. Pichon had spent most of his career as a protégé of his chief, and showed to him a subservience which Clemenceau repaid by an amused condescension. The Foreign Minister therefore reserved 'any decision of importance or even minor importance' for his daily conversations with the Premier,[5] whose preoccupation with military questions did not leave the Quai d'Orsay free to take an independent line. Within his Department, however, Pichon's failings as an administrator permitted his officials some of the latitude they had enjoyed under Briand, although they suffered from the aversion felt towards many of them by Clemenceau himself. Paradoxically, the chief object of that aversion – Berthelot – made himself irreplaceable to Pichon and won undisputed primacy among the Minister's advisers. In December 1917 the Secretary-Generalship was suppressed and Jules Cambon was shunted off to a face-saving post as Clemenceau's Counsellor on Franco-American affairs.[6] In June 1918 de Margerie collapsed from overwork and Berthelot became acting *Directeur politique*, with one of his admirers, Jules Laroche, succeeding him as *Sous-directeur d'Europe*.[7] Berthelot thus realized his long-standing ambition at the moment when his leading rivals were removed.

Under Clemenceau preparation for the post-war years continued in the Bourgeois Commission on the League of Nations, the *Comité d'études*, the *Bureau d'études économiques*, and the *Service d'Alsace–Lorraine* in the Ministry of War. More important was the planning in the Ministries: in Commerce, under Clémentel; in Colonies, under Simon; and, more intermittently, in Blockade, under Lebrun; Marine, under Leygues; and Armaments, under Loucheur. By contrast, while Clémentel dominated French economic diplomacy, the Ministry of Finance, under Klotz, did not specify its reparations claims.[8] And Clemenceau, much more than Painlevé, confined French military intelligence to the tasks of assembling and collating information. Poincaré, finally, was more rigorously deprived of influence than under any previous ministry. So strong was Clemenceau's antipathy against him that before November 1917 a Clemenceau Government was widely thought to be impossible without a constitutional crisis. Indeed, Poincaré called on the veteran statesman only because he feared that if the political disintegration of 1917 remained unchecked it would end with a Caillaux ministry pledged to a negotiated peace. But thereafter the President showed sufficient abnegation for a *modus vivendi* between him and Clemenceau to survive until the end of the war.

'My entire policy', the new Premier told the Chamber, 'has this sole objective: to sustain the morale of the French people through the worst crisis in its history.'[9] His methods of achieving this appeared to break abruptly with those used by his predecessors. In a succession of arrests and trials his Government struck at the revolutionary pacifist movement. It deterred the parliamentary advocates of compromise by imprisoning Caillaux. In its statements to the Chambers, it had little need to conciliate the Socialists, who were now out of office, and decisively outvoted. Behind the scenes, however, Clemenceau was in contact with the French trade-union leaders, and bought a measure of labour peace at the price of an accelerated growth in the money supply. French society polarized more sharply in 1918 than in 1917, but the pacifist minority was more isolated. The working-class opposition to the war took on a violent edge which culminated in an insurrectionary general strike in the Department of the Loire in May, but many fewer working days were lost in total than in the previous year. Above all, the troops' morale stayed firm, and civilian confidence, if jolted by the German breakthroughs in March and May, left behind the pessimism which was so pervasive before the spring.[10] After its difficult first weeks, the Government was liberated from many of Painlevé's and Ribot's anxieties about parliamentary and public solidarity, and relative to domestic opinion it enjoyed a freer hand.

2. The Bolshevik Revolution and the Fourteen Points, November 1917–March 1918

The ministry's heroic period was preceded by a loaded pause. During the winter of 1917–18 the Chamber still heatedly debated war aims, American diplomatic pressure was stepped up, and events in Eastern Europe grew more threatening. On 23 November, *Izvestiya* began publishing the treaties, including the Doumergue Agreement and its Polish codicil, made between the Allies and the Tsar. The Bolsheviks then opened ceasefire negotiations with the Central Powers, and invited the western Allies to take part: an invitation which Clemenceau's Council of Ministers indignantly refused.[11] None the less, on 15 December the Armistice in the east was signed.

The correct response to the events in Russia was debated at an inter-Allied conference in Paris from 29 November to 3 December 1917. For the first time there was a .powerful American delegation, whose leader – the ubiquitous Colonel House – believed the time had come for 'the announcement of general war aims and the formation of an international association for the prevention of future wars'.[12] This he saw both as an answer to the Bolsheviks and as a propaganda weapon against Germany. But in his first speech to the Chamber Clemenceau had cast doubt both on the League of Nations and on the likelihood of democratic revolution in the enemy camp.[13] At the Conference his Government followed the suggestions of the Polish National Committee and its sympathizers in the Quai d'Orsay, and proposed not a general declaration but one specifically about Poland. For a reunited Poland, argued de Margerie, would be not only 'the harshest blow' the Allies could strike against Prussia, but also, in association with the Romanians and the Czechoslovaks, the best barrier available against German influence becoming dominant in the Russian power vacuum.[14]

Neither the French nor the Americans got what they desired at Paris. Pichon introduced a declaration favouring the 'creation of an autonomous, united, and indivisible Poland, with every facility for political, military, and economic development, and with free access to the sea' as one condition of the peace.[15] Lloyd George objected that the Bolshevik Revolution had destroyed the very means of fulfilling such a promise, and the Conference could agree only on a formula so lukewarm that the Polish National Committee preferred it not to be published.[16] But when House proposed a telegram to the Bolsheviks denying that the Allies were 'waging the war for the purpose of aggression or indemnity', he found that 'England passively was willing,

France indifferently against it, Italy actively so'.[17] He had to be content with a statement that the Allies would be ready to discuss their aims when a regular Government had reappeared in Russia. Even this the French saw as a propaganda move which implied no commitment to revise their objectives.[18]

Clemenceau used the Conference to keep up pressure over two other subjects which Ribot and Painlevé had earlier raised. One passage in a speech by Wilson to the American Congress on 4 December suggested that the President had incorporated the Clémentel plan into his ideas.[19] Clemenceau told House that he 'fully accepted' Wilson's language, and urged that the Allies should immediately seek ways of placing their exports of commodities under central control.[20] The French Government had special reason to be optimistic because the Paris Conference had agreed in principle on machinery which would allocate the coalition's scarce reserves of shipping and raw materials according to need.[21] Henceforth, Clémentel's plan could be presented less as a radical innovation than as the continuation of an existing web of commitments in which the United States was already deeply enmeshed.

These high hopes, however, were offset by renewed French anxiety about Alsace–Lorraine, which Wilson did not mention in his speech of 4 December and over which House refused to be badgered into any public undertaking.[22] Lloyd George, too, 'much irritated' Clemenceau when in the Commons on 20 December he reverted to his former silence on the subject.[23] The Paris Conference was therefore indecisive, and even the more limited goals pursued by French diplomacy since the summer appeared to be again in jeopardy when in the first weeks of December Clemenceau turned his energies to a prolonged review of foreign policy.[24] The outcome was a major speech by Pichon to the Chamber on the 17th, in which the Foreign Minister proclaimed a unilateral French commitment to a Poland which would be 'united, independent, indivisible; with all the guarantees of its free political, economic, and military development, and all the consequences which may result'. In the west, he fell back on the Dumont resolution and its sibylline talk of 'guarantees'; but Alsace–Lorraine, he warned, with the evident intention of being heard in London and in Washington, was not 'a French territorial problem' so much as a universal, 'moral' question, the touchstone of the justice of the settlement.[25]

Clemenceau and Pichon therefore began by pursuing with bolder means the same ends as their immediate forerunners; and they encountered the same reticence on the part of the Anglo–Saxon Powers. This reticence would be harder to maintain in the weeks of rival declarations that lay ahead. The war was becoming more ideological, and for the first time since American entry the Bolsheviks represented a large, uncommitted quantity which suitable pronouncements might help to sway. The opposition within the Central Powers might also respond to such enticements. In January 1918 Germany was shaken by a vast strike movement, whose objectives included forcing the authorities to renounce all claim to annexations and indemnities. None the less, the rulers of the Central Powers threatened to gain a victory in the propaganda battle when on Christmas Day 1917 they accepted the general peace conditions laid down by the Bolsheviks in discussions at Brest-Litovsk.

The hollowness of this acceptance soon became apparent. But it challenged the Allies to respond in kind, with the risk that war-aims declarations would splinter their fragile unity and draw one or more of them into a compromise peace. The gains that could be set against this risk remained uncertain. In Paris the Bolshevik regime was considered abhorrent but ephemeral, and was expected to be overthrown by the conservative front which French agents were trying to create in southern Russia.[26] As for Germany, French military intelligence saw little chance that the opposition would prevail, and Clemenceau doubted that Allied declarations would have much effect.[27] All the same, Pichon asked his counterparts whether they thought a joint statement was called for. When it became clear that they did not, he withdrew his suggestion,[28] and the Allied reply to the Central Powers took the form of independent pronouncements from each of the main capitals.

Lloyd George was first off the mark. Convinced that a new statement of British aims was needed, he invited Clemenceau to discuss the 'overtures' made at Brest-Litovsk. The phrase stung Clemenceau into an angry refusal, whose wording was strengthened because of Pichon's fear that the British Premier wished to

begin peace negotiations.[29] The French claim to Alsace–
Lorraine was therefore impressed on Lloyd George only unofficially, by Albert Thomas.[30] Lloyd George was torn between
his wish to shore up French morale and his fear of being committed to prolonging the war for the sake of the two provinces
alone. When he spoke at Caxton Hall on 5 January, his reference to Alsace–Lorraine was still very elastic, although he balanced this by favourable allusions to an independent Poland, and
to the French claims for reparations and for priority in the
allocation of raw materials.[31] This was a bitter-sweet message,
although Clemenceau sent a laconic telegram of congratulation.[32]

The Caxton Hall speech was quickly overshadowed by the
address to Congress three days later in which Wilson unveiled
his celebrated Fourteen Points. Like Lloyd George, House and
Wilson were much exercised over what to say about Alsace–
Lorraine, and eventually opted for an inconclusive wording.[33]
They also followed him in confining the scope of reparation to
the 'restoration' of the invaded areas, and in envisaging a Poland restricted to its ethnic limits. Finally, again like the British
Premier, they gave no encouragement to any French pretensions
to the Saarland and the left bank of the Rhine. On the contrary,
one of Wilson's objects was to strengthen the Western European opposition against governments he distrusted as imperialist, and at first he succeeded in this aim. His speech deeply impressed the French Left, and helped to rally French civilian
morale after its depression in 1917, but at the same time it
brought Clemenceau's policies into disrepute. 'While criticisms
of our own diplomacy . . . are frequent,' the French postal surveillance agency reported, 'the approbation given President Wilson is without reserve.'[34]

Clemenceau's immediate opinion, none the less, was that the
Fourteen Points gave France 'satisfaction in all the vital questions which concern her', and that it was best to endorse them
'purely and simply', in order to throw the onus of dissent on to
the Central Powers.[35] He authorized Pichon to tell the Chamber
that 'all the Allies' declarations are in accord'; if not in form, at
least in substance. To this show of support for Wilson the Foreign Minister added the suggestion – of questionable sincerity –
that the Government's claims in Alsace–Lorraine were limited

to the frontier of 1870. But at the same time he betrayed his impatience with the Allies' vacillation on the subject of the plebiscite. Alsace–Lorraine, he said, could be settled only 'by making good the right violated in 1871, a right superior to any combination of plebiscitary duplicity and corrupted referenda . . . .'[36]

This note of irritation brought results, for in an interview on 18 January Lloyd George conceded that the French 'are the people who have to determine what they regard as fair . . . .'[37] As for Wilson, however, Pichon's first opinion was that the Fourteen Points did not go far enough and that Blumenthal's propaganda must continue. He relented only after Tardieu and Jusserand protested that the essential had been won and the claim to Alsace–Lorraine should not be exposed to further controversy.[38] For the first time since the alert in the summer of 1917 British and American policy towards the provinces ceased to rank among the foremost of the Government's concerns.

Clemenceau soon thought better of his precipitate acceptance of the Fourteen Points. Like Ribot in the previous September, he tried to draw his European allies into a rival manifesto that would reassert their independence from Washington. When the Supreme War Council[39] met at Versailles at the end of January, he and Pichon introduced a draft declaration which resembled Wilson's programme in its plan, but abandoned altogether some of the President's general points (open diplomacy, disarmament, the adjustment of colonial claims), and made others (freedom of the seas, reducing barriers to trade) much less explicit. Furthermore, if the draft seemed again to limit France's territorial claims to the Alsace–Lorraine of 1870, it also asked for more solid 'guarantees' than the mere signatures of the Central Powers could provide.[40]

The declaration ran up against objections from Lloyd George and Sonnino, and all that emerged from the meeting was a terse communiqué that made no attempt to catalogue afresh the Allies' aims. The communiqué did, however, observe that the enemy replies to the Allies' recent pronouncements were inadequate, and that the war must therefore be continued 'with the utmost vigour'.[41] Even this the Americans interpreted as an act of defiance.[42] Wilson's 'Four Principles' of 11 February were designed in part to counteract it, and were directed almost as much against his European partners as the Central Powers.[43] On the 19th Lansing read to the Allied Ambassadors in Washington a sternly phrased letter in which the President charged that by venturing into high policy the Supreme War Council had gone beyond its competence.[44] Clemenceau was incensed, and a reluctant Jusserand was ordered to press for an explanation until Wilson eventually made a partial apology.[45]

This display of disunity could occur because of the tendency of both Wilson and the Europeans to issue unilateral statements designed to present their associates with *faits accomplis*. Yet if the President had reacted so sharply to a statement which said nothing of war aims, he would have objected far more violently to the declaration Clemenceau and Pichon had originally proposed. Like the affair of the Papal Peace Note, the episode showed that retaining America's diplomatic freedom had a priority for Wilson second only to that of victory itself. The French were attempting to commit American power to the pursuit of objectives which they could no longer achieve unaided. But matters which for them were primary, such as Alsace–Lorraine and their raw material supplies, were only subsidiary for Wilson. They could co-operate little more effectively with a British Government whose views on many counts approximated more closely to those of Washington than to those of Paris. In these conditions the limits on their freedom of manœuvre were very great.

3. *Eastern Europe and Economic War Aims, March–July 1918*

In March 1918 the season of public declarations came abruptly to an end. At Brest–Litovsk the Bolsheviks signed away one-third of the Russian Empire's population and more than half its heavy industry in one of the harshest treaties in European history. The implications for what remained of the pre-war power balance on the continent were immense. Yet in the *Reichstag* only the Socialists, of the parties which had supported the Peace Resolution of July 1917, witheld approval. On the 8th, in one of the most electrifying performances of his career, Clemenceau drew what he considered the inescapable conclusions. 'The attempt at a democratic peace by the effect of persuasion on the

German revolutionaries' had now been made. Yet however hard
they listened for a cry of protest in Berlin, 'nothing replies except silence'.[46] On 21 March the enemy offensives on the Western Front began, and in the anxious months that followed the
friction between America and its European partners was re-
lieved. In a 'moment of utter disillusionment' at Baltimore on 6
April, Wilson, too, concluded that 'force without stint or limit'
must be left to decide the issue.[47]

By 1918 the great systems of trench fortification were no longer invulnerable, and the war of movement made a first, spasmo-
dic reappearance in the west. This was little comfort to the
Allies, whose 'crisis of effectives' was more intense than ever,
and with only a small numerical superiority the Germans twice
broke through deep into open country. At the end of March the
French and British Armies were on the verge of being separated, with Haig planning a retreat to the Channel ports while
Clemenceau and Pétain contemplated a stand in front of Paris.
Two months later, in Champagne, the Germans smashed
through a French line denuded of reserves and penetrated once
again to the Marne. Only in June–July, with the Germans' tactics being successfully resisted and the arrival *en masse* of the
Americans, did the tide begin to turn.

During the weeks of tension Clemenceau was preoccupied
with military events and French diplomatic action slackened;
though it was not suspended. The earlier objectives on Germany's western frontiers were neglected in favour of a programme that was both more and less ambitious. This was due
less to the military situation than to the policies of France's
allies. At a time when Amiens and Paris were in danger the
French made new promises to the Czechoslovaks and the Poles.
But over their own frontiers with Germany they did not press
the British and Americans to go beyond the cautious undertakings given earlier in the year. In the House of Commons Balfour withheld British support from any attempt to separate the
left bank of the Rhine from Germany or to claim the 1814 frontier in Alsace–Lorraine.[48] Wilson was less explicit, but passages
in the Fourteen Points and the Four Principles suggested his
view was the same. In Western Europe, then, French diplomacy
had come to a dead end.

In Eastern Europe the outstanding influence on French policy was Russia's reduction almost to a satellite of the Central Powers. Whatever Clemenceau's loathing of the Bolsheviks' domestic policies, his first concern was to halt the growth of German influence. In February, when Lenin and Trotsky appeared ready to resist the Brest–Litovsk terms, his Government offered them military and financial aid, and only after the Treaty had been signed did the French commit themselves unequivocally to supporting the Russian Whites and to pressing for Allied intervention against the Bolsheviks. France was quicker than Britain and America to make this choice. It acted as it did because the longer-term imperatives of checking social revolution and salvaging the remnants of France's political and economic influence coincided with the short-term ones of keeping the Eastern Front in being and denying Russian food and raw materials to the enemy.[49] Unlike Lloyd George, and certain members of their own General Staff and diplomatic corps,[50] Pichon and Clemenceau felt the stakes in Russia were so high that they were never tempted by a peace which would satisfy the Allies in the west at the price of a free hand for the Central Powers in the east. When Wilson confided his fear that his European partners might succumb to an offer of this kind, Pichon replied that he and the Premier were in 'complete accord' with the American President that any such proposal must be rejected. 'We would', he added, 'consider that abandoning Russia to the Germans would be to lose the war.'[51]

Undoing the result of Brest–Litovsk was therefore now a fundamental French objective. For it to be achieved, the settlement in Eastern Europe would have not only to provide a new counterbalance in replacement to the Tsar, but also to block German penetration of a Russia that was likely to be anarchic and enfeebled far into the future. Brest–Litovsk and the associated treaties created on Russia's western marches a vast *Raum* of nominally independent States which was intended to become an exclusive sphere of influence for the Central Powers. The need to prevent this added urgency to the debate in Paris between those who wished to strengthen Austria–Hungary in the hope that it would free itself from Germany and those who wished to break it up and rely on its successors. The first of these alternatives was now set aside, earlier than in London and in Washington, although the exact moment of decision is hard to isolate. Indeed, the notion of an Austrian counterbalance had attracted Clemenceau in the past,[52] and he began by allowing contacts with Vienna to resume. On 18 November 1917 he approved a fresh meeting betwen Armand and Revertera, on condition that this time Armand confined himself strictly to noting what the Austrian had to say.[53]

Armand found the Vienna Government committed to the pre-war status quo and unwilling to renew its undertaking of the previous year to plead with Germany to restore Alsace–Lorraine to France.[54] The same inference was suggested by a secret exchange of views between Wilson and the Emperor Charles which British and French intelligence intercepted in February 1918.[55] Finally, a series of competitive disclosures made in April by Clemenceau and the Austrian Foreign Minister, Czernin, brought the Sixte and Armand–Revertera conversations into the open.[56] From this point on Charles's independent diplomacy was at an end, and in the eyes of Clemenceau and of Pichon the Habsburgs' fate was sealed. It was time to choose between supporting the Eastern European subject nationalities and chasing the mirage of an Austrian separate peace.[57]

Until this point the Government had kept both options in the air. Even while contacts with Vienna were continuing, de Margerie told the Belgian Minister in Paris that Pichon, Foch, and Clemenceau wished to thwart the growth of German power in Russia by creating an eastern 'barrier', in which Poland, Czechoslovakia, and Romania would all take part.[58] The ministry responded to the news of Brest–Litovsk, as to that of the October Revolution, by urging on its allies a public undertaking 'to pursue the creation of a free, self-governing, and independent Poland, able to ensure its own economic, political, and military development, and with access to the sea'.[59] Pichon's final wording was more cautious than the original proposals of the Polish National Committee and its supporters among the Foreign Ministry officials.[60] It still went too far for the British and Italians, and the suggestion had to be withdrawn.[61]

Italian reservations about the Yugoslavs, and British and American ones about the Czechs, meant that the commitment to the Poles still took pride of place in French diplomacy in the spring of 1918. Once the Habsburgs had been written off, however, this expanded into more general support for national self-determination in the east. The Czechs had particular leverage with the Allies because of their ability to cause disruption in Bohemia and their authority over the Czech Legion, a body of former prisoners of war who now constituted one of the strongest military organizations in Russia.[62] In April and May Clemenceau privately assured Beneš of his Government's willingness to pledge itself to Czechoslovak independence, and Pichon urged the necessity of such a promise on a lukewarm British Government in London.[63] Only after America took the lead with a loosely worded statement on 29 May,[64] however, did the British, French, and Italian Prime Ministers declare their 'warm sympathy' for the Czechoslovaks and the Yugoslavs in 'their struggle for liberty and the realization of their national aspirations'. At the same time, they at last agreed that 'the creation of a united and independent Polish State, with free access to the sea, constitutes one condition of a just and solid peace. . . .'[65]

Although the fruit of over six months' effort, these utterances were still too weak to satisfy the French, who from now on gave their undertakings in Eastern Europe unilaterally. A public letter from Pichon to Beneš on 29 June conceded the Czech National Council's claims in their entirety. Not only did Pichon promise official French support for an independent Czechoslovakia 'within the historic limits of your provinces', and therefore including the Germans of the Sudeten Mountains; the Minister also voiced his hope that 'the Czechoslovak State may soon become, . . . in close union with Poland and the Yugoslav State, an insurmountable barrier to German aggression. . . .'[66] The idea of an eastern 'barrier' which would replace the Russian alliance and separate Germany from the Bolsheviks, an idea launched by the Czech and Polish nationalists and taken up by Quai d'Orsay officials such as de Margerie and Degrand, was now acknowledged public policy.

On the Czech question in the summer of 1918, as on the Polish question in the spring, France took the boldest stand within the Allied coalition. Before the war, Franco–German tension on the continent had been confined to Germany's western Marches;

afterwards, it extended to the eastern Marches also. French power spilled out into the vacuum left by Russia's collapse. Both Paris and Berlin now favoured a degree of national self-determination and territorial fragmentation in the east, but while the Germans wished to limit this to the Russian border-lands France desired it to apply in Austria–Hungary as well. The result would be a chequer-board of minor Powers whose likely solidarity was greatly overestimated in the Quai d'Orsay, and whose resistance to pressure from the Germans would depend on unremitting French support. Even in 1918 this support was far from absolute. Neither the Poles, the Czechs, nor the Yugoslavs, thought Pichon, expected from the Allies 'an engagement not to end the war before their national programmes are met in full'.[67] The crucial promise of Polish sea access, he explained to Sonnino, would not 'necessarily' imply a territorial corridor to the Baltic which would split Germany in two, and might mean as little as an international status for the Vistula.[68] That the more extreme solution also figured in his mind, however, suggests that in the east as in the west French purposes were flexible, and retained the option of expanding if better times should come. As ever, much depended on the willingness of France's allies to underwrite the pledges it distributed in Eastern Europe, and here French action had resulted super-ficially in success, if less complete success than had been hoped for. In reality, however, Britain and America had shifted ground because of changes in their own perceptions of what was necessary, and until this happened French lobbying was ineffective. Thus, in the sphere of economic war aims no less pertinacious French *démarches* met with nearly total failure.

The Clemenceau ministry began by cherishing similar hopes for economic war aims to those indulged by Painlevé and Ribot in the previous year. In the Senate, Clémentel defended his raw-materials proposals as a means of rousing popular pressures which would force the German leaders to seek terms.[69] Clemenceau himself was impressed by the argument that the threat of an embargo could, if not provoke revolution, at least demoralize the enemy business community.[70] But by April 1918 Allied confidence in the German opposition had been severely shaken, and henceforth it was omitted from official justifications of Clémentel's ideas. Instead, the Commerce Minister was increasingly alarmed by what de Fleuriau, the Counsellor at the French Embassy in London, described as the rise of an Anglo-American economic entente which would hold France in 'tutelage'.[71] The two men agreed that this danger could be averted only by placing the Allies' resources under the control of supra-national committees in which the French delegates could exploit the differences between the Anglo-Saxon Powers.[72]

Tardieu had given soothing assurances in January that House and Wilson approved raw-material controls in principle,[73] but the Americans did nothing to act on this in the months that followed. On 16 April Clémentel and Pichon formally proposed an inter-Allied conference to draw up plans for the centralized apportionment of food and raw materials,[74] only to be met with another prolonged silence from Washington. When Tardieu reported that Wilson had hung back because he feared the issue would be divisive in Congress, the two Ministers insisted: Tardieu must make 'repeated *démarches*' on the conference's behalf.[75] But at this point there came solace from another quarter. The British Government intimated that, subject to the approval of the forthcoming Imperial War Conference, it intended to control the Empire's commodity exports in future, and it might give special preference to France.[76] This was the first success in a campaign of agitation which had been going on since the previous October, and for the moment, pending the Imperial War Conference's decisions, diplomatic pressure on the subject was relaxed.

By 8 June the Bourgeois Commission on the League of Nations had completed its final report.[77] This was still little more than a sketch, which left unanswered such questions as how agreement would be secured in the 'International Council' of heads of government which it suggested. None the less, its requirement that each member should 'be bound to use in common agreement with the others its economic, naval, and military power' to enforce the Council's decisions pointed towards a stronger League than the one which finally emerged, largely under British and American inspiration, at the Peace Conference. Clemenceau's Government showed great reserve towards the report, and simply forwarded it to the Allies without comment.[78] For this the main responsibility lay with the Premier, who, according to Poincaré, had not read the dossier, completely misunderstood what Bourgeois was saying, and regarded the whole subject as a butt for his ironies.[79] The response in Washington was hardly more sympathetic, and House ignored the report when he prepared the first American draft 'Covenant'.[80] The League therefore played little part in French diplomacy until Clemenceau took up Bourgeois's ideas, largely for tactical reasons, after the Armistice.

4. *In Expectation of Victory, August–October 1918*

At the Second Battle of the Marne, in mid-July, the last German attack was halted and the Allied counter-offensive scored its first success. Under the nominal direction of Foch, who had been appointed Commander-in-Chief on the Western Front in April, the Allies moved forward less spectacularly than had the Germans earlier, but more steadily, and by September they were advancing all along the line. The victories at the front let loose a patriotic fervour both in the French Parliament and among the public at large, and Clemenceau's domestic base, always strong, became impregnable. In August he began conferring with the heads of the *Comité d'études* and the *Bureau d'études économiques*,[81] but neither the French military nor the civilian chiefs yet expected the war to end that year. Their thoughts were turning to the peace and their ambitions were extending, but the Armistice negotiations took them by surprise, with many of their war aims still inchoate.

France was now part of a coalition centred on the North Atlantic, a coalition whose immense reserves of strength had, until the spring, hardly begun to be exploited. For its first year the American war machine was idling; after March 1918 its every gear was engaged.[82] Yet as the threat from Germany receded so discord among the Allies again became more marked. The prodigious outpouring of American resources caused not only satisfaction, but disquiet. Clemenceau, confided to Lloyd George his fear that if America supplied too many of the effectives on the Western Front it would be able to decide the outlines of the settlement,[83] and he remarked morosely to Poincaré that

'We may not have the peace that you and I should wish for'. When Poincaré informed Pichon of this, the Foreign Minister protested: 'If we want it we shall have such a peace . . . the Alsace of 1790 and the neutralization of the left bank of the Rhine. As for Luxemburg, I have raised it with Clemenceau.'[84] The inner circle were therefore reverting to the programmes of the spring of 1917, even if this had not yet led to detailed planning in the Ministries, and Clemenceau in the Chamber avoided the contentious language of 'guarantees'.[85]

Other Western European aims, however, received closer scrutiny. A new *Service d'Alsace–Lorraine* under Jules Cambon was charged with examining 'the numerous political problems' that would follow the provinces' reoccupation.[86] Reparations, too, were made an urgent question by the devastation executed by the Germans as they retreated, and the Government warned on 4 October that those responsible would be held 'morally, penally, and financially' to account.[87] Interest was also focusing on the perplexities of the northern flank. In the summer and autumn of 1918 the Belgian Government seemed once again to be attracted by a separate peace concluded at its allies' expense, this time through the interest that it showed in overtures from Germany made via the Belgian Queen's brother-in-law, Count Törring.[88] The alarm caused by this episode reinforced the French authorities' desire that Belgium should follow a francophile policy in future. Clémentel wished to negotiate 'consortia' linking French with Belgian industries, in the hope that Belgium could thereby be kept out of Germany's economic orbit after the war.[89] Pichon promised to support the Belgians' wish to end their statutory neutrality, which would remove another obstacle to a closer association with the Allies.[90] When the Belgian Foreign Minister, Hymans, visited Paris in October, he found Clémentel conditionally prepared to give economic aid, and Poincaré made the unsolicited suggestion that Hymans might claim the German districts of Eupen and Malmédy. But Hymans's main objective was to turn Ribot's assurance of disinterest over Luxemburg into a promise of diplomatic backing for the Belgian claim, and this the French were unprepared to give. Disabused, Hymans concluded that French support would be forthcoming only if his Government agreed to a military union, on which point he evaded commitment.[91] None the less, although Franco-Belgian relations remained stuck in the familiar groove, the outlines were emerging of a barrier against Germany in the west which might complement that envisaged for the east.

In Eastern Europe also, the pace of French diplomacy was quickening. Conversations with the Czech National Council about the future Czechoslovak–German frontier resulted in a convention on 28 September which confirmed French support for the historic line.[92] But the great innovation of the last weeks of the war was that the same was promised to the Poles.

As usual, this owed something to French fears of being outpaced by Germany in the rivalry for Polish favour.[93] In addition, the Foreign Ministry was concerned by accusations in the other Allied capitals that the Polish National Committee was unrepresentative, imperialist, and anti-semitic.[94] A decisive memorandum by Georges Degrand, of the *Sous–direction d'Europe*, argued nevertheless that France should have no 'objections of principle' to the Committee's desire for the Polish frontier of 1772.[95] Yet these frontiers would give Poland the coveted land corridor to the Baltic at Germany's expense, as well as the port of Danzig with its mainly German population. In March Pichon had held this possibility in reserve, and he had still been undecided in July.[96] Now, however, Clemenceau promised the Polish National Committee that 'on the day of our victory . . . France . . . will spare nothing in order to revive a free Poland corresponding to the latter's national aspirations and bounded by its historic limits'.[97] About the Czechoslovak frontiers Britain and America had said nothing; for Poland, both Wilson and Lloyd George had advised in January that the ethnic boundary should be followed. France by contrast, now favoured the historic line for both. As victory approached, so implicit differences between the Allies became explicit also.

This was even clearer in the third sphere of French concern, which was also that in which the French came closest to collision with America in these weeks: economic war aims. In London at the end of August Clémentel was informed that the Imperial War Conference had not reached unanimity about controlling trade in raw materials. Before any formal inter-Allied conference the British wanted technical discussions between experts: discussions which Pichon sanctioned with evident impatience.[98] The British had been warned by Wilson that he might dissociate himself from any threats of 'punitive post-war measures' against German trade; the French, unaware of this, supposed the President was still undecided.

Indeed, French policy was broadening out from its near-exclusive concentration on the Clémentel plan into an economic programme comparable to that of 1916. Henri Hauser, Professor of Economic History at the University of Dijon, had been seconded to the Commerce Ministry, where he advocated a Western European economic union as an alternative to France being 'caught between two powerful groupings: a grouping led by Germany on one side and on the other a British grouping ... or even an Anglo-Saxon one'.[99] It was largely Hauser who prepared a letter sent by Clémentel to Clemenceau on 19 September, which soon afterwards became part of Government policy.[100]

The letter argued that victory was now close enough for France to define its economic aims, before proceeding to consult its allies. A new conference should supersede the resolutions of 1916, and create the nucleus of a future 'economic union of free peoples'. Its agenda should include 'the rational and systematic use of the raw materials arm as a means of compelling German industry to co-operate peacefully with that of other nations'. Such action, together with international legislation against dumping and false marks of origin, would prevent the post-war 'economic offensive' by Germany that had long been feared. At the same time, Clémentel and Hauser hoped to aid France's own reconstruction by reparations from the enemy and by loans and tariff concessions from their partners. Without such co-operation, they feared, France would be isolated in a world of closed economic blocs.

When Clémentel discussed the letter with Clemenceau, Pichon, and Tardieu on 28 September, the four agreed that Tardieu should use it as a basis for discussion on his next visit to the United States.[101] Reversing their earlier practice, the French now sought American adhesion before they had that of the British. These tactics derived from illusions about American intentions which were fast becoming untenable. Although Wilson had once considered using economic sanctions against an unregenerate German autocracy, his enthusiasm waned as the chances of decisive victory increased. Meanwhile, House suggested to the President that it was time 'to try to commit the Allies to some of the things for which we are fighting'. If America did nothing, the Colonel feared, the fever of nationalism caused by victory would render the liberal opposition in the European Allies powerless 'to compel the reactionaries in authority to yield at the Peace Conference to American aims'.[102] Impressed by these contentions, Wilson fired a warning shot across his allies' bows in a speech at New York on 27 September. In particular, he declared, there could be 'no form of economic boycott or exclusion', except in so far as such powers were vested in the League of Nations.[103] Although on most points Wilson's language was still too vague to contradict the French official statements, an embarrassing divergence over economic questions was therefore coming into view.

But on one thing there seemed to be complete agreement: that the war must go on until the enemy capitulated. On 14 September the Austrians took one last action in defiance of the Germans and appealed for peace conversations to begin at once, without hostilities being suspended.[104] In the Senate, Clemenceau was moved to one of his most bellicose orations: 'A military decision is what Germany desired and has condemned us to pursue . . . . So let it be as Germany has willed and Germany has acted.'[105] Wilson, Jusserand reported on the following day, agreed it was essential to cut short the Austrians' 'pacifist propaganda'. The enemy could not be trusted, and the Allies should not settle for less than 'absolute victory'.[106] These confident assertions were soon put to the test. For on 5 October the German Government asked Wilson to arrange for an armistice to be agreed at once, prior to the negotiation of a peace which should be based on the Fourteen Points and the President's subsequent pronouncements.

V

The Armistice, October–November 1918

1. The Decision

Within weeks of the turning-point of July 1918 the German High Command judged that it could no longer win the war. The most that might be possible was to moderate the terms the Allies could impose, by negotiating before the German Army had been broken in the field. The *démarche* at the beginning of October, however, came not after an improvement in Germany's fortunes but at a moment of exceptional danger, and its objectives included not only peace negotiations but also a cease-fire. It was made by a new ministry, which was pledged to make the German constitution representative, and enjoyed the confidence of the *Reichstag* parties that had passed the Peace Resolution of July 1917. The *démarche* took this form because of a loss of nerve by Ludendorff, the German Chief of Staff, who prompted both the change of Government and the appeal for hostilities to end. Within a few days the High Command realized that the danger on the Western Front was less acute than it had feared, and it reverted to favouring an armistice only on conditions that would enable it to move its troops to new positions on the German frontiers, there to negotiate from strength. As late as 15 October the Berlin Cabinet still supposed it could obtain a peace which would entail no loss of territory and might leave Germany in possession of some of its Eastern European gains.[1]

The Allies therefore faced a complex of exacting judgements. Were the Germans any longer able to resist? How important was the change of rulers in Berlin? The task was made more delicate because the negotiation of the Armistice was bound up with the terms of peace. The Germans asked not only for the suspension of the fighting but also for a settlement on Wilson's principles; they approached not the Allies collectively but the President alone. From 5 to 23 October there was a public dialogue between America and Germany from which Wilson's partners were excluded, although they forwarded their views to him in confidence. From 23 October to 5 November there followed bargaining within the Allied coalition, during which the clauses of the Armistice were decided and the United States compelled its associates to do lip-service to a peace programme about which they had never been consulted and many of whose elements they profoundly disliked. Finally, the compromise that resulted was accepted by the leaders of a Germany which was close to military collapse and now erupted into revolution.

Because the Armistice came into being in this way, the Clemenceau Government was confronted by an American question as well as a German one. It also had to bear in mind the advance of revolution westward. Since the abdication of the Tsar the control of the European Chancelleries and Cabinets over foreign policy had been under threat. At first the Bolsheviks were seen in France as a bizarre but transient phenomenon, and only from the summer of 1918, when Lenin and Trotsky showed their ability to withstand the Allied intervention forces and to survive independently of German collusion, did the full significance of events in Russia strike home. 'This new and monstrous form of imperialism', wrote Clemenceau, 'places over Europe a menace all the more formidable for coming precisely at the moment when the approaching end of war will inevitably cause a grave social and economic crisis in every country.'[2] Official characterizations of the Bolsheviks abound with the imagery of disease: with likenesses to a malignant bacillus in the European body politic whose spread it was imperative to contain.

The fear of revolution complicated assessment both of external and internal events. In policy towards Germany it raised the question which Russia had presented in the previous year: whether French war aims should be reduced in the interests of preserving social order. In France itself it added a new urgency to Clemenceau's long-standing preoccupation with public morale. The questions the Government had to answer were three. Should the German request be refused outright? If not, on what terms should a ceasefire be conceded? Finally, could Wilson's speeches be accepted as the basis of the peace? French public opinion answered the first two of these questions unusually clearly. The revolutionary pacifist movement had shot its bolt with the May strike in the Loire, and its agitation subsided after the Allied victories began. According to the postal surveillance authorities, only five per cent of the public wanted peace at any price. A much larger body of opinion thought that it was still too early for an armistice, either because this was seen as a trick designed to win the German Army breathing space, or because it was thought that the horrors of war must be brought home to enemy civilians by an invasion of their soil. But the biggest, if most amorphous, grouping did not oppose the principle of a ceasefire as long as measures were taken to prevent the Germans from using it to strengthen their position, and there was security that France's war aims could be fulfilled. This was the judgement even of the Socialists. Although the former *minoritaires* took over the leadership of the *SFIO* at the party congress of 6–9 October, the same gathering called on Wilson to grant an armistice only on condition that it contained the necessary 'diplomatic and military guarantees'.[3]

It was some time before these attitudes towards the German question became clear to the authorities, and Clemenceau at first supposed the public to be less firm than it was. His Government was also anxious to keep its hands free in dealing with the Americans, and it censored open criticism of Wilson.[4] Accordingly, French commentators approved the President's actions, although more warmly as the demands he made on Germany were toughened.[5] Even so, beneath the surface many viewed American arbitration with exasperation and alarm.[6]

During the negotiations the opinion of the Government's military advisers necessarily played a larger part than in foreign policy hitherto, as did that of Clemenceau himself, as Premier and Minister of War. Military opinion came in part from Pétain and Mordacq, but far the most important voice was that of Marshal Foch. Although nominally an inter-Allied commander, Foch persistently expressed a French viewpoint when he advised on the conditions of the Armistice, and he was sharply conscious of those conditions' political as well as their military significance. His exceptional prestige made him one of the Government's greatest assets in dealing with its partners.

French policy towards the Armistice, therefore, was made largely by Foch and Clemenceau. The latter still dominated his Ministers, and Poincaré, condemned to fume in impotence, made only one attempt to have a say: an attempt which irreparably harmed his relations with the Premier. At the Quai d'Orsay

the leading influence was that of Berthelot, who shared with
Pichon the task of expounding policy in the telegrams sent to
guide French diplomats abroad. He also had some influence on
the drafting of the Armistice clauses, through his work in liais-
ing between the Government and Foch and the confidence
which the Marshal placed in him.[7] All the same, once German
resistance began to fail and Clemenceau turned his mind from
the problems of war to those of peace, French priorities altered.
Colonies, raw materials, and even Eastern Europe mattered less
to the Premier than did reparations, Alsace–Lorraine, and,
above all, France's claims to British and American support and
to security in the north-east. Clemenceau, wrote Mordacq, was
'hypnotized, like all who had seen the defeat of 1870,
by . . . the question of the Rhine. There, for the men of his
generation, was the real danger, the weak point *par excellence*;
there we must concentrate all our resources, all our efforts, all
our thoughts.'[8]

2. *The First Paris Conference and American Arbitration*

When the German armistice request was published, the British,
French, and Italian leaders were in conference in Paris, for-
tuitously assembled to discuss the recent capitulation of Bulgaria. They quickly agreed that for the sake of Allied public opinion they should not treat the new approach so cavalierly as they
had that of the Austrians three weeks earlier. 'Whatever the intentions of the enemy *démarche*,' felt Clemenceau, 'I do not
think we should leave it unanswered . . . . The attitude we
take will be of the highest importance for the opinion and
morale of our peoples.'[9]

With this point of principle decided, the Prime Ministers drew
up an outline of the possible armistice conditions. Clemenceau
was unprepared for this, his Western European war aims still
half-formed, and he was slow to see how the clauses of the
Armistice might impinge upon those aims. He agreed to a proposal by Lloyd George that although the Germans should
evacuate Alsace–Lorraine and the left bank of the Rhine, no
Allied occupation forces should replace them. Only after consulting Foch did he secure an alteration, so that the Conference
ended by agreeing provisionally on an occupation of Alsace–

Lorraine, although no territory beyond. In general, Clemenceau's tone was cautious: he wanted 'to demand what is necessary and no more. We must not lay ourselves open to the charge of having, by excessive demands, prolonged the war and caused the deaths of hundreds of thousands of men.'[10]

This restraint was under challenge from within Clemenceau's Government. The leading French Ambassadors advised unanimously that the Germans faced disaster and their note must be rejected.[11] A letter from Poincaré took issue not merely with the terms the Prime Ministers had agreed but also with the principle that the fighting should yet be stopped at all. Only after saying this did the President add that any armistice should at least give the Allies bargaining counters for the peace negotiations and enable them to enforce what they decided. Clemenceau responded to the letter with a paroxysm of rage, and offered his resignation.[12] Relations between the two men were poisoned for the rest of the Government's life. Yet within a fortnight the second part of what Poincaré had written became Clemenceau's policy: in part because of an intervening change in Germany's position, but more because the same view was being urged on the Premier by Foch.

The Marshal's recommendations were presented to the Conference by Clemenceau on the 8th. They rested on a characteristic mixture of military and political justifications. Alsace–Lorraine, considered Foch, was a 'wrongfully invaded area', analogous in status to German–occupied Belgium, Luxemburg, and France. The Allies should occupy all such areas, in addition to three bridgeheads east of the Rhine opposite Alsace, which they could use as jumping-off points if the Armistice broke down. They should also occupy the left bank north of Alsace–Lorraine, as a 'surety for reparations'.[13] In short, although Foch was careful not to say so, his proposals would install the Allies along the coveted military frontier on the Rhine.

Foch's note was the first sign of a distinctive French approach to the Armistice negotiations. He had chosen a scheme which would place the Allies in control of a maximum of German territory. Yet this was not the only possible solution to the problem, even in its technical, military aspect. The 'Collective Opinion' of the permanent Allied service representatives on the Supreme War Council envisaged much more drastic disarmament of the enemy than had Foch, but wished to occupy no more than a few strategic points in Alsace–Lorraine.[14] The French political judgement of what could be imposed on Germany was also hardening. In the Conference sessions of 8–9 October the British and Italian spokesmen felt that both Foch's proposals and the 'Collective Opinion' went beyond what the Allied public would stand for. Clemenceau and the Marshal, however, suggested it might soon be possible to make harsher stipulations than any being considered now.[15]

Thus far the Conference had deliberated in ignorance of Wilson's views. Before replying to the Germans on 8 October the President consulted the Europeans neither about the wording of his message nor about his basic decision to answer in a way that would keep the conversation open rather than terminate it. Once again, therefore, he broke the Alliance's diplomatic unity. Although he could not foresee at the outset how events would develop, these principles of action were clearly in his mind. De Billy, the French Consul-General in New York, warned that 'this note is the expression of a very old-established attitude of the President, which is . . . to retain for the United States alongside its position of belligerent its position of arbiter'.[16]

Wilson's reply caused a difference of interpretation at the Paris Conference between France on the one side and Britain and Italy on the other. The reply's phrasing was ambiguous, and could mean either that a ceasefire could be *granted* if the Germans evacuated Allied soil, or that such an evacuation was the precondition for a ceasefire even to be discussed. Clemenceau accepted the latter reading, and therefore considered Wilson's note was 'excellent'. It had saved the European Allied Governments from embroiling themselves with their domestic opinion by having to insist on stiff armistice terms, and the best course now was to keep silent.[17] Unlike Lloyd George, Clemenceau and Pichon feared neither that the note would allow the Germans to withdraw unmolested to a more favourable line nor that it would start a process which would hustle France into accepting the Fourteen Points and compromising its own war aims.[18] On the contrary, Wilson's intervention appeared to have saved Clemenceau from an embarrassing dilemma and to have made a ceasefire more remote.

For a while, events bore out the French interpretation of Wilson's views. True, he was indignant that the Paris Conference had drawn up armistice conditions without referring to him.[19] But there was no suggestion yet that he was clinging to his diplomatic independence in order, as Lloyd George suspected, to conclude a *fait accompli* with Berlin which would coerce the European Allies into a premature cessation of hostilities. Instead, Wilson protested to Jusserand on the 10th that an armistice at present would be 'against our interest'.[20] His second note to Germany, four days later, complied with a request from the Paris Conference, by stipulating that the conditions of any armistice must be decided by the coalition's military advisers, and must guarantee 'the present military superiority' of its armies. Such terms would destroy German bargaining power as completely as would a capitulation; and the authorities in Berlin were dismayed. Pichon concluded that Wilson had rejected the enemy 'request for mediation . . . he is not making proposals that Germany can accept'.[21] The Foreign Minister told the Senate of his 'entire confidence' in Wilson's judgement, and of his belief that the note of 14 October marked the final American refusal to negotiate a ceasefire.[22] So far from believing that the time was ripe to end the war, therefore, the Government was mainly concerned to see the burden of rejection fall on Wilson. What it felt inhibited from doing itself was welcome to it if achieved through the agency of the United States.

By the middle of October the French Government judged the chances of an armistice to be lessening, and Pichon reaffirmed that it was too early for peace discussions even with the British.[23] Even so, the approach of peace caused subtle shifts in inter-Allied diplomacy, and especially in the uses the coalition partners perceived for military power. It was supposed, except perhaps in Washington, that the deployment of the Allies' forces on the ground would go far to shape the territorial clauses of the Peace Treaty. To Clemenceau's fury, the British had long been accumulating manpower for the offensive which won them control of Syria in September–October 1918. All that France could do to underline its own claims in the region was to land a detachment of sailors at Beirut.[24] In Europe, the Belgians hoped to further their designs on Luxemburg by sharing in any Allied occupation of the Grand Duchy: a request which Clemenceau and Pichon adroitly sidestepped by referring it to Foch.[25] The French High Command hoped to exploit the reversal of fortunes on the Western Front by returning to a *stratégie des gages*, and Pétain's staff prepared an offensive which would strike into Lorraine towards the Saar.[26] Foch, however, was slow to approve these plans, and his strategy in the autumn of 1918 took little account of French territorial ambitions. Instead, he saw as early as the first Paris Conference that these might be fulfilled through the clauses of the Armistice, and he argued this even more explicitly in a decisive memorandum to Clemenceau on the 16th.

At the moment when Clemenceau and Pichon supposed the armistice request had been rejected, Foch raised the most explosive of all the problems of peace. What, he asked, would happen to the left bank of the Rhine? Would France annex all or part of it, or would it set up neutral and autonomous buffer States? The question was urgent, he persisted, for the ceasefire clauses must 'put in our hands sureties which will guarantee that in the peace negotiations we obtain the conditions that we wish to impose upon the enemy, and it is evident that only the advantages established by the Armistice will remain assured; *the only definitive territorial sacrifices will be those conceded by the enemy when the Armistice is signed*'.[27] Clemenceau replied by forwarding a letter by Pichon as 'the doctrine of the Government'. In it, the Foreign Minister reprimanded Foch for trespassing on political concerns, but he acknowledged that 'the necessary guarantees of the peace must have *points d'appui* in the clauses of the Armistice . . . .'[28] From now on this crucial clarification was at the heart of official policy. What lay behind it?

The Government was altering its assessment of both Germany and the United States. At the Paris Conference Clemenceau had supposed the enemy was unlikely to accept severe terms, and persistent evidence was reaching him that the Germans were acting in bad faith: even that they thought it compatible with the Fourteen Points for them to keep Alsace–Lorraine.[29] But Dutasta, the French Ambassador in Berne, reported on 15 October that the German leaders now feared 'the weariness of the troops and the advance of Bolshevism might cause disaster'.[30] And the Swiss authorities, it appeared, were certain that Germany would have to accept any conditions it was offered.[31] By the 18th Foch judged the enemy army no longer able 'to present for any length of time a serious resistance', and Pichon told the British Ambassador that the Germans 'would accept practically any terms we liked to impose'.[32] Although uncertainty did not die entirely, it seemed that the eventuality Foch and Clemenceau had envisaged at the Paris Conference had been realized. The German predicament was so desperate that the Allies could win an armistice that would place the enemy at their mercy and would contain the 'sureties' necessary for the Peace Conference. At the same time the Berlin Government was losing faith in Ludendorff, and after a momentous Crown Council on the 17th most of its members were convinced that nothing could be gained from further bloodletting. On 20 October a German note accepted Wilson's conditions of the 14th. The dialogue between Washington and Berlin had, after all, been resumed.

Now, at last, the French fell prey to alarm about American intentions. Events in Eastern Europe acted as a catalyst. On 18 October Wilson informed the Habsburg Government that the condition he had laid down in the Fourteen Points of autonomy for the Austro-Hungarian subject nationalities was no longer adequate. The nationalities must decide their future for themselves. The effect was dramatic, and the note did much to bring on the Danube Monarchy's disintegration two weeks later. In Paris also it caused consternation. If Austria–Hungary broke up, the way would be open for an *Anschluß*, or union, between the Austrian Germans and their fellows to the north. Having ignored this danger earlier, the Government recoiled at the eleventh hour before the possible consequences of its policy.[33] Pichon pleaded with Jusserand that Wilson must consult his allies before accepting commitments of such gravity. He amplified this with a warning that after losing 1,700,000 dead the French nation could not accept 'a premature peace which would deprive us of our victory . . .'. It had full confidence in its Government's refusing 'any armistice which does not assure the guarantees and reparations indispensable to the conclusion of a lasting peace'.[34]

Wilson's third note to the Germans, on 23 October, ended the dialogue between the President and Berlin, and opened that between him and his Allies. It was understandable that the note should leave Clemenceau 'very much annoyed',[35] for it was the clearest statement yet of Wilson's conception of the Armistice as a contract, under which the Germans would reduce themselves to helplessness in return for being promised a peace 'upon the terms and principles indicated' in his speeches.[36] Yet, commented Clemenceau and Pichon to their Ambassadors, once the Americans passed on the Germans' armistice request 'we shall have no cause to enter into retrospective considerations of the correspondence between President Wilson and the German Government'. All that would be called for as a reply to Wilson would be not (as he requested) a profession of willingness or otherwise to make peace on the basis of his speeches, but simply a list of armistice conditions, drawn up in consultation with the Government's military advisers.[37] It was therefore in a mood of defiance that the French leaders entered the second stage in the making of the ceasefire.

3. *The Second Paris Conference and the German Revolution*

An interlude of preparation followed, before the Paris Conference of 29 October–4 November 1918. Clemenceau's Government used this interlude to draw up a set of armistice clauses for the Western Front which went well beyond Foch's programme of 8 October. At Senlis on the 25th, the Marshal consulted the national Commanders-in-Chief: Pershing (for the USA), Pétain, and Haig. Foch and Pétain held out for the occupation of the left bank and of bridgeheads east of the Rhine; Pershing wanted an unconditional surrender. Haig, sharing his Government's high assessment of Germany's powers of resistance, wished to occupy no more than Alsace–Lorraine.[38] Foch took little account of either the British or the American view in his recommendations to Clemenceau on the following day, which the two men converted into the terms finally presented by the Marshal to the Paris Conference as, ostensibly, an apolitical, technician's appraisal.[39]

Foch paid more attention, however, to the advice reaching him from the Foreign Ministry. Robert de Caix, the editor of the *Journal des débats*, had been seconded to the Ministry, and had become an influential figure. On 20 October he argued that an Armistice should give many more 'sureties' than those re-commended by Foch: French occupation of Alsace–Lorraine and the Bavarian Palatinate, the exclusion of Belgian troops from Luxemburg, an Allied presence in the rest of the left bank and in the Ruhr basin as a guarantee of reparations, and similar occupations of Schleswig-Holstein,[40] of German Poland, and of Czechoslovakia and German Austria in the south.[41] These ideas were adopted in more moderate form by Berthelot[42] and by Pichon himself, who urged Clemenceau to occupy not only the left bank and bridgeheads opposite Alsace, but also bridgeheads further north and the whole of the Ruhr, as well as to establish a 'supervision' of the German mines and railways.[43]

Foch's proposals to the Paris Conference were milder than these suggestions, although influenced by them. He and Clemenceau ignored the Quai d'Orsay's suggestions for Eastern Europe. They kept the Marshal's original stipulations of an occupied left bank and a special status for Alsace–Lorraine, but dropped the claim to bridgeheads opposite Alsace in favour of three at Mainz, Coblence, and Cologne. At the same time, they envisaged a neutral zone of thirty to forty kilometres' width along the remainder of the right bank. The effect would be to leave most of Frankfurt and the Ruhr undefended, and the Germans constantly exposed to pressure through the vulnerability of two of their key industrial areas.[44] This document was far the most important work of preparation by the Government for the Conference, and the Council of Ministers accepted that the Premier would similarly dominate the negotiations themselves. It gave a blank cheque to him and to Pichon, 'accepting, for the moment, to be informed of nothing'.[45] In effect, this was to give Clemenceau alone a mandate to decide his country's destiny at this historic moment.

On 29 October the British, French, and Italian leaders pro-ceeded to preliminary conversations with House, who acted once again as Wilson's envoy. The mood was stormy. Clemenceau introduced the clauses he had agreed with Foch; Lloyd George questioned the need to occupy the left bank, and House, too, with express authority from Wilson, was sceptical.[46] When discussion moved to the Fourteen Points, Clemenceau ob-jected to abolishing confidentiality in diplomacy and to forming a League of Nations which included Germany.[47] House tried to reassure the Europeans with the aid of the Cobb–Lippmann memorandum, a gloss that made the Fourteen Points more palatable and enjoyed Wilson's provisional approval. It did not prevent a dramatic clash with Lloyd George over the freedom of the seas, in which Clemenceau, who supported the British position, was also implicated.[48] Should the European Allies not accept the Points, House warned, the President might continue discussions with Germany alone, and eventually make a separate peace.[49]

That evening Mordacq found his chief anxious and depressed, and afraid that Lloyd George's opposition to Foch's terms showed that Britain was renewing 'its traditional hostility towards us'. Clemenceau instructed Pichon to prepare a note, in which the Foreign Minister expressed his indignation, not to say incredulity, at the implications of House's menaces. For America to present simultaneously to its allies and its enemies peace conditions on which the former had never been consulted was 'irregular, illogical, and unjust'.[50] Before this note could be presented, however, Anglo-French solidarity against the Fourteen Points disintegrated. Early on the 30th Lloyd George gave House a note accepting peace with Germany 'on the terms' contained in Wilson's speeches, but with two qualifications, both conceived from a British standpoint. The first was an absolute reservation about the freedom of the seas; the second an interpretation of the 'restoration' of invaded territories which would allow the Allies to claim compensation for all the damage done to their civilian population and its property by the German land, sea, and air forces.[51] Pichon objected to the vagueness of the Fourteen Points because it would allow Germany to cavil. Yet for Lloyd George the same vagueness was a reason for accepting them; and House no longer faced a united front.

When Clemenceau arrived it soon transpired that he was having prepared a memorandum of dissent. House warned again that American support might be withdrawn, and in the face of this Clemenceau accepted the document presented by Lloyd George.[52] That afternoon the Italians, isolated, gave way in their turn, and the British memorandum, with little alteration, was forwarded by Wilson to the Germans as representing his

Allies' point of view.[53] In American eyes, the three Govern- ments were now bound by a contract, which circumscribed the claims they could bring forward at the Peace Conference. Alone, and in a matter of minutes, Clemenceau accepted almost the entirety of a programme which he and his Ministers consid- ered dangerously vague and a menace to the objectives for which France had made the greatest sacrifices in its history. But he had a stratagem in reserve, and what he had lost through his precipitate acceptance of the Fourteen Points he attempted to make up for in the remainder of the Conference through the clauses of the Armistice itself.

The most important clauses were those for the Western Front. When discussion of the French proposals resumed, Lloyd George persisted in his opposition. If Alsace–Lorraine and Lu- xemburg were occupied, he observed, 'you would have in hand everything you desired in the west at the Peace Conference and, if the Armistice broke down, it would not be necessary for you to attack but for the enemy to do so'.[54] The implication was clear: that the French were risking further bloodshed for the sake of unavowed political ambitions. Foch stuck his ground, however, insisting that the bridgeheads were strategically indis- pensable, and Lloyd George finally gave way. When the Su- preme War Council convened formally on the afternoon of 1 November the terms prepared by Foch and Clemenceau went through almost without comment.

This French triumph was made possible by Anglo-American disunity. House had initially been doubtful about the French conditions; but on 30 October he was silent, and on 1 Novem- ber he supported Foch against Lloyd George.[55] According to the normally well-informed Mordacq, Clemenceau saw House on the morning of the 30th and won him round to Foch's terms.[56] Yet on the same morning, according to House himself, the Colonel made his arrangement about the Fourteen Points with Lloyd George. House may have played off the two Prime Ministers against each other, by giving way to one over the free- dom of the seas, and to the other over the occupation of the left bank. Yet it seems also that the American, who similarly allowed the Italians to occupy the territory they desired from Austria, was blind to the political significance attached by the Europeans to the Armistice terms.[57]

During the remainder of the Conference the French attempted to repeat for Eastern Europe and the financial clauses their success over the arrangements for the west. The Allies were militarily weak in Eastern Europe and their decisions were made harder by the Bolshevik advance, as well as by the break-up of Austria–Hungary even as the Conference was in session. Clemenceau adhered to the policy established in the spring: the Treaty of Brest-Litovsk must be abrogated and Germany's influence destroyed by the withdrawal of its troops from Russian territory. House and Balfour, fearing that the Bolsheviks would fill the resultant void, stipulated that the withdrawal should proceed gradually, as the Allies should determine.[58]

The other main question in the east was Poland, part of which was already in revolt against the Central Powers. On 1 November Pichon urged that the Conference should demand 'the evacuation of Poland in its limits of 1772 with Danzig', in order to ensure that an independent Poland in its historic frontiers was included in the Peace Treaty. This dramatic proposal was in line with Quai d'Orsay thinking on the subject; but neither Foch nor Clemenceau supported it, and Pichon was obliged to acquiesce in a British suggestion that the Germans should pull back merely to their frontier of 1914.[59] It was Balfour and not Pichon who kept open the possibility of sending troops to Poland, when he successfully put forward what became Article XVI of the Armistice.[60]

It appears that Clemenceau was ready to give way in Eastern Europe in order to retain British and American goodwill towards France's own claims on Germany in the west. In economic questions, similarly, the Clémentel plan was compromised when Wilson's speeches were accepted as the foundation of the Peace Treaty. Instead, the Premier concentrated on the matter closest to his own heart: reparations. On this, he succeeded in inserting in the Armistice a clause which became the point of departure for the French claims at the Peace Conference.[61] The combination which emerged from Paris of the Armistice conditions with the Allies' qualified acceptance of the Fourteen Points seemed to Clemenceau to be reconcilable with the fundamentals of French interests. It remained to be seen whether the Germans would accept it in their turn.

On 3 November the German Revolution was sparked off by the sailors and munitions workers who took over Kiel. Insurrection spread to the Rhineland and the cities of the North German plain, and on the 9th it reached Berlin. The Kaiser abdicated, and a provisional Council of People's Commissioners, representing the *SPD* and the *USPD*, or Independent Socialists, was created in his stead. These events vindicated Foch's judgement against Haig's, but they raised the question of whether the Armistice should be moderated in order to help the German authorities prevent the extreme Left from gaining power. Clemenceau and Pichon were not insensitive to the danger of universal social upheaval: even before the German Revolution the Foreign Minister considered that 'Bolshevism is very contagious', and feared that it might spread to France.[62] French press coverage of events in Germany was therefore heavily censored.[63] Yet Clemenceau was more inclined than the British and Americans to consider the danger from German imperialism as even greater than that of revolution. This was shown during the discussion of the Eastern European section of the Armistice, and when House suggested a more general moderation of the clauses the Premier 'stoutly refused to recognize that there was any danger of Bolshevism in France'.[64] In the end, Foch was authorized to make only slight alterations to help the German Government keep order.[65] Clemenceau was afraid that no authority would survive in Berlin which was able to enforce a ceasefire, and that the revolution might facilitate an *Anschluß* between Germany and what was left of Austria.[66] But he and Pichon seem also to have believed that the Bolshevik threat was purposely being magnified by the German rulers,[67] and they were not prepared to sacrifice to it the crippling of the enemy's military power.

Uncertainty persisted until Foch presented the Armistice conditions to the Germans on 8 November. Once the tension eased, the French leaders' more visceral feelings surfaced. On the morning of the 9th, Mordacq, Clemenceau, and Foch conversed in an atmosphere of jubilation: 'We spoke naturally of 1870, of this revenge at last obtained, the supreme object of our existence, the dream so often cherished . . .'.[68] And on 11 November itself, Paul Cambon wrote, 'Great difficulties lie ahead for

us; I hardly dare envisage them, but whatever happens I shall
have seen the revenge for 1870 and I can leave this earth without regrets'.[69]

It was often argued later that the Armistice had been 'premature'. Pétain's offensive in Lorraine, scheduled to begin on 14
November, might have enabled the French Army to strike decisively against the German lines of communication and to
break through to Luxemburg, the Saarland, and the Rhine. In
the longer run, by penetrating to the heart of Germany and
proving to the enemy civil population that it had truly been defeated, the Allies could have stifled the 'stab-in-the-back' legend
whose diffusion played a part in Hitler's rise to power. But this
part was only a subsidiary one, and it would be far-fetched to
conclude that the circumstances of the Armistice made even the
failure of German democracy inevitable, let alone a new world
war. By contrast, it *was* inevitable that to prolong the fighting
would cause the death and mutilation of some tens of thousands
of men. Seen in this light, the standpoint of Foch and
Clemenceau – who were not indifferent to the satisfactions of *la
revanche* – appears both statesmanlike and humane. Although
Clemenceau himself later wondered if the Armistice had been
too mild, in the event the Germans were compelled to sign the
Treaty of Versailles and Foch's judgement proved to have been
sound.

A combination of military success with the collapse of the
German home front had given the Allies sufficient superiority to
be able to dictate their terms. For this reason, as Foch and
Clemenceau acknowledged, the fighting had succeeded in its object and need not be continued. But the decisive, smashing victory which had been proclaimed so often as the only satisfactory
outcome of the war – *that* had not been achieved. Instead, the
conflict had been ended through the arbitration of one of the
belligerents. In what appeared as a spectacular, if unorthodox,
triumph of American diplomacy, the guns had fallen silent far
sooner than expected, and with both sides apparently submitting
to Wilson's desires for the European settlement.

The French leaders were caught off-balance by these events,
and were slower than their British and Italian counterparts to
perceive the drift of Wilson's intervention. By October 1918

American aid was indispensable to the European Allies, and there is evidence that Wilson had intended all along to use their dependence as a lever.[70] Yet to attempt this would have been to risk a political crisis in the United States, where, even before the electoral successes on 5 November of Wilson's Republican critics, much of Congressional and press opinion vehemently opposed an armistice being signed at all. House believed that opinion in Western Europe, on the other hand, would have deserted its own leaders and supported Wilson in an open confrontation. This might have been true of the Socialists and the labour movement; but whatever the early misgivings of Pichon and Clemenceau, the evidence reaching them was that the mass of French opinion would have backed them in refusing an armistice with insufficient 'guarantees'.[71]

The conflict between Wilson and his allies was held below this dangerous level by the divisions of the Europeans themselves. Both Britain and France aspired to a special relationship with the United States; both harboured a profound contempt for the Italians. The French representatives in London twice approached the British, but neither time did consultation between the two Governments result.[72] At the Paris Conference, once House admitted the British reservation over the freedom of the seas, his antagonists' resistance crumbled. At a deeper level still, the American effectives on the Western Front already outnumbered those of Britain, and in a few more months they would have outnumbered those of France itself.[73] The longer the war went on, the more the Americans would dominate the Allied effort in every sphere. Clemenceau and Foch may therefore not have been unhappy that the fighting ended when it did, particularly as they expected the Peace Treaty to be determined more by troop movements on the ground than by any adherence to the ambiguities of Wilson's speeches.[74]

The key to the Government's policy towards the Armistice was therefore its acceptance of Foch's note of 16 October. Suddenly it seemed the Allies could impose what terms they liked, and the claim to a strategic frontier on the Rhine was abruptly resurrected. If the French leaders had never ceased believing that such a frontier was essential, they had been inhibited by the need to preserve the alliance with the Anglo-Saxon Powers. Wilson's arbitration in October 1918 threatened to make actual the latent conflict between these systems of security; Foch offered a method of evading choice, at least until after victory had been won. Both Clemenceau and Wilson desired the Armistice and the Peace – the 'military' and the 'political' questions – to be compounded. But Wilson did so openly and imposed his views by *force majeure*; Clemenceau resorted to a strategy of stealth. Once his conditions for the Armistice had been accepted a public clash with the Americans was not only hazardous; it was also unnecessary, and the conflict between the rival conceptions of the settlement could be delayed until the Peace Conference was convened.[75]

VI

From War Aims to Peace Aims,
November 1918–March 1919

1. *Stability and Security*

With the signing of the Armistice it was time for French war aims to pass from the realm of aspiration to that of action. For the next eight months, the Western Powers debated how the preponderance of force their victory had won should be applied. It was a preponderance gained at a moment when the European economy had been dislocated, and the political structures of the continent were more malleable than they had been for decades. These months were also a strange interlude between the heightened popular emotions of wartime and the more humdrum normality of peace. During them the sinister extremes of Left and Right which dominated inter-war Europe were already visible. All the Allied Governments were aware of the power that public opinion was acquiring in international politics, but they were uncertain either how to interpret it or to channel it to their own ends.

In this atmosphere of expectancy the policies of the victors came into conflict. The fundamental antagonism at the Peace Conference was between competing views of how best to safeguard Europe against any repetition of the holocaust it had witnessed in the four preceding years. This was in part a conflict between President Wilson, with his concern to restore political stability to the continent as a whole, and his allies, all of whom intended to construct local systems of security running more or less directly counter to his aims. Separated from the turbulence of Europe by three thousand miles of ocean, Wilson could rely as could no other Allied leader on solutions of abstract 'justice': on the, in reality, far from infallible opinions of the military, academic, and business specialists who staffed the American Delegation. For many of these men, the Conference was an unparalleled opportunity for American power to weld the industrialized nations into a community of interest, based on shared loyalties to representative government and the market economy, expressed by membership of the League of Nations, and in which territorial and economic causes of tension would have been removed. In the short term this implied policies of food relief and industrial reconstruction which would undercut support for political extremism and incidentally benefit the American economy. In the longer term it implied a territorial settlement which as far as possible would make political and ethnic boundaries coincide, and an economic one which would ensure equal access for all nations to the commodity and export markets of the world. European frictions would thus be dealt with at their root, disarmament could begin, and such dissensions as remained could be settled peacefully through the League.

Strict adherence to such a programme was possible only for a Power without more specific and immediate needs in Europe to cut across the remoter aim of restoring stability to the continent. Wilson came to Paris ill-prepared and with the League far higher among his priorities than any detail of the settlement. Before the Peace Conference began, however, he conceded sufficient of the British Government's objectives to be sure of its support in many of the controversies that lay ahead. Although without land frontiers in Europe, the British retained their traditional concerns with the continental balance of power and naval security in the narrow seas, as well as with their world-wide commerce and imperial lines of communication. They had their programme of security, but it violated national self-determination less obtrusively than those of the continental Powers, and much of it was accomplished in advance. At the Armistice Germany lost control of its navy and Wilson gave way over the freedom of the seas. In the President's first big concession at the Conference itself, the British Empire won *de facto* ownership of the leading German colonies. From now on the British had outstanding against Germany only one claim which was pressing and direct – reparation – and they pursued it with a determination equalling and surpassing that of France. Haunted by the fear that Germany would inevitably regain Great-Power status, they were otherwise prepared to make concessions, although concessions, as the French were quick to comment, which were planned to be at other Governments' expense.

British support for Wilson was therefore neither unconditional nor disinterested. Among the continental Powers, even this much sympathy was absent. 'Through centuries of conflict', wrote Harold Nicolson, 'the Europeans had come to learn that war is in almost every case contrived with the expectation of victory, and that such an expectation is diminished under a system of balanced forces which makes victory difficult if not uncertain. The defensive value of armaments, strategic frontiers, alliances, and neutralizations could be approximately computed: the defensive value of "virtue all round" could not be computed.'[1] The histories of the continental Allies, unlike those of Britain and America, had been dominated by land frontiers and the great defensive systems created to maintain them. After the renewed experience of massacre and invasion which had just ended, a heightened value also attached to the sources of industrial might: to coalfields, steel mills, and railways. From one end of Europe to the other the victors hoped to cocoon themselves in local structures of security: Greece in the Aegean, Italy in the Adriatic, Poland on the North European Plain, Belgium on the lower Rhine. All ran the risk of challenge from Britain or America, but none more than the structure spanning almost the entire continent which was being elaborated in Paris.

After the Armistice as before it the French leaders therefore had to balance their other aspirations against the need for continued friendship with the Anglo-Saxon Powers. They also faced an explosion of public debate at home. French policy at the Peace Conference was moulded by the State in greater isolation from unofficial currents of opinion than had been Briand's aims in 1916–17. The crucial programme for the Franco-German frontier was worked out by a small circle of Clemenceau's intimates, and the same circle decided on the compromises that steered the programme through. But if unofficial opinion did not form policy directly, it was constantly present at one remove in the French negotiators' calculations. This was not because of the danger from the Left, although the Socialist and labour movements were growing fast and edging further into revolutionary extremism. Rather, it was because the great majority of articulate French opinion was determined that the peace should impose the greatest possible restrictions on Germany's influence and power. The Government shared this determination; but because of its need to accommodate Britain and America it had to cope with both internal and external pressures of unprecedented strength that more clearly than ever before were acting in opposite directions.

During the winter of 1918–19 Clemenceau's ministry made ready for the Peace Conference by establishing a negotiating platform and by seeking advance approval for it from the Allies. But policy towards Germany after November 1918 no longer showed itself merely in the quiet labour of Government officials or even in the hurly-burly of inter-Allied bargaining; equally important was action on the ground, far from the conference-chamber walls. It is with that action that this chapter will begin.

2. Faits accomplis, *November 1918–March 1919*

The historic empires which before the war had brought stability to a vast arc of territory extending from the Rhineland to Siberia and Baghdad had yielded to a chaos of revolution and uncertainty. Whatever order emerged from this maelstrom might determine the European balance for years into the future. Yet even to interpret the intelligence coming from the region was difficult enough, and to shape events there the Allies disposed of instruments which, though powerful, were inadequate. None the less, for France this was a time of opportunity. Clemenceau had already tried to anticipate the peace conditions through the armistice: he now attempted new *faits accomplis*, designed to fix Germany's boundaries in advance and even to alter its domestic political structure.

France had little to spare for ventures unconnected with these concerns. In Syria, despite entreaties from Pichon and Poincaré, Clemenceau released only 1,300 men after the Armistice to back up France's claim by joining the British and Arab occupation forces.[2] In Russia the stakes were much higher, less because of the presence of the Central Powers, who were now retreating, than because of the Germanophilia and revolutionary contagiousness which were attributed to the Bolsheviks. The French Government hoped in the long run to see Russia reunited, but its immediate priority was to keep the Bolsheviks out of the Ukraine, and to this end it gave financial support and military advice to the local Whites, as well as landing a small expedition at Odessa in December.[3] The confusion in Russia also made more urgent the long-planned barrier along Germany's eastern frontiers, and here the French could act with more effect. This was most evident in the Sudetenland. Among the German minority in the newly established Czechoslovakia there was agitation for union with the Austrian Republic. Beneš, now Czechoslovak Foreign Minister, feared that a secession of this kind would deprive Bohemia of defensible frontiers and of much of its industry. The French responded by sending military instructors, and with a convention that allowed Czech veterans to be transported from France and Italy. As a result, the authorities in Prague quickly brought the Sudeten rimlands under their control.[4] At the same time, France warned the Parliament in Vienna that the Czechoslovaks would have jurisdiction within their historic boundaries until the final decision of the Peace Conference.[5] The other Allies did not challenge this, and the fate of two and a half million Germans in a region of great strategic importance was quietly pre-empted.

The Sudeten question was bound up with that of the *Anschluß*: the possible annexation by Berlin of the seven million German-speaking Catholics in what was left of Austria. On 12 November the Austrian Parliament voted for such a union. In Paris, a maverick opinion, represented by Laroche, argued that this was inevitable and indeed preferable to the influence an independent Austria would retain in south-eastern Europe. It might also paralyse Germany by creating insuperable tensions between an evenly balanced Protestant north and Catholic south.[6] Clemenceau himself, however, considered an *Anschluß* 'absolutely inadmissible',[7] and an official communiqué on the 19th denounced the Viennese Parliament as unrepresentative.[8] The Premier wanted to follow this with a 'march of honour' into Vienna and Budapest by French troops, although he abandoned the enterprise when the British Government refused to take part.[9] Indeed, not until March 1919 did the French send to Vienna even a diplomatic mission, whose leader, Allizé, was instructed to warn the Austrians against union with Germany, and to seek ways of restoring them to economic independence.[10]

In Austria, therefore, the combination of military and diplomatic action which had been applied in the Sudetenland misfired. Initially, this was also true in Poland, which remained the corner-stone of the French defensive system in the east. Clemenceau's Government gave *de facto* recognition to the expatriate Polish National Committee, and suspected Pilsudski, the new Head of State in Warsaw, of sympathizing with the Central Powers.[11] In January 1919, however, Pilsudski accepted Paderewski, a member of the Committee, as his Prime Minister. Pichon assured the new Government of France's continuing support for 'a Polish State with its historic frontiers and free access to the sea',[12] and the Pilsudski–Paderewski regime turned out to be as unyielding over the frontier with Germany as the exiles had been earlier.

The French were quick to press for military assistance to the new State. In December 1918 the Polish National Committee asked for General Haller's Polish troops in France to be brought home via Danzig and the Danzig–Thorn railway, with the latter being occupied by Allied troops. In this way, Article XVI of the Armistice could act as a cover for establishing control over the vital corridor to the Baltic. Pichon and Clemenceau recommended the suggestion to the British,[13] and the French Delegation brought it up again early in the Peace Conference.[14] Indeed, on 22 January, Foch went beyond it, and argued that the Allies should forestall any enemy resistance by fixing the Polish–German frontier before Haller's troops were sent.[15] Lloyd George and Wilson refused their approval, but the subject was forced back to the Conference's attention by persistent clashes between the Poles and the Germans in the Prussian eastern provinces. Finally, despite American misgivings, the convention renewing the Armistice on 16 February stipulated that the Germans should end hostilities and retire behind a line to be decided by Foch.[16] In this way, the territorial settlement in Poland, as well as in the Sudetenland and on the Rhine, was at least partially anticipated by the movement of Allied troops.

In Western Europe Clemenceau's Government attempted similar initiatives, with the twin focuses of attention remaining as ever the left bank of the Rhine and its northern fringes. New Franco–Belgian negotiations after the Armistice were intended on the French side to create the closest possible association between the two countries short of a customs union. In parallel conversations the French proposed an exporting cartel which would embrace the two iron-and-steel industries as well as those of Luxemburg and the Saar, and be based on an exchange between Lorraine iron ore and Belgian coal.[17]

These projects suffered from the continuing fear in Brussels that French action might eventually 'imperil the full independence . . . of Belgium'.[18] There were also more specific causes of dispute. The Belgian Government had hopes of annexing South Limburg from the Netherlands, but when it suggested that Allied troops should occupy the province Pichon and Foch refused.[19] For Belgium to acquire this territory and Luxemburg, Foch believed, would 'compromise the security of continental Western Europe'. If Belgium annexed Luxemburg its population would rise by barely one-thirtieth but its frontier with Germany would more than double in length. The result would be an invasion corridor into northern France even more exposed than that of 1914.[20]

The Marshal had a ready instrument for frustrating the Belgians' claim. He offered them participation in the occupation of the Grand Duchy only on such terms that they preferred to stay aloof.[21] Instead, he moved his own headquarters to the city of Luxemburg, where his officers took part in francophile propaganda.[22] Many of the Republican and Socialist opposition leaders in the Grand Duchy wanted closer ties with France, whereas the reigning dynasty had been tainted in Pichon's and Clemenceau's eyes by its wartime complaisance towards the Germans. At the end of December, Pichon ostentatiously protested against having to receive a delegation from the Luxemburg Government,[23] and by so doing he galvanized the opposition into preparing a *coup d'état* which the authorities lacked the military strength to resist.

When the *coup* was attempted, however, on 9–10 January, the French failed to press their advantage home. The local Commander, de La Tour, was ordered neither to intervene nor to resist *'faits accomplis'*,[24] but instead he placed his troops at the Luxemburg Government's disposal, and cleared the insurgents out of the Parliament building. A report to Clemenceau condemned de La Tour's action as 'thoroughly regrettable',[25] and when news arrived that a second *coup* was planned the Premier ordered that in no circumstances should French troops aid the authorities again.[26] The plans never came to fruition, and the existing Government remained in power, although, as a result of a French and Belgian *démarche*, unrecognized by any of the Allies.[27] This, however, was not the last that the Peace Conference would hear of Luxemburg.

Further south, there were fewer restraints on the French occupying forces. Alsace–Lorraine was gallicized in disregard of the provisions of the Armistice with a speed that made some of the French leaders themselves afraid that autonomist sentiment would revive.[28] The Government also approved a plan of Foch to reinforce the significance of 'line no. 2', by making it the northern limit of the French customs zone.[29] This was only part of a much larger project to remould the political allegiance of the occupied area by redirecting its commerce. It was soon decided to reduce to a minimum the trade between the left bank and the rest of Germany,[30] and in December more ambitious arrangements were worked out to 'direct' the region's economy in the triple interest of maintaining social order, cultivating the inhabitants' goodwill, and assisting France's own reconstruction. Britain and America gave approval to two inter-Allied committees, which would carry out these tasks with the aid of a local inspectorate.[31]

This economic hierarchy was superimposed on the existing military one. Foch had placed most of the French troops in the south of the occupied zone, where they controlled the Saarland, the Bavarian Palatinate, the southern tip of Rhenish Prussia, and a bridgehead opposite Mainz. Within this region the Tenth Army was commanded by General Mangin and the Eighth by General Gérard, with over-all responsibility falling on General Fayolle. At the summit remained Pétain, as French Commander-in-Chief, and ultimately Foch himself. The emerging French economic policy on the left bank was the work of Jacques Seydoux, the *Sous-directeur des services commerciaux* at the Quai d'Orsay, and, more particularly, of Foch's chief civilian adviser, Paul Tirard.[32] Tirard was a formidable bureaucratic empire-builder who was skilled in disguising political designs as uncontentious technical regulations. His past included service in Morocco, and the outlook of the colonial administrator stamped his attitude towards the Rhineland.

Early in 1919 the policies of Foch and Tirard were cleared at the highest level. French planners generally took for granted that German nationalism was coarser, more superficial and materialistic, than their own.[33] It was therefore primarily by economic inducements that they considered Rhenish sympathies could be won. Passing on a report by Pétain which argued this, Foch requested Government authority to encourage the industries of the left bank to 'turn towards France'.[34] Clemenceau replied by forwarding a letter from Pichon which gave broad but emphatic support to what the Marshal had proposed. 'We must', wrote the Foreign Minister, 'try as hard as possible to create among the population of the left bank of the Rhine a state of mind favourable to France.'[35] On 15 January French citizens were permitted to trade with the occupied zone, and large quantities of French merchandise were sold there in the following months.[36] Tirard prepared a memorandum in which he argued that unless France made its viewpoint clear the separatist politicians in the Rhineland would not risk themselves by campaigning in public, and that a signal could best be given in the economic sphere. When Pichon at length gave his 'entire approbation' to this doctrine, Foch and Tirard could proceed in the assurance of being covered, at least in general terms, by their superiors.[37]

By now, however, as in Luxemburg, the moment of opportunity had slipped by. Immediately after the Armistice, when Germany was defeated, its economy at a standstill, and its social hierarchy under threat, there was a groundswell of enthusiasm for a Rhenish Republic which would be separated from Prussia while remaining in the *Reich*. Catholic political organizations provided the backbone of this movement, and its leaders included the pivotal figure of Adenauer, the Mayor of Cologne. Yet as early as January 1919, with the defeat of the left-wing Spartakist rising in Berlin and the holding of national elections, support for Rhenish separatism was dwindling.[38] Not until the revolutionary wave of March did it revive; not until May did contacts between the French occupation forces and a new generation of separatist leaders move towards decision. At first, therefore, the repercussions of the new policy in the Rhineland were slight.

The fluctuations of opinion in the occupied zone followed developments on the larger German stage. In January 1919 a Constituent Assembly was elected and the Government of the new

Republic was broadened to include non-Socialist parties. Although there was food only for a few months, the distribution system did not break down, and the mechanisms of command in the army and the civil service continued to function. None the less, in December, January, and March the authorities' control of their own capital was challenged, and it was uncertain whether they would avoid the Russian Provisional Government's fate.

The French leaders were less anxious than the British and Americans to arrest the Revolution, and readier to risk its taking an extreme form. Its 'main object', thought Pichon, was 'to obtain more moderate peace conditions from President Wilson by giving him the impression that he controls the destiny of a people whom he can either plunge into Bolshevism or save from this scourge'.[39] In Clemenceau's view, the German democrats had similar intentions in foreign policy to their predecessors, and he insisted that the threat of Bolshevism was a form of 'blackmail', to which the Allies must not submit.[40]

No Allied Government in 1918–19 wished to extend the occupation over all of Germany and embark on an exercise in social engineering on the scale of that attempted after 1945. Except on the country's fringes, their power over Germany was more a power to threaten than a power to act, and their strongest means of influence were economic more than military. Even so, they could at the least powerfully influence German politics, and possibly cause a far more sweeping transformation of German society and institutions than had so far occurred. A struggle developed over food relief, which the American leaders considered the most effective instrument at their disposal to halt the spread of Bolshevism, and were determined to keep under their control.[41] The French did not oppose relief in principle, although they believed the Germans were exaggerating their economic difficulties in order to obtain easier treatment.[42] They also feared that a German economy which had suffered much less wartime damage than their own might steal a march in the race to lift production back to peacetime levels. For France to consent to America supplying Germany freely with food and raw materials, wrote Tardieu, would both remove one method of forcing the enemy to sign the Peace Treaty and 'ruin a second time our factories in the north and east'.[43] As a result of these anxieties France objected, first, to the United States having exclusive responsibility for food relief, and, second, to a series of Anglo-American plans for easing the blockade.[44] Neither of these objections prevailed, and, as will be seen, the French were shown to be equally powerless on the one occasion when they attempted, as the Americans had feared, to make the programme of relief serve their own political ends.

The German Revolution raised for the first time for many years the possibility that the unity of the *Reich* would founder. Although the French leaders hoped for this, they appear to have believed at first that it was most likely to occur if the Allies showed restraint and let matters take their course. When the Americans suggested that the victors should accelerate the creation of a regular Government in Germany by refusing to negotiate until a Constituent Assembly had met, Pichon protested that such an intervention would benefit 'the centralizing tendency . . . of Prussia against the autonomous and federal tendency of other States, notably of Bavaria'.[45]

By the spring of 1919, with German separatism on the ebb, French attitudes were changing. In February a mission was dispatched to Berlin under Professor Haguenin, who from now on was the Government's most important and incisive source of intelligence on German intentions. Haguenin wished to use propaganda and control of food and raw materials 'to keep Germany under surveillance, to dominate, to educate it'.[46] Bavaria, he reported, if given preferential food supplies, could act as the 'lever' which would prise German unity apart.[47] On 28 March Pichon put forward precisely such a scheme in the Peace Conference's Supreme Economic Council, hoping privately to encourage the formation in Munich 'of a ministry which would have supported our interests'. But 'an absolute opposition from the United States' obliged him to retract,[48] and when the next French attempt to aid the German separatists began in May, economic penetration was no longer the favoured means.

In the six months since the Armistice the French had tried to engineer a series of *faits accomplis* which would help to shape the Peace Treaty in the sense that they desired. These attempts were most successful when co-operation from France's allies was unnecessary. Thus the Sudetenland had been subdued, the Belgians kept out of Luxemburg, the German bureaucracy expelled from Alsace–Lorraine, and the left bank flooded with French goods. But when such projects had depended on British shipping – as with the transport of Haller's army to Poland – or American food – as with the preferential revictualling of Bavaria – they had generally been stillborn. By March 1919 the map of inter-war Europe was coalescing after the upheavals of the two preceding years, and the most favourable moment had passed. It was too late for action on the ground to save France from head-on conflict with its allies at the Peace Conference.

3. *Sounding out the Allies, November 1918–March 1919*

The second influence on the Clemenceau Government's negotiating position was its assessment of its partners. This meant largely its assessment of Britain and the United States. The links being planned with Belgium and in Eastern Europe were potentially as much a drain on French resources as a supplement to them, and could not replace a guarantee of France by one or more Great Powers. Some French statesmen – Poincaré most notably – hoped for as close an association with Italy as with the Anglo-Saxons.[49] But French rivalry with Rome was even more acrimonious than that with London,[50] and Italy's financial weakness and military incompetence made the value of its friendship dubious. British and American support, by contrast, was needed to uphold the Treaty clauses and deter renewed German aggression, and to permit France to regain financial stability and reconstruct its devastated regions. Anglo-American intentions on both counts were sounded out at the end of 1918.

While not abandoning the option of collaborating with the United States, Clemenceau began by seeking a prior understanding with London. He had been shocked by American conduct in the Armistice negotiations; he regarded Wilson as the greatest obstacle to French objectives[51] and on 15 November he suggested to Lloyd George that they should attempt to reach agreement before the President arrived in Europe.[52] In addition, he approved an 'Examination of the Conditions of Peace', which Paul Cambon presented to the British on the 26th, and which explicitly portrayed itself as the basis of such an understanding.

The 'Examination' was the first formulation of the ministry's peace programme, and had been carefully prepared. It was both

more and less ambitious than its predecessors of the spring of
1917. The financial section, based on a Finance Ministry memorandum of 18 November, gave a foretaste of the sweeping
French reparations claims put forward at the beginning of the
Peace Conference. The territorial section incorporated a recommendation by Foch of 21 November for a strategic frontier
along the northern watershed of the Saar basin which would require France to annex more than a million Germans on the border of Alsace–Lorraine. The other territorial clauses were prepared by Cambon himself, with revisions by Berthelot. They envisaged that France would take possession of the main Luxemburg railway system, the *Guillaume-Luxembourg*, and that Poland
would gain not only the frontiers of 1772 but also the German
industrial province of Upper Silesia. Towards the left bank of
the Rhine, however, the document was more moderate, suggesting a prolonged occupation, but no change in the region's political status.[53]

Clemenceau entrusted his hopes for an Anglo-French combination primarily to the conference of the European Allied
leaders held in London from 1 to 3 December 1918.[54] No such
combination was agreed in the formal sessions of the Conference, in which Lloyd George refused to discuss territorial questions in the absence of the American leaders.[55] But in an informal meeting with the British on 1 December Foch argued not
merely for a military frontier on the Rhine but also that German sovereignty over the left bank should cease and that its inhabitants should be conscripted for a Western European army.[56]
This went well beyond the 'Examination', and Clemenceau, who
stayed away on this occasion, withheld official backing from the
Marshal's ideas. In another conversation in London, however,
he agreed with Lloyd George to modify the 1916 Sykes–Picot
Agreement in order to give Palestine and Mosul to Britain. The
quid pro quo – so Tardieu later asserted – was a British promise
to support the French over the left bank of the Rhine. The
affair was characteristic of Clemenceau's business methods:
nothing was written down, and Lloyd George was subsequently
able to deny that he had promised anything in Europe in return.[57] There is other evidence, however, that in December
1918 Lloyd George favoured the prolonged occupation of the
Rhineland which at the Peace Conference he tenaciously

resisted.[58] Clemenceau, on the other hand, believed by March 1919 that his entire negotiating strategy had been undermined by Lloyd George giving his word over the left bank and then reneging.

It was perhaps, therefore, because of an assurance from the British Premier that a fortnight later Clemenceau was emboldened to tell London of a major extension to his aims. He adopted Foch's views, not to the extent of wanting to conscript the population of the left bank, but to that of desiring 'an independent State whose neutrality should be guaranteed by the Great Powers'. 'I can see', reported the British Ambassador, 'that he intends to press that very strongly . . . .'[59] It soon became apparent that although the British and American Governments could accept a demilitarized Rhineland under Allied occupation, a change of sovereignty in the area was a far more serious challenge to their ideas. None the less, Clemenceau now authorized his Generals to soften up the Rhinelanders by economic measures, and, as will be seen, entrusted Tardieu with the defence of the buffer-State demand.

Meanwhile, what of the Americans? Clemenceau so distrusted Wilson that at first he wanted to exclude him from the Conference altogether.[60] House as usual seemed more amenable, and Clemenceau broached with the Colonel the subject of the Saar, as well as promising disingenuously to 'discuss no question of any importance' with Lloyd George at the London Conference.[61] This cautious approach was interrupted by a long telegram which Pichon dispatched on 27 November for delivery in Washington. Based on a series of notes by Berthelot, it was an attempt to wriggle out of France's commitment to the Fourteen Points under the cover of certain concessions to Wilson's thinking. It proposed abandoning simultaneously the Allies' wartime 'secret treaties' and the pre-Armistice agreement. The President's speeches would be replaced as the terms of reference for the Peace Conference by a new scheme, whose terse phrases would allow French claims to the 1814 frontier in Alsace–Lorraine, to the demilitarization of the left bank of the Rhine, and to the occupation of part of the right bank.[62]

The telegram was a grave miscalculation, which grossly underestimated the importance Wilson attached to the Fourteen

Points, and gratuitously offended the Italians. Jusserand reluctantly delivered it, but the Americans never replied.[63] It appears that Pichon had made a rare attempt to act independently of Clemenceau, who subsequently told Paul Cambon that he had not been consulted about the telegram and thought Berthelot's ideas 'absurd'.[64] In the event, the French Delegation at the Peace Conference both stood by the 'secret treaties' and did obeisance to the Fourteen Points. The telegram's main consequence was therefore further to discredit the Quai d'Orsay in Clemenceau's eyes.

Possibly because the advances to Lloyd George had been indecisive, Franco-American relations improved at the end of 1918. This was partly due to Tardieu, who returned from his work as High Commissioner in the USA on 20 November, and tried to blunt the anti-American edge of Clemenceau's diplomacy. It was probably he who urged on the Premier the danger of pursuing a *fait accompli* with Britain in Wilson's absence, and the opportunity presented by 'the entry of America into the world two generations earlier than if the war had not intervened, and also the possibility of drawing the United States into the idea of an alliance under the cover of the League of Nations . . .'.[65] When Wilson arrived in Paris in December his first meetings with the French leaders were unexpectedly amicable, and Clemenceau, concluding that 'on the whole he will not give too much trouble', dropped his earlier opposition to the President participating in the Peace Conference.[66] Finally, in a proposed agenda made ready by Tardieu on 5 January, the Government accepted the pre-Armistice agreement and Wilson's speeches as the Conference's terms of reference.[67] Even this document, however, remained broad enough for the whole gamut of French territorial and economic claims to be brought forward under its provisions, and, like Pichon's telegram before it, the agenda was rejected by the British and Americans.[68] As a result, the French claims had to be advanced piecemeal, without the authority they might have gained from being included in a negotiating schedule sanctioned at the start.

One final indication of Clemenceau's thinking came when he addressed the Chamber on 29 December. In what the American Delegation interpreted as a deliberate challenge to Wilson's principles,[69] the Premier admitted that he still saw virtue in the defensive system now condemned by 'certain high authorities': that of strategic frontiers, armaments, and alliances. And yet he gave an even clearer admonition to those who thought that French objectives should be pursued without regard to France's partners. His 'directing thought' in the negotiations would be that 'nothing must happen which might separate after the war the four Powers that were united during it. To this unity I will make every sacrifice.' Clemenceau did not hide that if the Government's more tangible demands – whose substance he refused to disclose – came into conflict with the needs of the alliances, he would give priority to the latter.[70] Thereby he covered his line of retreat relative to the Chamber, which gave him a resounding vote of confidence; but he also publicly admitted the weakness of his bargaining hand.

In ascertaining British and American economic policy, the French began from a position of great vulnerability. In the fiscal year 1918–19 Government spending was more than double Government revenue, and the value of French exports in the first half of 1919 was barely one-quarter that of French imports.[71] The French State was heavily in debt both to London and to Washington, and when the British Treasury suspended its monthly subsidies Paul Cambon won a reprieve only by pleading that otherwise his Government would be reduced in days to 'bankruptcy'.[72] France had little chance of regaining financial independence until it reconstructed the invaded regions, with their disproportionate share of the nation's exporting industries. Because Britain, America, and Germany had escaped invasion, their Treasuries would be spared what promised to be a crushing burden, and they would enjoy a head start in what Loucheur, now Minister of Industrial Reconstruction, expected to be a post-war 'race for foreign markets'.[73] 'In industry and commerce,' warned Clemenceau, 'between France and Prussia, victory for the moment rests with the latter.'[74]

Given this, the French Ministers agreed, the first essential was to keep in being the wartime inter-Allied controls on shipping and on trade in food and raw materials, less now as the instrument of plans to regulate the world economy than as a way of staving off immediate disaster. If France were left as the weakest bidder in an unregulated sellers' market, its industrial reconstruction and even its social stability would be endangered.[75] In consequence, Clémentel approached the British for assurances that his country would have access to sufficient credit, shipping, and commodities to escape 'a situation of inferiority resulting from the war.'[76] The British acceded to this in principle, but subject to the policy adopted by the USA,[77] and a similar French approach to Washington was left, as usual, without reply.[78] As in the dispute over food relief, French expectations conflicted with the Americans' determination to end controls on international commerce and regain full sovereignty over their merchant navy and their exports of goods and capital. They were willing to preserve the vestiges of an inter-Allied system during the transition from war to peace; but that was all. As evidence of this accumulated, French economic objectives began to change profoundly.

4. The Definition of French Negotiating Aims, November 1918– March 1919

By the time the Peace Conference opened, the French had neither formed a duumvirate with Britain nor secured American backing for any territorial or economic dispositions going beyond a strict interpretation of the Fouteen Points. Nor had their attempted *faits accomplis* saved them from weeks of hard bargaining over almost every aspect of the Treaty with Germany. None the less, Clemenceau's Government brought before the Conference a programme that was not only clearer and more comprehensive than those of the spring of 1917 but also more exacting. In the Government's rear, French opinion was engaged in a vast and acrimonious controversy about the conditions of peace, and was losing its solidarity of 1918. The legislature, too, was becoming more difficult to manage, and Clemenceau's support there was eroded both by defections to the Left and by sniping from an intransigent and well-connected Right.[79]

In spite of this, Parliament had little success even in eliciting what the Government's bargaining position was, and had no direct part in that position's formulation. The Chamber's External Affairs Commission, although it drew up a programme of its own, was hardly better informed than were the other

Deputies.[80] The political parties which supported Clemenceau began by leaving him the free hand that he requested, and the running in public debate was made by their rivals and by independent pressure groups. The Socialists, in combination with a portion of the left-wing intelligentsia and the *CGT*, campaigned on behalf of principles akin to those of the Fourteen Points. The colonialists tirelessly defended French rights in Syria, without agreeing among themselves about the ranking order of their other claims.[81] The *Ligue française* also drew up a peace programme, and Barrès renewed his arguments for economic and military dominance over, and ultimate annexation of, the left bank of the Rhine.[82] The most effective patriotic group, however, was the *Comité de la rive gauche du Rhin*, which prompted resolutions in favour of its ideas by Chambers of Commerce and local councils, and was responsible for the meeting of the 'French National Congress' from 28 February to 2 March. The Congress implausibly asserted that it represented twelve million citizens; it was certainly the largest gathering of patriotic, economic, and veterans' organizations on a foreign-policy question that had yet occurred.[83]

By comparison, economic pressure groups were less prominent than in 1916, although most of them expressed their views. The *Association de l'industrie et de l'agriculture française* concentrated on tariffs and reparations;[84] the *Comité central des houillères de France* argued that France must safeguard its energy supplies by establishing control over the Saar basin and through forced coal deliveries from the Ruhr.[85] The *Comité des forges*, however, made no special effort to present its case, and later complained bitterly of not being confided in during the peace negotiations.[86] It is possible that heavy industry exerted its influence more through private contacts with Loucheur, who became Clemenceau's leading economic adviser at the Conference.[87] Yet de Wendel, who knew Loucheur well, also felt he had not been adequately consulted,[88] and the Minister was quite capable of putting what he deemed the national interest before an industrial one when the two conflicted.[89]

There is less evidence about the millions of separate individuals who formed 'opinion' in its broadest sense. Military surveys suggested that Wilson's ideals had only a limited diffusion, and that most of the public still deeply distrusted Germany and had a burning desire for reparation.[90] The pro-Government dailies accounted for well over half the circulation of the French press; of the remainder, most belonged to newspapers which considered Clemenceau too indulgent towards the enemy, and the Socialist and pacifist journals took only a small fraction of the whole.[91] Both unorganized and articulate opinion, however, were bemused by Wilson's great, if ambiguous, prestige. On the Left, it was hoped the President could introduce an international order based not on threats and force but on amicable discussion and the peaceful arbitration of disputes. Elsewhere, it was hoped that under a smoke-screen of arrangements for international co-operation Wilson could be brought to guarantee a peace which would be based on French conceptions.

More serious than this was the tendency of French opinion to overestimate the country's contribution to the Allied victory, and hence to lose patience with obstacles to the full French programme being attained. Most press and parliamentary spokesmen included in this programme both security against German attack, and reparations which would enable France to liquidate its wartime debt and meet the needs of reconstruction without a heavy contribution from the taxpayer. Clemenceau's own awareness of dependence on Britain and America was not widely shared among his countrymen, and differing assessments of that dependence helped to divide him from his critics.[92]

French opinion therefore spoke in strident, if discordant, voices. This did not weaken Clemenceau's determination to keep the peace negotiations under the control of his immediate circle. Not only did he leave Parliament in the dark; even the Council of Ministers did not discuss the subject at length until after the main decisions of the Peace Conference had been taken.[93] Senior politicans outside the ministry, and the leading pressure groups, had less chance to state their views at the highest level than under Briand two years earlier. Even so, at first Clemenceau was supported by most political tendencies except the Socialists. Only after he retreated from his initial bargaining position, in March–April 1919, did crises in Parliament and in civil–military relations briefly result.

The Government's own preparations for the Peace Conference fell into two phases. The first was a largely abortive attempt to collate the views of the interested Departments while a programme was drawn up in the interests of an understanding with the British. After December, however, the official machinery was bypassed. Much of the final negotiating platform was the work of Clemenceau's intimates, and, in particular, of Tardieu.

On 15 November Pichon invited the Ministries to submit position papers on the Treaty, together with drafts of the clauses they desired.[94] The response was belated and incomplete. Economic affairs were well served by Clémentel and Klotz,[95] while the Colonial Ministry and the Quai d'Orsay both drew up sets of extra-European aims.[96] But the War Ministry never summarized its security requirements,[97] and Clemenceau's leading military adviser continued to be Foch. Still more striking was the failure of the Quai d'Orsay to act as a clearing-house, or to present a departmental point of view on European questions. Paul Cambon's 'Examination of the Conditions of Peace' on 26 November was the closest approximation to this;[98] but the claims set out there had been modified by the time the Conference began.

Early in December Clemenceau instructed Tardieu to draw the views of the Ministries and the independent research bodies into a coherent whole. Tardieu died an unfulfilled man, but at this stage in his career he was at the height of his powers and to all appearance destined to become the outstanding French statesman of his generation. Prodigiously endowed with energy and intellect, he combined unflagging stamina with a gift for lucid, if tendentious, exposition. It was Tardieu, chain-smoking into the small hours, who more than any other man prepared and then defended the Government's negotiating aims. Few areas of policy escaped his ubiquitous supervision. Colonial claims were one; the League of Nations, which Clemenceau left to Léon Bourgeois, and German disarmament, which was left to Foch, two more. These were peripheral, however, compared with the financial and economic clauses, Germany's boundaries in the east, south, and north, and, above all, the Franco-German frontier itself.

Of these three areas, departmental preparation was most thorough in the first. In the draft Conference agenda which he prepared on 5 January Tardieu took over with little change of substance the main elements of what Klotz and Clémentel proposed.[99] From the Finance Ministry's memoranda of 18 November and 27 December 1918 it was clear that Klotz placed on 'reparation' a drastic and uncompromising construction. As far as possible, the Ministry recommended, Germany should make restitution in kind for the pillage and destruction in the occupied zone; the balance should be paid in cash, along with the reimbursement of the French State both for disablement and widows' pensions and for the entire cost of the war. Germany should also repay the indemnity it had exacted from France in 1871, with accumulated compound interest for the intervening years. The Ministry offered no assessment of the value of these sums; or of Germany's capacity to make the raw-materials deliveries and pay the cash annuities envisaged.[100] None the less, its ideas were submitted to the British on 26 November, and formed the basis of the stand taken by the French negotiators at the beginning of the Conference.

Clémentel and Hauser drew up France's more general economic aims against a background of continuing lack of reassurance from Britain and America. The Commerce Minister advised Clemenceau that the terms imposed on Germany could be moderated if the Allies would agree to keep the wartime pooling arrangements in being. The irreducible minimum was limited to 'integral reparation' for the damage in the occupied regions and 'guarantees' against dumping and the other unfair commercial practices employed by Germany before 1914.[101] But, significantly, the Commerce Ministry prepared its detailed programme on the assumption that Allied economic co-operation would *not* continue. For this reason, it desired an 'enormous' debt burden to be imposed on Germany, as well as the annexation of the Saar, and coal deliveries of up to thirty-five million tonnes annually for the next twenty-five years.[102]

Unlike the Ministry of Finance, which needed to regain budgetary equilibrium without levying heavy supplementary taxes, Hauser and Clémentel did not think large cash payments desirable in themselves. On the contrary, Hauser feared such payments would vitiate the French economy through inflation, while benefiting German exports through a forced depreciation of the mark.[103] Large cash exactions were considered rather as a second-best, high-risk strategy, designed to meet the emergency caused if the wartime co-operative arrangements ended before the industrial north and east could be reconstructed. The convergence of view between the Finance and Commerce Ministries at the end of 1918 was therefore to some extent fortuitous. Neither, however, had entirely abandoned hope that Allied commercial and financial aid would eventually be forthcoming. Once these illusions had been shattered, in the spring of 1919, the predicaments of the two Departments had much in common.

On territorial questions, Tardieu began with much less detailed guidance. He wrote a long position paper for Clemenceau, in which he came down firmly against an *Anschluß*.[104] Most of the remaining problems, except for that of the Franco-German frontier itself, were considered at a series of meetings that he convened early in 1919, which were attended by his secretary, Louis Aubert, by General Le Rond, of Foch's staff, and by spokesmen for the Quai d'Orsay and the *Comité d'études*. The latter's reports were uncompleted when the Peace Conference opened, but Tardieu used what was available, and sometimes incorporated its evidence bodily into his memoranda. More than this had never been expected from the *Comité*.[105]

A first session on 29 January took as axiomatic that Poland must be strong enough to serve as a 'buttress against German expansion' and a 'screen between Russia and Germany'. For this reason, it favoured the boundaries proposed by the Polish National Committee, and in particular the annexation of a broad corridor to the sea at Danzig. It conceded that the 'internationalization' of Danzig and the corridor might have to be accepted as a second-best, out of deference to Britain and America.[106] But most of the Polish nationalist programme – which had been defended in a particularly ruthless position paper from the Quai d'Orsay[107] – was now to be supported by the French Delegates at the Peace Conference. Similarly, a second meeting agreed to encourage the Czechoslovak claims, and recognized once again the economic and strategic indispensability of the Sudetenland.[108]

The Belgian programme called for more delicate judgement. A final session decided to support the Brussels Government's controversial demand for the Dutch territories of South Limburg and the left bank of the Scheldt, for which Holland would be 'compensated' at Germany's expense in Guelderland and on the lower Rhine. Over Luxemburg, the need to avoid antagonizing Brussels conflicted with France's economic and strategic interest in the Grand Duchy's fate, as well as its supposed 'sentimental' claim on the inhabitants' affections. After contemplating a partition which would give France the steelmaking district and leave the rest of Luxemburg to Belgium, the meeting eventually broke up without reaching a solution to its dilemma.[109]

Tardieu and his associates took over most completely the work of preparation for the Franco-German frontier. The main questions to consider were the northern border of Alsace–Lorraine and security arrangements on the Rhine. Berthelot had already drafted arguments in favour of the 1814 boundary; Laroche went further, and desired the strategic frontier to the north of the Saar basin which was also recommended by Foch.[110] As for the Rhine, the 26 November 'Examination of the Conditions of Peace' had advocated a demilitarized left bank under Allied occupation; Clemenceau wanted a buffer State, and Foch wanted to conscript the inhabitants as well.[111] It was time to decide which of those possibilities to take up.

On 25 January Tardieu marshalled his thoughts about the northern frontier of Alsace–Lorraine in an '*Exposé* of the Saar Question and its Possible Solutions'.[112] He drew on Foch's note of the preceding 21 November, and on a characteristically shrewd contribution from Aubert.[113] On the one hand, Tardieu felt, France's claim to the coal deposits themselves was indisputable, both as compensation for the destruction of its collieries in the Nord and the Pas-de-Calais and as a means of preventing the acquisition of Alsace–Lorraine from so worsening the country's coal deficit as to make it a 'tributary' of Germany. On the other, it would be difficult to take possession of the subsoil without annexing the surface, and here the best defensive frontier was Foch's line. But to take that line would mean annexing one million people, of whom all but 120,000 were culturally German. For this reason, France must in any event give generous autonomy and perhaps be content to acquire the coalfield area narrowly defined. Whereas Foch had conceived his strategic frontier as a *supplement* to a military presence on the Rhine, Tardieu wished to claim it only if the latter could not be obtained.

Following Aubert, Tardieu had used the arguments of economic and strategic *Realpolitik*: France's historical and sentimental claims seemed unlikely to cut ice with the Americans, and the 1814 frontier, in particular, he considered valueless. On 6 February, however, Clemenceau finally asked the British for precisely that frontier, including the Landau salient north of Alsace, together with a nominally independent republic under French occupation which would cover the remainder of the coalfield.[114] The Premier therefore aimed towards the middle of Tardieu's range of options; but he allowed his emotional attachment to the 1814 line to override the logic of his adviser's arguments.

Tardieu's thinking on the broader frontier question crystallized in the aftermath of a new initiative by Foch. In a note to the Allied Governments on 10 January 1919 the Marshal renewed his advocacy of a prolonged occupation of the Rhine and of a buffer-State system on the left bank, while dropping his earlier idea of conscripting the local population.[115] Clemenceau instructed Tardieu to reinforce and clarify these contentions for presentation to the Peace Conference.[116] Tardieu accordingly stated the essential of the French demand in three memoranda on 20 January,[117] and elaborated the supporting argument in a 'Summary Note' on 19 February [118] and a culminating 'French Government Memorandum on the Fixing of the Rhine as the Western Frontier of Germany and on the Inter-Allied Occupation of its Bridges' six days later.[119]

For all the subtleties of Tardieu's exposition, the substance of this claim was simple: that German sovereignty over the left bank should cease, and that Allied troops should be stationed on the Rhine, with both provisions to apply indefinitely. Tardieu's most considered attempt to reconcile this with national self-determination appeared in his note of 20 January on 'The Political Status of the Rhenish Territories of the Left Bank'.[120] In it, he dwelt less on the historic loyalties to France which supposedly lingered in the region than on the reports of the French occupying forces. According to these, the left bank 'places its material interest above all else', and, if independence would bring better economic prospects and security from Bolshevism, 'separation from Germany will no longer meet with obstacles'.

The political arrangements for the area therefore mattered less than the attendant economic incentives. It should be divided into one or more independent States, disarmed, neutral, and with no diplomatic representation of their own. Their prosperity would be assured by the abolition of military service, partial exemption from reparations payments, and preference over the rest of Germany in the supply of raw materials. They would be included in the 'Western European customs zone', and be spared from the depreciation of the mark by means of their own central bank and note issue. The whole of this ingenious argument, therefore, depended on the French occupying forces being right in their impression that German nationalism in the Rhineland was a calculating nationalism, whose allegiance would shift as it perceived the balance of material advantage.

Tardieu's second task was to defend an indefinite Allied presence on the Rhine. He relied in part on the technical considerations adduced by Foch: that the Rhine was the only natural barrier of its kind available, that it could not be outflanked, that it was an obstacle to tanks.[121] Further, the German railway system permitted infantry deployments, prior to an invasion of Western Europe, either on the left bank or on the line of the river itself, and only Allied control of the Rhine bridges could prevent both.[122] Germany, Tardieu asserted, might be able to evade disarmament measures, and, if there were no obstacle on the Rhine, to seize the exposed French and Belgian industrial regions before the unwieldy League of Nations machinery could give assistance to the victims. Such hypotheses could be persuasive, however, only in conjunction with Tardieu's explicit assumptions that the leaders of 'the so-called German democracy' were as devious and implacable as their predecessors.[123] This was the view of Germany as a hardened criminal, unreformed and perhaps unreformable. If it was correct, to weaken Germany by the proposed arrangements in the Rhineland would be a general Allied interest, compatible with the spirit of the League of Nations, and a cure for rather than a cause of war. But if Britain and America remained unimpressed, Tardieu warned, France would insist on preventing at least one possible German deployment by acquiring Foch's strategic frontier north of Alsace–Lorraine.[124] This was a bargaining threat that in the last resort France might present even more embarrassing demands.

Although divided by personal animosities, the French leaders were united behind Tardieu's Rhenish programme. Pichon and Clemenceau approved the memorandum of 25 February with little alteration;[125] Poincaré lauded it as 'quite remarkable and in most felicitous agreement with those of Foch'.[126] Because most of Tardieu's work was designed for presentation to the Allies, however, it left out one element of the French élite's innermost thinking. In his note of 10 January, Foch let slip the hope that the left bank might eventually desire political union with its western neighbours,[127] and Poincaré suggested an amendment to Tardieu's 25 February memorandum which would leave this possibility open.[128] Clemenceau himself told a delegation from the Senate that, 'In reality, we shall occupy until the country is willing to unite itself with France'.[129]

Whatever *arrière-pensées* lurked behind the Rhenish programme, Tardieu's apocalyptic reading of the German mind was sincere. Both the French leaders and much of French opinion viewed Germany with abhorrence, as an enemy of a peculiarly odious kind. In London in December 1918, Clemenceau himself pleaded for the Kaiser and his 'accomplices' to be tried for 'the greatest crime in history'.[130] As well as territory and reparations, punishment for German war crimes was under study as the Conference approached.[131] Out of this mood there grew what some observers took as a concerted plan to grind down Germany in every sphere, whose result would be 'nothing less than the domination of Europe by France'.[132] The French Delegation at the Peace Conference did indeed have a sharper and more detailed knowledge of what it wanted from the European settlement than did either of the Anglo-Saxon Powers. Repeatedly, as the Conference proceeded, French drafts acted as a basis for and set the limits of discussion. But this had been achieved at the expense of consultation with unofficial French opinion and with the slow-moving and factionally divided officials of the War Ministry and the Quai d'Orsay. Furthermore, no blueprint set out the French conception of the Peace Treaty as a whole, and if any concerted plan existed it was only in Tardieu's capacious memory. No one else, not even Clemenceau, was so familiar at once with policy in Western Europe, in Eastern Europe, and in economics and finance.

How did the elements of a French programme that had emerged by February and March 1919 compare with the Briand Government's thinking two years earlier? Outside Europe there had been little change. The Government claimed its share of the German colonies in West Africa which it had partitioned with the British. From the Sykes–Picot Agreement it retained powerful but still ill-defined aspirations in Syria.[133] Inside Europe, however, the French negotiators wanted *de facto* control of the whole of the Saar, and were strongly attracted by Foch's 'strategic frontier', which went well beyond it. The Doumergue Agreement had envisaged an occupation of the left bank pending reparations; Clemenceau asked for a permanent occupation which would also take in bridgeheads east of the Rhine. While uncommitted over Luxemburg, his ministry favoured German 'compensations' to the Netherlands for annexations at Dutch expense by Belgium. It also wished to see an Eastern European system of alliances that would pivot on a Poland and a Czechoslovakia equipped with frontiers going well beyond what ethnic criteria would justify. Finally, Clémentel and Hauser had drafted arrangements for restraining German economic growth, and Klotz had defined the French financial claims in uncompromising terms. Privately, Ministers cherished hopes that the left bank could be annexed and German unity dissolved. These, however, were velleities that could not be converted into proposals for the Treaty clauses, both because the French leaders were reluctant to violate national self-determination too nakedly, and because of their need to conciliate the Anglo-Saxon Powers.

The true nature of the French demands can be understood only by reference to this need. The claims that were presented fell short of some of the French leaders' deepest desires; but they were also a maximum programme, an insurance against being left in isolation with Anglo-American assistance totally withdrawn. Should the Allies be more tractable, much of the programme could be modified, and not all of it was regarded as intrinsically of value. Concessions might be possible, for example, over Danzig and the Polish corridor. But if no agreement were forthcoming Foch's frontier in the Palatinate and enormous reparations demands remained as an alternative. On the threshold of the conference chamber, the ministry conserved its options: some of its members inclining to economic and security co-operation with the Allies, others wishing rather to maximize France's independent strength. As the Heads of Government converged, the moment had come for French preparations to be put to the test.

VII

France and the Making of the Treaty of Versailles, January–June 1919

1. *The Peace Conference*

The Peace Conference opened in Paris on 18 January 1919. For the next five months the Allied leaders wrestled with the task of making peace with the defeated Powers. In the process they debated Asia and the Middle East as well as Poland and the Rhine, and the settlement with Germany formed only one component of a larger diplomatic edifice. It was, however, that edifice's corner-stone, and was overwhelmingly the most important part of it for France. Yet until March little of the German Treaty was decided. Then, in six weeks of often strenuous bargaining, its outlines were agreed in time to be presented to the German Delegation on 7 May. In the final phase, of exchanges between Germany and the Allies, the fragile compromise attained between the Western leaders was jolted by the attempts of each of them to change it in their favour. At last, however, the Berlin Government submitted, and on 28 June the Treaty of Versailles was signed.

The Conference's initial forum of decision was the Council of Ten. This comprised the two most senior representatives from each of America, Britain, France, Italy, and Japan, together with phalanxes of officials and advisers. From 25 March it was superseded by the Council of Four, in which Wilson, Lloyd George, Clemenceau, and the Italian Premier, Orlando, conversed alone, except for a note-taker and interpreter. An additional feature of the Conference was the multitude of specialized commissions on economic, territorial, and other questions, which the Allied leaders set up in January and February and whose recommendations they considered in March and April. In this many-layered structure, the different national Delegations could work effectively only if clear guidance was given by their chiefs and internal disagreement avoided. None found it easy to present a consistent front in every portion of the Conference machinery.

Of the three most powerful Allies, the French seemed to many observers the most successful in surmounting these problems and in incorporating their objectives in the Treaty. None the less, Clemenceau's tactics caused heated argument in his Government and among the French negotiators, and actions which to the British and Americans seemed concerted from the centre often had in reality only a fortuitous harmony. Clemenceau's choice of plenipotentiaries – himself, Pichon, Klotz, Tardieu, and Jules Cambon – aroused recrimination. This was exacerbated when the usual discrepancy appeared between the holders of formal and of effective power. Jules Cambon served on some important specialized commissions, but was not among the Premier's intimates. The unfortunate Klotz earned Clemenceau's ridicule, and Loucheur replaced him as the leading author of French policy both towards reparations and in economic questions generally.[1] As the Conference progressed, even Pichon was frequently excluded from the inner circle's deliberations.[2] Loucheur and Tardieu, more than any other members of the Government, spoke with Clemenceau for France in the most vital Paris debates.

Despite Clemenceau's scorn for the diplomatic corps – which he demonstrated once again by appointing his protégé, Dutasta, as the Conference's Secretary-General[3] – he could not do without its services entirely. At first, while he and his assistants concentrated on reparations and on Western European security, Eastern Europe and colonial questions were in the domain of the career officials.[4] After the territorial commissions had reported and the Council of Four began its sittings, however, the Quai d' Orsay was kept in almost total ignorance of the Allied leaders' discussions.[5] Poincaré, whose jealousy of Clemenceau had become almost deranged, was better informed, but little more influential.[6] Some members of the Council of Ministers could help to shape detailed sections of the clauses,[7] but the Council was not consulted on the Treaty as a whole until it was presented with a virtual *fait accompli* in its sessions of 25 April and 4 May.

The Premier's methods led to the formation of a coalition of the excluded, which eventually mounted the most serious challenge to Governmental control of foreign policy since 1917. The challenge did not, however, come from the same direction as before. 1919 was a year of social unrest, in which days lost through strikes reached a record level. Violence in the streets of Paris on 1 May caused some in authority to fear that revolution would advance from Central Europe.[8] But the danger from the Left mattered less to Clemenceau than the restiveness among his nominal supporters in Parliament, who were encouraged not only by Poincaré but also by Foch. The Marshal was the one man in public life whose prestige rivalled the Prime Minister's, and the possibility that conflict between the two might culminate in military defiance of the civil power could not, in the troubled atmosphere of the time, entirely be ruled out.

2. *Opening Moves, January–March 1919*

Like many statesmen of his years, Clemenceau husbanded his strength by delegating to trusted lieutenants and by focusing his own attention on what he considered primary. Although of formidable judgement, courage, and intelligence, he was impatient with legal, financial, and even military technicalities, and regarded professional opinions with suspicion. Inevitably also, for much of the negotiation, he was feeling his way. He began the Conference with 'his own ideas on two or three essential points: the rest let him indifferent'.[9] Crucial among these points was that of ensuring French security by some combination of an Anglo-American guarantee with a physical presence on the Rhine. He planned to achieve such a combination by 'making concessions to the Allies in order to win their co-operation over the essentials', and by postponing discussion of the territorial questions that concerned France.[10] This was to risk that the unilateral renunciations which he made in order to cultivate British and American goodwill would, at the critical moment, go unrequited.

In its opening weeks the Conference awaited the reports of the specialized commissions and attended to urgent executive tasks. These included disarming and supplying food to Germany; as well as considering successive British and American proposals for a negotiated settlement to the undeclared war between the Allies and the Bolsheviks. Whereas Foch argued for a vast crusade in Russia, Clemenceau envisaged no more than limited military and economic pressure of the sort already being applied. He was, however, far more hostile than were Wilson and Lloyd George to seeking compromise. He reluctantly approved a conference on Prinkipo island in the Sea of Marmara which all the Russian factions were invited to attend, but the Quai d'Orsay helped to defeat this by encouraging the Whites to refuse. French policy therefore contributed to the Allies' dilemma of being unable either to overwhelm the Bolsheviks or to come to terms with them. Meanwhile, the uncertainty in Russia complicated almost every decision that the Conference had to take.[11]

The main clauses of the German Treaty to be agreed on in these weeks were those for the German colonies and the League of Nations. Syria and the Ottoman Empire remained a loose end which embittered Clemenceau's relations with Lloyd George until long after the Treaty of Versailles had been signed. German influence in Morocco and in sub-Saharan Africa, however, was expeditiously destroyed. Clemenceau's Minister of Colonies, Simon, defended France's right to annex its share of Togoland and the Cameroons, but Clemenceau was willing to hold these territories under a League of Nations mandate on condition that their inhabitants could serve in France's depleted European armies.[12] Indeed, far from opposing international institutions on principle, the French began by hoping that these would elicit British and American commitments to help solve the country's security, economic, and financial problems. The first phase of the Conference saw the disappointment of these hopes.

With encouragement from House, Clemenceau viewed the League of Nations as a device which might prolong indefinitely the wartime alliance. He therefore gave full backing to his representatives on the Conference's League of Nations Commission, Bourgeois and Larnaude.[13] Bourgeois's proposed amendments to the Anglo-American draft Covenant for the League could be construed both as an attempt to give it a coercive power which it would otherwise lack and as a design to convert it from a body of genuinely universal scope into a disguised alliance of the type Wilson hoped to make superfluous. With an obvious reference to Berlin, Bourgeois wanted no State in the League that could not give 'effective guarantees it would honour conventions in good faith'. The organization from which Germany would thereby be excluded would both 'exercise an international surveillance over armaments and effectives' and have a permanent military and naval planning staff.[14] The Commission voted down these suggestions, however, and the Covenant which emerged on 14 February deprived Wilson of much of his support among the internationalist Left in France. It also disabused those conservatives who had hoped that he would acquiesce in French objectives under an idealistic veneer.[15]

The French economic negotiators were similarly frustrated. In January Clémentel regained optimism that Britain and American would agree to France being supplied with raw materials on special terms. He and Loucheur were therefore willing to limit reparations to compensation for the pillage and destruction in the invaded zone.[16] But in the Economic Drafting Commission of the Conference and in its successor, the Supreme Economic Council, Clémentel again failed to win American acquiescence in his desires.[17] This was the final disillusion, and the Commerce Minister's projects at last ceased to dominate French economic diplomacy.

A third setback was financial. Informal contacts with the British suggested they would support a French proposal for the Allied Governments to redistribute amongst themselves the debts they had incurred during the war.[18] In the Conference's Financial Drafting Commission, Klotz supported an Italian request for this to be discussed, only to be warned by the American Treasury that it would suspend loans to any Government which favoured such a plan.[19] The Financial Drafting Commission did approve in principle an idea of Klotz for a 'Financial Section of the League of Nations', which would have made the League an Allied debt-collector, charged with enforcing the Treaty's economic and financial clauses.[20] But this, too, failed to gain approval at a higher level.

French enthusiasm for inter-Allied economic and financial institutions had been genuine, if far from altruistic. The League, by contrast, although possibly a substitute for an Anglo-American guarantee, had never been considered as able to replace a military frontier on the Rhine. It proved to be no equivalent even to a guarantee, and Tardieu's memoranda in the following weeks made this plain.[21] Wilson's resistance to

French pretensions caused an about-turn in Clemenceau's negotiating strategy, and early in February the French began preparing to force decision on the major questions while the President
was absent on a visit to America scheduled for later in the
month.[22]

On the 6th, Clemenceau and Tardieu revealed to the British
leaders their desires for the Saarland and the left bank, while
keeping the American Delegation uninformed.[23] In the Commission on the Reparation of Damage (or CRD), meanwhile, Klotz
advocated claiming all the categories of 'reparation' his Ministry
had defined.[24] Above all, this meant war costs, which Britain
and most of the Allies also wanted to include, in opposition to
the United States. In addition, French and American ideas conflicted over the 'fixed sum': the valuation of Germany's debt to
be entered in the Treaty. If no figure were stated, the Americans feared, the Berlin Government's credit-worthiness would
be so uncertain that it would be unable to raise in the New
York capital market the loans needed to restore prosperity and
political stability in Germany and, indirectly, in Europe as a
whole.[25] This danger seemed less pressing to the French than
that of German liability being determined prematurely and
hence, perhaps, set at too low a figure. In the CRD's second
sub-committee, Loucheur appeared to contemplate an even
higher valuation than did the British, although he admitted that
it would be difficult to find a mechanism for the Germans to dis-
charge their debt.[26]

By the time Wilson departed, on 15 February, the French had
aligned themselves with Britain against him over reparations,
and apparently were trying to do the same over Germany's
western frontiers. Clemenceau and Tardieu understood the
ethical and even strategic objections to their Rhenish programme, but they felt obliged to pursue it in the absence of any
Anglo-American commitment outside the League.[27] Klotz's reparation claims were a similar response to the demise of his and
Clémentel's initial hopes. In late February and early March
there was an interregnum, during which Lloyd George and Wilson were absent, and were represented by the more conciliatory
Balfour and House. Although Clemenceau himself was badly
wounded by a would-be assassin on 19 February, his Delegation
now tried to capitalize on the general impatience with the Con-

ference's slow progress in order to score negotiating *coups* over reparations and the Rhine.

Foch began the new French onslaught. He urged that Germany's frontiers in the west and east should be fixed without delay, with the object, as he hoped, of terminating Berlin's sovereignty over Danzig and the left bank of the Rhine.[28] The French civilian chiefs supported him, and impressed on House and Balfour the idea of a lightning settlement.[29] Tardieu made known to the Americans his proposals for the left bank, and his outpouring of memoranda reached its height.[30] Confidentially, he hinted that neither the buffer States nor the Allied occupation need be permanent, and he won the personal approval of the Colonel and the Foreign Secretary for his ideas in his form.[31] But at a meeting with Lloyd George and House on 7 March, Clemenceau, reasserting himself after his illness, rejected in any circumstances 'the principle of self-determination' on the left bank.[32] The Allied leaders were still far from compromise, and the Conference was approaching the first of successive deadlocks over French security.

This was made plain when Germany's frontiers were considered on 11–12 March by a special committee of Tardieu, of one of Lloyd George's closest advisers, Philip Kerr, and of the American, Mezes. Wilson had at last unambiguously instructed his representatives to agree to nothing about the Rhine until he returned,[33] and for most of the discussion Mezes kept a guarded silence. Kerr, however, attacked the ideas of a permanent occupation and of buffer States. Tardieu in turn considered Kerr's alternative – a German army limited to 100,000, a demilitarized left bank, and a possible Anglo-American undertaking to defend these provisions by force – to be inadequate. He also warned that France might have to claim Foch's strategic frontier to the north of the Saar, and thereby annex more than a million Germans.[34]

The French had failed to force a settlement in Wilson's absence, and a common front with Britain was more remote than ever. Clemenceau was enraged that Lloyd George had, as he supposed, gone back on earlier promises to support him over the Rhine, and the difficulties encountered in parallel Anglo-French negotiations over Syria drove a further wedge between the two Prime Ministers.[35] When on 14 March Lloyd George and Wilson jointly spelled out to Clemenceau their opposition to his Rhenish claims, it appeared that the entire French negotiating strategy had been abortive. But at least both sides' illusions were definitively removed, and the real bargaining could now begin.

In late February negotiations over reparations, too, entered on a phase of spurious concord. In contrast with the Rhineland, however, the French made large concessions, at the expense of their initial solidarity with the British. Yet reparations were the subject over which French domestic opinion pressed the Government most strongly, and the motives for the change of direction remain obscure.[36] Clemenceau was willing to compromise on his financial claims if it would strengthen his hand over security,[37] but at this stage the two sets of negotiations seem still to have been proceeding independently.

One reason for the new approach was the growing influence of Loucheur. Loucheur's background – like Tardieu's – was that of a politician of the Fifth Republic more than one of the Third. A graduate of the *École polytechnique*, he had made his fortune as a civil engineer and armaments producer before being brought into government in 1916. As the Conference proceeded, Clemenceau drew on his advice in matters as diverse as reparations, German disarmament, and the left bank of the Rhine. Loucheur shared Clémentel's preference for raw-material deliveries and moderate cash payments rather than Klotz's more extreme position, and he recognized the technical difficulties of recouping the Allies' entire war costs from Germany.[38] For this reason, he may have been impressed by the American argument that France would have a larger share of what remained if war costs were omitted. At all events, by early March the French claim to war costs had been dropped.[39] At the same time, in the CRD's second sub-committee, Loucheur reduced his estimate of Germany's capacity to pay. He fell below the British figure and almost reached the American one.[40] In the report of the 'Committee of Three' which he signed on 15 March with Montagu for Britain and Davis for the USA he dropped even further,[41] and Britain more than France now seemed the biggest obstacle to a moderate reparations settlement. Like Tardieu, however, Loucheur was overstepping his mandate from Clemenceau. The

Premier had no time for the intricacies of the negotiation, but he was more sensitive than was his Minister to French domestic feeling,[42] and at the end of March his position was again to harden.

Over two remaining aspects of the German Treaty the Conference made more progress in its opening phase: the military clauses, and Germany's frontiers other than with France. The first of these was complicated by the dual meaning given to disarmament: the narrow one of rendering Germany helpless, and the broader one of a general reduction in the armaments of the Powers, as conceived of by the Fourteen Points. During the Armistice negotiations Clemenceau had accepted Foch's view that occupying the Rhineland was a more important security than was disarming Germany, and this remained his doctrine at the Conference.[43] Perhaps because of this, the military clauses were another area in which he was willing to give ground.[44]

When German disarmament was discussed in early March disagreement centred on one question. A commission under Foch recommended a small German conscript army; Lloyd George desired an even smaller one which should consist entirely of volunteers.[45] Behind the finely balanced technical considerations, Lloyd George suspected that the Marshal had, as usual, an ulterior motive: that of keeping a large, trained population in Germany as a pretext for not diminishing France's own armed forces.[46] Foch, and with more caution, Clemenceau, certainly intended to keep a powerful standing army in being,[47] and there might be circumstances in which such a force would give France political leverage. Nor did the French representatives sympathize with the Anglo-American view that great conscript armies contributed to international tension irrespective of who controlled them. But the dispute was quietly interred when Clemenceau accepted the voluntary principle,[48] and Germany was left with an army barely sufficient to keep order in a revolutionary period, as well as being deprived of a General Staff and of the right to equip itself with aircraft, poison gas, and tanks. In defending their programme for the Rhine, however, Clemenceau and Tardieu attempted to discount this by referring to the problems of inspection and enforcement. It was on these problems that the later history of the military clauses would turn.

Between January and March Germany's frontiers other than with France were examined by specialized commissions. The French delegates on these bodies followed the lines agreed by the Quai d'Orsay, Tardieu, and the *Comité d'études*, and championed the claims of the smaller nationalities against the Germans. Where dispute arose, they gave greater weight to the nationalities' economic and strategic interests than to the principle of self-determination. The British and American experts, lacking adequate guidance from their superiors, generally did not resist, and the French were able to obtain a succession of favourable decisions, which the Allied leaders often sanctioned later without argument.[49]

In the Commission on Polish Affairs, Poland's right to annex Danzig and the corridor was not contested. The Commission accepted French proposals for departures from the ethnic line in the Bartsch and Schneidemühl regions farther south, and reached a compromise between the French and Anglo-American views about the corridor's eastern edge.[50] In the Commission on Czechoslovak Affairs, similarly, Jules Cambon and Laroche quickly won agreement that the Sudeten Germans must remain in Czechoslovakia. They also resisted an American suggestion that the Rumburg and Eger salients should be ceded to Germany, although on this unanimity was not attained.[51]

The French task in the Commission on Belgian and Danish Affairs was less straightforward. Clemenceau's Government got on badly with the Danish authorities, who feared there would be permanent friction between themselves and Germany if the latter were forced to cede too much of the disputed province of Schleswig. Nevertheless, the Commission approved a report by Laroche which provided for a plebiscite in a larger part of Schleswig than the Danish Government had wanted.[52] As for the Belgian–German frontier, the British and American experts acquiesced in Belgium gaining Malmédy and neutral Moresnet, and eventually accepted Tardieu's arguments for Eupen to be transferred as well. In addition, the French were the strongest advocates of Holland being 'compensated' by Germany for ceding land to Belgium, and the Commission forwarded this project to the Allied leaders with a cautious imprimatur.[53]

In spite of these successes in the territorial commissions, little of the French programme against Germany had been accepted or rejected at the highest level by mid-March. That programme had been fully disclosed, in the Conference's specialized agencies and in conversations between the Allied leaders. On some points – reparations, colonies, the League – compromise had begun. But the core of the future Treaty was barely visible even in outline. Two things, however, were clear: France could not mobilize a general Allied combination against Wilson, or make him yield over substantive issues by internationalist gestures. The time had come for concessions over major and not merely minor issues if the alliances were to be preserved.

3. *The Crucial Compromises, March–May 1919*

Once Wilson and Lloyd George were back in Paris, the Conference worked with breakneck speed. The decisions it took in March and April determined much of the agenda of European politics for twenty years to come. At the heart of its deliberations was, as always, French security, which from now on depended not only on the Rhineland clauses but also on the terms of an Anglo-American guarantee. At the same time, the Rhine and reparations questions became so closely linked that the settlement of each depended on that of the other. Meanwhile, the problem of the Saar was resolved only after bringing Clemenceau and Wilson nearer to a breach than over any other issue of the Conference. Finally, agreement was achieved over Germany's other European frontiers and over the commercial and economic clauses. The Treaty and the Anglo-American guarantee together represented a formidable accumulation of restraints on Germany and an unprecedented chance for France to arrest its long relative decline. Even so, before the compromise could be adopted Clemenceau had to surmount civil–military tension and a parliamentary challenge at home.

On the afternoon of 14 March, Wilson and Lloyd George made to Clemenceau their historic offer of a joint guarantee of France against German attack. But they would concede only a brief occupation of enemy soil; and they insisted on the buffer-State proposal being abandoned.[54] Clemenceau decided his response in two days of conversations with Tardieu, Pichon, and Loucheur. In his view, they had to choose: 'Either France alone on the left bank of the Rhine, or France regaining the 1814 frontier . . . and Britain and America our Allies'.[55] But were the alternatives so stark? Of course, Tardieu acknowledged in a private memorandum, ultimately the alliance mattered most, but France should not renounce its right of occupation unconditionally, and it might yet consider 'provoking' unilaterally the creation of left-bank buffer States.[56]

The result of these discussions was a note to Britain and America on 17 March which set the French negotiators' course from now on. It accepted the Anglo-American offer, and made large renunciations in return. The buffer-State demand was dropped, and Foch's strategic frontier, which Tardieu and Loucheur had wanted to bring forward in compensation, was jettisoned as well. The left bank and the Rhine bridgeheads should no longer be occupied indefinitely but, in a new formula, evacuated 'in accordance with the guarantees needed to ensure at least the partial execution of the financial clauses'. The note also required the left bank and a fifty-kilometre zone on the right bank to be demilitarized, with a French right of reoccupation if this were violated. Finally, it renewed France's claims to the 1814 frontier and to the occupation of the whole of the Saar, and requested an Anglo-American guarantee of Belgium. In this way, it tried to tie reparations together with all the Western European territorial questions into a single interconnected whole.[57]

The guarantee was therefore acceptable to Clemenceau only on conditions, and disagreement over these conditions caused renewed deadlock at the end of March. Wilson's first written statement of his offer, on the 28th, accepted that the left bank should be demilitarized, and promised American assistance to France against 'any unprovoked movement of aggression by Germany'. But it made no concession to the French claims to the Saar, to a right of reoccupation, and to a continuing presence in the Rhineland while reparations were being paid. Nor did it admit a French demand for the League of Nations to have permanent inspection rights, as this would once again have made the League appear the instrument of the victorious Allies rather than an impartial guarantor of peace.[58]

Negotiations with America had thus frozen hard when a new passage of arms took place with the British. Lloyd George's Fontainebleau Memorandum of 25 March failed to influence the detailed bargaining, and its importance was rather in causing a brief dialogue about ends. It was the most sustained argument yet advanced in favour of a settlement designed above all to remove the causes of economic instability and of nationalist and Bolshevik extremism in Europe.[59] Wilson gave it broad support; Clemenceau, however, challenged its concept of a 'just' peace which would seem legitimate in Germany. On the contrary, he felt, *any* settlement acceptable to the Allies would have to be imposed.[60] Besides, as a written reply to the Memorandum pointed out, Lloyd George had suggested no naval or colonial and few commercial concessions to Germany, with the effect that he was proposing appeasement at the continental Powers' expense.[61] This was a good polemical riposte, although even if the British had gambled with their maritime supremacy it is unlikely that the French would have acted similarly in Europe. At bottom, Lloyd George's hopes for a continent free of irredentist frictions influenced them little more than did the Americans' concern to rebuild a stable system of international trade and credit. Rather, Clemenceau and Tardieu asserted and believed that Germany would resent any limits placed upon its power, and that the essential was for those limits to be strong enough to prevent resentment from being converted into action.

While this exchange of views proceeded, French conceptions of the Rhineland question were subtly changing, in a way that made possible a final compromise. Even if the British and American guarantee could deter an invasion of France, an occupation would still be needed as 'the only direct means of applying pressure' if the Germans threatened Poland, Czechoslovakia, or Romania. The same would be true if they failed to execute any of the clauses of the Treaty, and the financial clauses in particular. From now on, indeed, the difficulties of enforcement were never far from the French leaders' thoughts. If Germany did show good faith, however, the Government had in mind a three-stage evacuation of the Rhineland which would leave the French Army established in the Palatinate until the last moment. France would thereby keep the option of advancing up the Main valley to join hands with the Czechs and split Germany in two.[62]

Clemenceau therefore had a new proposal ready when Lloyd George briefly absented himself in London and Wilson gave what seemed to be a signal by slightly moderating his position in a note of 12 April.[63] The French replied by accepting Wilson's definition of the guarantee; and House induced the President to agree to a three-stage evacuation over fifteen years, or half the period reparations payments were generally expected to continue.[64] 'Now', Clemenceau telephoned to a sceptical Poincaré, 'I consider that the peace is made.' The latter, characteristically, offered not a word of congratulation.[65]

The Franco-American compromise was confirmed by an exchange of notes on the 20th. As well as containing the draft Treaty of Guarantee, these met the French demands for the left bank and a fifty-kilometre strip on the right bank to be demilitarized, and provided for a general right of inspection by the League of Nations. They also stipulated that the occupation should continue 'as a guarantee of the execution by Germany of the present Treaty', and provided for a phased withdrawal over fifteen years if execution did take place and a right of reoccupation if it did not.[66] Lloyd George therefore returned to Paris to find himself outnumbered, and on 22 April he acquiesced in what had been agreed.[67]

Clemenceau's famous victory was supplemented by one final French success. An amendment accepted in the last week of April allowed the occupation to be prolonged if after fifteen years the Allied leaders still considered France to be inadequately safeguarded.[68] In principle, France gained a power of veto which would enable it to stay on the Rhine indefinitely. According to Tardieu, he and Clemenceau took this precaution because they feared the Anglo-American guarantee might not be ratified:[69] a danger the Premier certainly understood.[70] Until this point, however, Clemenceau had first given ground over other questions in order to secure his objectives on the Rhine, and then, after 14 March, compromised on these objectives, too, for the sake of agreement on the guarantee. He had doubts about the military value of the occupation, and understood that it might inflame German nationalism.[71] Yet precisely because the guarantee was such a radical departure from the traditions of British and American diplomacy it was more of an unknown quantity than if it had been given by a Power inured to continental politics. For these reasons – as well as the need to win approval for the settlement from the Chambers – the Government needed to combine elements of the deterrent provided by British and American support with the more direct constraints on Germany it had originally envisaged. Finally, by keeping its options open in this way, it might yet be able to use the occupation in the sense conceived of by Tirard, as a wedge that would force open the cracks in German unity.

When Wilson returned to Paris in mid-March, the British, French, and American Delegations appeared close to agreement on demanding a moderate fixed sum as reparation.[72] By the end of the month they were so far apart that the attempt to determine such a sum was abandoned altogether. Although the British appeared the most intransigent in their claims, the French supported them in pressing for the cost to the Allies of war pensions and separation allowances to be included in the categories of damage.[73] By contrast, after 26 March it was Clemenceau and Klotz who took the lead in arguing that no figure for Germany's liability should be stated in the Treaty.[74] When the British lent their backing to this view, the American negotiators gave way. Next, and once again with the support of Clemenceau himself, Klotz tried to overturn the hitherto accepted principle that reparations payments should not go on for more than thirty years.[75] On 5 April House, deputizing for an ailing Wilson, conceded the French objection to a time-limit.[76] Finally, it was agreed that the Allied Governments must unanimously approve before any portion of the German debt could be cancelled, and once again, as in the question of prolonging the occupation of the left bank, France acquired a right of veto.[77]

By 10 April Clemenceau had gained the bulk of what he wanted from the reparation section of the Treaty. The so-called 'war-guilt clause', which prefaced it, was designed to mollify British and French public opinion by asserting Germany's integral liability for the loss and damage its 'aggression' had inflicted on the Allies. But this was qualified in what followed, and dealt more with the cosmetics of the reparation claim than with its substance. That substance was a requirement for Germany to reimburse the Allies' expenditure on war pensions and separation allowances, as well as to pay compensation under a variety of other headings, among which civilian death and injury and the seizure and destruction of property were the most important. The value of this liability would be decided by an inter-Allied Reparation Commission before 1 May 1921, and the French Government retained the power in theory to insist on being paid in full however long the process might last. This compromise could be interpreted in two ways. For Poincaré, a sum determined in two years' time was likely to be smaller than one determined now; for Clemenceau, to omit a figure was a method of evading American pressure for a low fixed sum, and dropping the time-limit made it possible for payments to continue for longer than thirty years.[78] It did more. The duration of reparations payments might decide how long French troops were present on the Rhine.

During the protracted bargaining over reparations, French policy went through vagaries which had little internal logic. Initially cautious, it hardened once it appeared that France would have to reconstruct its industry without British and American aid. It was moderated by Loucheur in early March before finally being exerted in favour of large, but undefined, claims. For most of this time the contrasting approaches of Klotz on the one hand, and of Clémentel and Loucheur, on the other, were allowed to run in parallel. Only in the final phase did a strong lead come from Clemenceau. The eventual arrangement – a decision not to decide – had been favoured from the start by portions of the French business community.[79] For the Premier, however, it took on particular importance because of its implications for the Rhineland settlement.

The Doumergue Agreement had already stipulated that the left bank should be occupied until the Peace Treaty had been executed in full. At the Conference, the idea of holding territory as a surety against default was launched by the Ministry of Finance, and taken up in the French Rhineland memorandum to Wilson and Lloyd George on 17 March.[80] In spite of this, during March and early April Clemenceau underwent a long period of doubt about the value of an occupation.[81] It was only *after* the reparations agreement had been reached that he overcame these doubts and seized on an open-ended financial settlement as a means of staying on the Rhine indefinitely without violating the Treaty or directly challenging the Allies.[82] The Franco-American Rhenish compromise of 20 April gave France not only the initial fifteen years but also the right of reoccupation if Germany failed to meet its obligations: a failure more likely over reparations than any other Allied requirement.[83] 'I shall', the Premier told his Ministers, 'make a prediction: Germany will default and we shall stay where we are, with the alliance. Remember that, so that you can remind me of it on my tomb . . . .'[84]

Reparations and the Rhine were indissolubly connected at the centre of the 'French crisis' of the Conference: the long period of tension in March and April caused by British and American resistance to Clemenceau's programme. But the tension reached its climax over a French interest which was much less primary. In his collision with Wilson over the Saar, Clemenceau was driven less by his concern with coal and with strategic frontiers than by his sentimental attachment to the border of 1814 and his illusions about the Saarlanders' supposed sympathy for France.[85]

The French claim was made known to Britain and America in February, and in the Rhineland memorandum of 17 March it figured as a *quid pro quo* for the left-bank buffer-State proposal being dropped. Tardieu presented a final, comprehensive statement to the Allies ten days later. Abandoning his earlier strategic arguments, he concentrated on the lingering francophilia of the basin, France's need for access to the coal, and the undesirability of dividing an economic unit by a political frontier. He concluded by demanding ownership of all the coal deposits, annexation up to the 1814 line (including Landau), French occupation of the coalfield north of that line, and the right to exploit the mines and keep public order in this latter region as well as to incorporate it in the French monetary and customs zone.[86]

It was the economic arguments that had the greatest impact in the Council of Four. Even Wilson agreed to temporary French access to the coal, and Lloyd George accepted that the mines should enter French possession. But both protested that the 1814 frontier had never been raised with them during the war, and in effect charged Clemenceau with bad faith.[87] Within the French Delegation itself, Tardieu thought the 1814 frontier 'a third-rank gain', over which it would be unpardonable to cause a rupture with the Allies.[88]

Isolated, Clemenceau conferred with Tardieu and Loucheur, and agreed to major concessions with, as yet, little in return.[89] A new 'Note on the Saar Question' retained the economic aspect of the French demand: ownership of the coalfield and an administrative regime which would enable France to exploit it freely. But the sentimental claim to Landau and the 1814 frontier in the Saar was abandoned. Instead, the Saarlanders should decide their fate in a plebiscite, after fifteen years of autonomy during which France would occupy the basin and have a right to veto the local Parliament's decisions.[90] The rationale for this arrangement was that the German officials in the Saar must be removed before the population could experience the political awakening needed for its true allegiance to be ascertained. Until the plebiscite, however, France would have its own means of pressure comparable to those that Germany had lost. As over the left bank two weeks earlier, Clemenceau and his intimates found concessions easier because of their faith in the French occupying forces' ability to mould German hearts and minds. In part the change of position was tactical, with a similar line of retreat being selected as before the Armistice.

These concessions had the additional advantage of exploiting the differences between Wilson and Lloyd George. The latter was consistently more sympathetic to Clemenceau's position, and was willing to admit an autonomous Saar under French control.[91] The President, however, while consenting to French ownership of the coal deposits, objected to Germany even temporarily losing sovereignty in the region.[92] For the moment, the task of working out the economic arrangements was entrusted to a committee of Tardieu, of Headlam-Morley for Britain, and Haskins for the USA. The committee accepted the majority of a draft prepared by Tardieu and the French technicians,[93] and advised that for France to work the coalfield was impracticable without some accompanying 'special political and administrative regime'.[94] The Four were once again confronted with the issue – that of sovereignty – over which compromise was hardest to achieve.

This time, however, it was Wilson who was on his own. While Lloyd George accepted the experts' recommendations, the President insisted that German sovereignty should continue on the surface even when France owned the mines, with disputes being resolved by a Permanent Arbitration Commission.[95] He also raised the stakes by ordering his ship to sail for Brest, and thereby suggested that he might leave the Conference. Tardieu objected that the new proposal would make the Saar a 'European Morocco', the source of endless Franco-German friction,[96] and Wilson, not the French, eventually gave way. On 9 April he suggested that for the fifteen years until the plebiscite the Saar should be administered by a Commission of the League of Nations, while France should have the economic rights that the committee of experts had agreed.[97] On this basis one of the hardest-fought negotiations of the Conference reached its end.

Although the Saarlanders kept German nationality in name, all the more concrete attributes of Germany's sovereignty in the basin were lost. But the French would have only minority representation on the League of Nations Commission, and if the plebiscite went against them they would lose even the perpetual ownership of the coal deposits that they had initially been offered. For the first fifteen years, however, while the Saar was occupied, and formed part of the French monetary and customs area, there would be opportunities to woo its population. It was to keep such opportunities open that the French negotiators ran such risks. Their interest in the Saar was not in a defensible frontier, for the 1814 line was no such frontier and the border to the north that Foch desired was abandoned after the middle of March. Nor was it purely in the coal, although they needed this to lessen their dependence on Germany during the difficult economic transition that lay ahead. Above all else came the pretension based on the sympathies that had supposedly outlasted France's historic presence in the region: sympathies that were paramount for Clemenceau, and that even the more sceptical Tardieu hoped could be revived. The Saar claim, with its flimsy economic and still more flimsy ethnographic base, was the closest to a French demand of sheer unreason, unsupported either by convincing arguments from national self-determination or by the logic of a broader strategic design.

The Saar was so sensitive for France in part because it was the northernmost extension of Alsace–Lorraine. Between 24 April and 1 May a committee again composed of Tardieu, Haskins, and Headlam-Morley approved with certain alterations the

French draft clauses for the regained provinces. Most of the issues of principle had been decided long before, and controversy centred on two points. The first was the German Rhine port of Kehl, a potential rival to Strasbourg, which it was agreed to place under French administration for up to ten years. More important were the powers needed by the French authorities to secure the allegiance of a population whose goodwill could not be taken for granted, and included a large minority of German immigrants. The French Government was determined to prevent this minority from gaining statutory protection of the kind assured to other such minorities by the Treaty, and it won for itself greater authority than was enjoyed by any other recipient of German territory. Thus, it had discretion to eject the German immigrants, and to liquidate German holdings in the provinces' metallurgical and mining industries. Conversely, the Kehl clause, special German tariff concessions to Alsace–Lorraine, and secure supplies of Saar coal would help to prevent the transfer from arousing economic grievances.[98] The Treaty included many of the carrots and the sticks that the Government would need to consolidate its hold on France's biggest territorial gain.

The Allies were obliged to determine Germany's eastern frontiers in ignorance of how the Russian Civil War would end. The Treaty of Versailles confirmed the decision of the Armistice, by abrogating the Treaty of Brest-Litovsk and requiring the German troops in Russia to be withdrawn.[99] In May 1919, however, attempts to reach agreement with the Bolsheviks ceased, and the Allies gave partial recognition to Admiral Kolchak, the leader of the Whites in Siberia. Clemenceau acquiesced in these decisions, having lost much of his independent striking power when the French Black Sea Fleet mutinied in April and Odessa was evacuated.[100]

The mutiny formed part of a more general resurgence in March and April of the revolutionary threat. Evanescent Communist regimes appeared in Munich and, under Béla Kun, in Budapest. The dispute over the Fontainebleau Memorandum revealed differing interpretations of these events. Lloyd George feared that the defeated Powers might succumb to Bolshevism unless the Allies' demands on them were reduced; Clemenceau and Tardieu, by contrast, professed to fear this danger rather in the States which composed the eastern barrier if the latters' desires were unsatisfied.[101] Clemenceau's attitude towards Béla Kun resembled that towards the Bolsheviks: he gave no support to Foch's plans for Allied military intervention, but he was also less prepared than Wilson and Lloyd George to negotiate with the Hungarian leader.[102] Despite the anxiety which the turbulence in Central Europe caused in the British and American Delegations, French policy towards the German eastern frontier continued on its previous course.

The settlements in west and east were linked by more than being decided in the same, crowded weeks of April. The Polish claims in the Baltic and the French ones on the Rhine were similar enough to set precedents for each other; and Clemenceau wanted to prolong the Rhineland occupation in part to restrain the Germans from aggression on their eastern borders. Poland remained the key to the projected 'barrier' in Eastern Europe, but Polish independence was thought to rest on the country's access to the sea at Danzig. The French Delegation therefore supported the recommendation of the Polish Affairs Commission that Poland should annex not only the port itself but also the two railways which led into the interior via Thorn and Mlawa.[103] The second of these traversed the predominantly German district of Marienwerder.

Danzig and Marienwerder became the objects of an Anglo-French dog-fight, in which Lloyd George, fearful of creating a new seedbed of xenophobia, contended that the Polish corridor should be drawn irrespective of strategic and transport considerations in order to include the fewest Germans possible.[104] Clemenceau, who shared most of his officials' thinking about Eastern Europe, disputed this, at first with Wilson's cautious sympathy.[105] But on 1 April the President accepted Lloyd George's main proposals, and Clemenceau grudgingly followed suit. Agreement was reached in principle two days later for Danzig to form a small, independent State under League of Nations protection, and for Marienwerder's destiny to be settled by a plebiscite.[106]

The Poles won control of Danzig's railways and foreign relations, and brought the city into their own customs zone. Both French and Polish commentators had forecast that such economic links might eventually alter Danzig's political loyalties.[107] None the less, the corridor would be diminished if the Germans won in Marienwerder (as they did), and a central portion of the French programme in the east had been compromised. Clemenceau understood this, and shared the traditional French benevolence towards the Poles. But he was unwilling to press the Conference so close to breaking point over Danzig as he was over the Rhineland and the Saar, especially once American support had been withdrawn. As in the Armistice negotiations, he was readier than the Quai d'Orsay to waive the Polish claims if his objectives in the west could be secured.

Over Czechoslovakia, the French were spared a painful dilemma of this kind. This was in spite of a spirited debate in the Council of Foreign Ministers on 1 April, in which Lansing criticized the report of the Commission on Czechoslovak Affairs and contested the principle of drawing frontiers on strategic rather than on ethnic lines. Pichon and Jules Cambon objected equally unambiguously that national self-determination could not be applied without qualification.[108] In the Council of Four three days later Clemenceau offered what appeared to be a compromise: simply to follow the Bohemian–German frontier of 1914, in defiance both of the American experts, who had wanted Czechoslovakia to have less than this, and of those of the other Delegations, who wanted it to have more. The Czechs would thereby win the control of the Sudetenland which France had desired for them all along. Lloyd George and House, who was standing in for Wilson, agreed almost without discussion.[109] The American President had failed to give his subordinates a lead, and Lansing's stand on the point of principle was an isolated incident. With this exception, the necessity of giving Czechoslovakia the Sudeten Germans was not denied.

Clemenceau's remaining concern in Central and Eastern Europe was negative: an Allied undertaking to prohibit an Austro-German union. According to the fullest statement of the French position, the movement in Austria for an *Anschluß* had no local roots and was an artificial German creation. If successful, it would worsen the demographic imbalance between France and Germany, and place Czechoslovakia in extreme peril.[110] Clemenceau won Wilson's agreement to forbid an *Anschluß* as part of the understanding between the two men reached on 20

April.[111] A clause accepted by the Council of Four on 2 May required Germany to respect Austria's independence not indefinitely – for this had met with Wilson's disapproval – but in the absence of a contrary decision by the League of Nations.[112] Not for the only time, the League lubricated inter-Allied frictions by allowing the President to deviate from his principles without losing face.

The final area of territorial uncertainty was the north, where Germany bordered on Denmark, Belgium, the Netherlands, and Luxemburg. Over Denmark, the French experienced setbacks in the later stages of the bargaining. The plebiscite zone in Schleswig was reduced,[113] and the French Ministry of Marine's proposals for the Kiel Canal to be completely demilitarized and placed under international sovereignty were defeated.[114] But these were minor difficulties compared with the deepening imbroglio in the Low Countries, where Clemenceau's entire Rhenish strategy could be compromised by a false move.

Although the Government's main objective was still a close association with the Belgians, the economic discussions with Brussels made little progress in the spring and summer, and military conversations had yet to begin. Afraid of being 'encircled' by a French sphere of influence in the Rhineland, the Belgians failed to give Clemenceau the backing he desired during the crisis of the Conference in early April.[115] Nevertheless, the French supported Belgium's claims for priority in receiving reparations and for its treaties of 1839 with Holland to be revised. This latter was a lost cause. The British and American Governments objected both to German territorial cessions to the Dutch and to putting pressure on the Netherlands to surrender lands to Belgium.[116] The Council of Four approved the Belgian gains of Eupen, Malmédy, and neutral Moresnet from Germany, but this did not assuage the Government in Brussels, and its disappointment exacerbated the festering dispute over Luxemburg.

The relevant section of the Peace Treaty confirmed Luxemburg's departure from the German railway and customs areas, but otherwise left its future undefined. Even while the Conference was sitting, this future was the stake in a subterranean conflict between Brussels and Paris. Although reluctant to displease the Belgians, Clemenceau and his advisers felt they were under pressure from the French Parliament,[117] and they were sensitive to the evidence that the Luxemburgers, if they could not remain autonomous, would prefer association with France. Indeed, Clemenceau warned Balfour and House that if the Luxemburgers voted for annexation by Paris he could not refuse them.[118] The Belgians, conversely, sought the Conference's public approval for a 'friendly *rapprochement*' between themselves and the Grand Duchy.[119] The British, and still more the Americans, were reserved towards this claim, but it was primarily Clemenceau who prevented such approval from being given. He did not, he said, oppose stronger ties between Belgium and Luxemburg, but they must not be established in a way that seemed a public setback for France.[120]

The French combined this ambiguity over the political status of the Grand Duchy with an attempt to replace Germany as the predominant influence on its economy. For a while, Clemenceau tolerated economic discussions between Belgium and Luxemburg, but at the end of May he suddenly reversed himself and suggested tripartite conversations between the three capitals.[121] His Government was aware of plans made in January and February for a Franco-Belgian group to purchase the Luxemburg interests of the German *Gelsenkirchen* steel concern, possibly with Loucheur's support.[122] More conclusive, however, is its policy towards the *Guillaume-Luxembourg* railway network, the principal system in the Grand Duchy, which had been administered by a French company before being transferred in 1871 to the German authorities in Alsace–Lorraine. France therefore had a claim to regain ownership, which it was able to insert not in the Luxemburg clauses of the Treaty of Versailles but in Article 67 of the Alsace-Lorraine section. The Belgians retaliated with a spoiling claim to the Kleinbettingen–Wasserbillig portion of the railway, for which they failed to gain similar recognition.[123] In June 1919 the Franco-Belgian rivalry was therefore still unresolved. Clemenceau had kept his options open, but at a heavy price in Belgian goodwill, and not until 1920 did his successor obtain the military convention with Brussels that was needed to complete the French defences in the north.

The restraints that the Versailles settlement imposed on Germany were in part traditional, in the shape of strategic frontiers and systems of alliances and guarantees. They also included a novel series of devices to hinder German economic growth. Of these, the commercial clauses were the one remaining sphere in which Clémentel could leave his mark after the eclipse of his earlier plans. The draft he proposed to the Conference's Economic Commission proposed international action against what he considered the peculiarly German sins of dumping and using false marks of origin. It also allowed the Allies to impose whatever tariffs they liked on Germany during the post-war transition period, while requiring Berlin unilaterally to concede most-favoured-nation treatment to the Allies in perpetuity.[124] Finally, taking up a project that had originated in Tardieu's fertile brain, Clémentel wanted to protect the invaded countries' reconstruction by placing Germany's imports of industrial raw materials and exports of manufactures under the surveillance of the Allies and later of the League of Nations.[125]

No trace of this last proposal found its way into the Treaty, and Clémentel's other ideas were implemented only in diluted form. The sole permanent German obligation was to protect Allied commerce against 'all forms of unfair competition', and especially against false marks of origin. After haggling with Wilson in the Council of Four, Clémentel was able to impose a unilateral most-favoured-nation clause on Germany for, at maximum, a decade.[126] Alsace–Lorraine won the right to export duty-free to Germany for five years, not ten as Clémentel had wanted. Even this would help the French steel industry to absorb the huge increment to its capacity represented by the former German Lorraine, while correspondingly impeding German readjustment. But the commercial section of the Treaty gave France negligible advantages in the longer term.

The combined effect of the commercial, reparations, and territorial clauses was much more severe. By the time the territorial transfers were completed, in 1921, Germany had lost eighty per cent of its 1913 iron-ore output and thirty-six per cent of its steel-making capacity, with all the former and much of the latter going to France.[127] The cash payments under the reparations section would delay Germany's economic recovery,[128] and their effects would be augmented by the reparations paid in kind. Loucheur and Clémentel respectively had pressed particularly hard for the most damaging of these: coal deliveries, and the

cession of most of the German merchant navy.[129] Loucheur's
original demand for up to sixty million tons of coal annually
until reparations had been paid in full, with half the total
going to France, would have hobbled for a generation an economy that was already to lose the Saar and much of upper Silesia.[130] The eventual provisions followed Loucheur's conception,
but were much more modest. France would be the main ben-
eficiary from deliveries by Germany which would average over
thirty million tons a year for a decade after 1919, and then
cease.

In their final form, therefore, the coal clauses were no more
able than the commerce clauses to paralyse German industry into the indefinite future. The French negotiators acted with little
consultation of French industry, and sought to meet a strategic
as much as an economic need.[131] They were largely neglected by
Clemenceau, and it is questionable whether they were able to
make the best of what was anyway a weak bargaining hand.
None the less, they had done enough to put Germany at a disadvantage in the post-war decade and perhaps to enable France
to enter on a virtuous circle of expansion which would leave it
permanently in a stronger relative position than before 1914.
Much would depend on the ingenuity of the French steelmakers
and the success with which reparations could be imposed. It was
on the transition period and the Franco-German balance that
the French negotiators concentrated, and more remote concerns
with the longer-term equilibrium of the Atlantic economy they
left, perhaps sensibly, to the British and the Americans. In Tardieu's memoranda on the Rhine the 'West' (excluding Germany) already figured as a cultural and, it was hoped, a military
unit. The idea of the West as an *economic* unit, whose political
stability depended on trading and financial harmony between its
members, had yet to register.

By mid-April the 'French crisis' of the Conference had passed
its peak, and the even more intractable Italian one could begin.
But no sooner had the outlines of the Franco-German settlement been agreed than they were challenged by Foch and by
Clemenceau's political rivals. Apart from Poincaré, these included some of the more prominent members of the Chambers
and even of the Council of Ministers itself.[132]

Foch, Clemenceau, and Poincaré had been united in supporting the Government's initial bargaining position. It was after
Clemenceau abandoned the buffer-State demand that Foch disputed his priorities, and on 6 April asked to be consulted before
the Council of Four had taken irreversible decisions.[133] This
Clemenceau effectively refused,[134] and after the Premier settled
for a fifteen-year occupation Foch protested that this would
leave France 'in the most complete insecurity' and was
'impossible'.[135] Poincaré, with his usual constitutional scruples,
refused the Marshal's urgings that he should take over the
negotiations,[136] but Foch put on a brief display of insubordination by refusing to pass on a message inviting the German plenipotentiaries to Versailles. By the time a partial apology from
the Marshal on 19 April had smoothed this over, Parliament was
rebelling in its turn.[137]

Unrest had been growing in the Chambers since the uproar
caused in February by Klotz's suggestion of a capital levy.
Enough was known about Clemenceau's difficulties at the Conference for demonstrations of intransigence plausibly to appear
as an assistance to the Government rather than a hindrance. On
10–11 April, many Senators and over three hundred Deputies
signed a 'Manifesto' that required Germany to pay full war costs
and give 'territorial guarantees'.[138] In this atmosphere, prompted by Foch's press attaché, Bardoux, Senator Paul Doumer introduced in the upper Chamber a resolution calling on the Government to insert in the Treaty the 'military guarantees indicated by the Commander of the Allied Armies'.[139]

This was both the climax of the agitation and the point at
which Clemenceau's critics overplayed their hand. The resolution was of doubtful constitutionality, and by threatening to
force a vote of confidence, Pichon and Clemenceau were able to
replace it with an anodyne substitute.[140] On 25 April the Council of Ministers unanimously approved the terms submitted to
it,[141] and the preliminary Treaty could now be revealed to the
Germans and the public.

Clemenceau was always ready to summon up French opinion
as a Mr Jorkins at his elbow, but Foch's protests and the turbulence in Parliament made little difference to the Premier's conduct in the Council of Four. The public was more deeply stirred
by reparations than by the Rhine; Poincaré and even Foch in

the last resort respected the constitutional limits on their power; and Parliament refrained from causing a ministerial crisis. With the Treaty still in gestation, and revolutionary currents running fast even in France itself, the outcome of such a crisis was sufficiently unpredictable for all sides to draw back from one,[142] and this left the initiative in Clemenceau's hands.

A shift in the nature of the argument facilitated compromise. By April even Foch and Poincaré no longer demanded left-bank buffer States or a permanent presence on the Rhine. Instead, they contended that the occupation should continue until reparations had been paid in full.[143] Clemenceau rejoined that Germany was so likely to default on reparations that the Treaty would in fact give France *both* an Anglo-American guarantee and an indefinite occupation.[144] Yet after their resistance to such an occupation, could Britain and America really be expected to acknowledge a lawyer's argument of this kind? They might; but France would impair the substance of the alliance if it made itself seem guilty of bad faith. Clemenceau argued retrospectively that it *had* been necessary to choose between the alliance and the Rhine, and that his preference for the former had divided him from Foch.[145] Yet the urge to believe the incompatibles could be reconciled was immensely strong, and both Clemenceau and Tardieu intended to keep the possibility of reconciliation open. Hard and painful sacrifices had been demanded from the Allied leaders for the April compromise to be arrived at, but the path was smoothed by continuing ambiguities. These ambiguities were a difficult legacy to European statesmen in the coming years.

4. *To the Hall of Mirrors, May–June 1919*

Even before the Treaty of Versailles was signed, the struggle between French, British, American, and now also German, attempts to revise it had begun. During the weeks between the Treaty's presentation to the German Delegation on 7 May and its signature on 28 June the characteristic themes of inter-war diplomacy began to assert themselves. The Berlin Government – defeated, insecure at home, reviled abroad though it was – returned as an autonomous agent in international politics, and used skilfully such leverage as it possessed. After the minutiae of the March and April compromises, the Allies were forced to reassess the problems of Germany as a whole: of whether the new Germany differed in intentions from the old, and whether chances to foster its division should be seized. The German Delegation at Versailles bombarded the Allied leaders with objections to the preliminary Treaty, backed up by the threat that Germany might refuse to sign. The French reverted to attempting *faits accomplis* on the ground. And, partly in response, Lloyd George pressed once again in favour of concessions. Not until mid-June did equilibrium return and the exhausted Heads of Government stand fast until German resistance to signing had been broken.

Throughout the tumult Clemenceau insisted in the Council of Four on the vanity of seeking reconciliation; the German Delegation under Brockdorff-Rantzau correspondingly judged France to be its most inveterate enemy.[146] None the less, the possibility of Franco-German *rapprochement* did not remain wholly unexplored. In the early stages of his mission to Berlin, Professor Haguenin made contact with the German governmental and business leaders, and invited their suggestions for the Treaty's economic clauses and for co-operation in post-war reconstruction. Although Haguenin professed to have authority from Clemenceau and Poincaré, his overtures met with little response.[147] He concluded that the Socialist Ministers in Germany were 'the servants . . . of the old regime, . . . the artisans . . . of a militarist reaction', against whom France would still need 'guarantees'.[148] Although Haguenin believed that a victory for the German extreme Left would be a disaster and that Germany's prosperity was necessary for France's own, he recognised the danger to French security if the German economic recovery were not kept strictly under Allied control.[149] By the end of April he believed that this might best be done by an Allied 'surveillance' of and possible participation in the leading German private firms.[150]

This idea reappeared in secret conversations during May and June between members of the German Delegation at the Conference and René Massigli, who reported his experiences to Pichon and Tardieu. Massigli caused a flurry of German interest by suggesting that the Saar clauses could be revised if coal supplies could be guaranteed by joint Franco-German ownership of

the mines and industries in the basin.[151] This suggestion evident-
ly went too far for his superiors, and the conversations ended
without result.[152] If highly placed members of the Government
were willing to investigate economic co-operation with Germany, they were not willing to sacrifice France's Treaty gains as
the price. And their understanding of co-operation, if Haguenin
is representative, was highly one-sided. In short, both the
Haguenin and Massigli affairs confirmed the French belief that
in spite of the Revolution little in the German rulers' mentality
had really changed.

During May and June the Allies had to reckon with the possibility that Germany would refuse to sign and the war would be renewed. The result might be a second political upheaval in which
the existing German Government would be replaced by the
more amenable Independent Socialists, and centrifugal tendencies would be reinforced. Partly for this reason, French interest
in German separatism revived. In the Conference's Verification
Commission, Jules Cambon argued that Bavaria, and perhaps
other German States, should be required to sign the Treaty
separately from the Federal Government.[153] Pichon admitted
subsequently that this initiative had 'purely political' motives.[154]
Cambon, however, found himself in a minority of one, and a
memorandum which Clemenceau encouraged him to submit to
the Council of Four was equally ineffective.[155]

Baulked in Paris, the French were meanwhile returning to a
forward policy in Germany. In contrast with the previous winter, they now opted not for economic pressures but for direct
contact with the separatist leaders. A first meeting, with the
Four's approval, took place between Dr Heim, of the Bavarian
People's Party, and General Desticker, of Foch's staff.[156] A
second, about which the Allies were not consulted, brought
together General Mangin and the Hanoverian leader, von Dan-
neberg, who asked for armed assistance to his movement if the
Germans did not sign.[157] Even so, although these broader perspectives should be kept in mind, French aspirations fleetingly
became reality only, as ever, on the Rhine.

In mid-March Clemenceau had apparently abandoned his
claim to a buffer State on the left bank. Yet he did not rescind
the authorization he had given to efforts by the French occupy-

ing forces to win the Rhinelanders' allegiance. The British and Americans now regarded Tirard's economic commission at Luxemburg with well-founded suspicion, and on 21 April the Council of Four approved a British suggestion for a civilian Inter-Allied Rhineland Commission which would supervise the occupation's political and economic aspects. As the French member – and President – of the IARC, however, Clemenceau appointed the unrepentant Tirard, who attempted to obstruct its work.[158]

In the occupation zone itself, Mangin had made contact with the activists in Rhenish Prussia led by Dr Hans Adam Dorten, at the same time as General Gérard was in touch with a rival southern faction whose aim – a separate Palatinate – Dorten's group opposed.[159] Since the beginning of the year, the Rhenish movement had lost much of its popular support, as well as the sympathy of the local Establishment, and it suffered another blow when the preliminary Treaty published after 7 May made no mention of a change in sovereignty north of the Saar. For those who recovered from the shock, the implication was that peaceful lobbying was no longer adequate, and some wished to pursue not autonomy within Germany, but independence.[160]

The first attempt to act on this miscarried. After conferring with the separatists on 17 May Mangin informed Liggett, the Commander of the American occupation forces, that a *coup* was imminent, and urged him not to oppose it.[161] Liggett, however, refused to co-operate, and promptly informed Wilson, who forwarded the information to Clemenceau.[162] In the Council of Four on the 29th, the President read out a letter from the American representative on the IARC, Noyes, which argued that both the numbers and the powers of the occupation forces should be reduced to a minimum. Lloyd George attacked the very principle of an occupation lasting fifteen years. Outnumbered, Clemenceau resisted the British contention, but accepted a commission which would take Noyes's letter as its terms of reference.[163]

How could this French discomfiture occur? There is little doubt that Mangin had told Foch of what was brewing, and he promised Dorten that he had support from Clemenceau himself.[164] It appears that Mangin reached general agreement with the Premier during a trip to Paris in early March,[165] but between that time and May the Government gave negligible guidance to its Commanders on the spot.[166] When news of the Liggett episode reached Clemenceau, he deplored Mangin's action,[167] and it is likely that the latter had taken the Government's general endorsement of a forward policy as authority for more drastic measures than Clemenceau yet intended. The Premier, however, was anxious to avoid 'a disavowal of any attempt at independence on the left bank',[168] and he sent Mangin only the mildest of reproofs. He urged the General to show 'a complete neutrality' between the Rhineland parties;[169] but this neutrality had a special meaning, as a circular Foch sent out with Clemenceau's approval made clear. The occupation forces, Foch instructed, should neither encourage nor impede separatist movements; but they should also ensure that the local Prussian and Bavarian officials did nothing to prevent the Rhinelanders from expressing 'on posters *or by any other means* their political demands'.[170] In any future incident, the German local authorities could be rendered powerless. And on 1 June Dorten tried again.

The *coup* unfolded in the towns of Mangin's zone after fresh collusion between Dorten and the General.[171] Poincaré urged Clemenceau that nothing should be done to hinder it.[172] But by the 4th Dorten had won so little support that he abandoned the attempt, and a rival insurrection in the Palatinate failed even more ignominiously. After another scene with Wilson and Lloyd George Clemenceau sent out his assistant at the War Ministry, Jeanneney, to make clear that French support for Dorten's venture must be liquidated.[173] The débâcle was complete.

The Dorten fiasco came at a moment when the Conference was once again hovering on the verge of breakdown. The Treaty had been assembled section by section and rushed into print without its cumulative effects on Germany being considered. During May the experts in the American and British delegations built up pressure on Wilson and Lloyd George in favour of alleviating these effects. Lloyd George in particular treated far more seriously than Clemenceau the implications of a German refusal to sign, and feared a military adventure whose consequences would be incalculable and which might be repugnant to British opinion. The French Army's activities in the Rhineland were the last straw, and on 1 and 2 June Lloyd George's colleagues authorized him to withhold British naval and military co-operation from any attempt to enforce the Treaty in its present form.

In the Council of Four, Lloyd George therefore proposed concessions to the Germans on four points: alterations to their frontier with Poland, more definite reparations requirements, a shorter occupation of the Rhineland, and speedy admission to the League of Nations if they executed the Treaty in good faith. Clemenceau retorted that the British were as usual pressing for concessions at other Governments' expense, and that the more the Allies gave to Germany the more it would demand. He offered to reconsider the costs of the Rhineland occupation, but no more.[174] The position of arbiter therefore lay with Wilson, and, as in March and April, the British and Americans only rarely launched a combined assault on Clemenceau's position. He was able to preserve the essentials of the compromise agreed two months before, and to keep it as the basis of the final settlement.

Over the League, Clemenceau was able to avoid concessions, and it was Lloyd George's other points that caused the main debate. The biggest French reverse came over Poland. Lloyd George wanted a plebiscite in Upper Silesia, which had been scheduled for annexation by the Poles despite its large German population and its importance to the *Reich* as a centre of coal extraction and heavy industry second only to the Ruhr. As with Danzig, Lloyd George was able to win over the American President, and Clemenceau faced a united front in favour of applying national self-determination at Polish expense.[175] In the Eastern Frontiers Commission, which considered the matter in detail, the French were less able to steer the deliberations than in similar bodies earlier in the Conference.[176] Their only compensation was that the plebiscite would be held after an intermediary Allied occupation, during which a hitherto suppressed Polish nationalism could mobilize. Grudgingly agreed to by Clemenceau 'in order not to create difficulties',[177] the plebiscite was the largest single inroad into the arrangements made in April. It demonstrated once again Clemenceau's helplessness when Wilson and Lloyd George combined, and his reluctance to push the Conference to a breach over something that concerned French interests only at one remove.

The controversy over reparations, by contrast, ended in Anglo-French co-operation against Wilson. Lloyd George's amendments were largely superficial, and Clemenceau shrewdly accepted them.[178] But they were the signal for the American Delegation to renew its efforts on behalf of the fixed sum. Tardieu conceded that this might be possible, and Loucheur even suggested a figure, to be arrived at by forcing abnegation on Italy and the smaller States.[179] But once Clemenceau in the Council of Four objected point-blank to specifying Germany's liability his assistants abandoned their initial moderation.[180] Even a plea by Wilson himself that the fixed sum was essential to German and European recovery failed to shake Clemenceau's and Lloyd George's stand.[181]

Clemenceau exploited this success in order to refute the British argument that because France would be safe from Germany for the next fifteen years it would have no need to occupy the Rhine. On the contrary, he explained, the main purpose of the occupation was to ensure not merely reparations but also Germany's submission to a complex of provisions that offered innumerable opportunities for calculated defiance.[182] Wilson failed to support Lloyd George, and in the *Arrangement rhénan* of 13 June Clemenceau escaped with an Allied promise to withdraw early if Germany demonstrated its good faith.[183] This was a concession in appearance only which left intact a French power of veto.

Clemenceau's Generals had so compromised his position, however, that he did not emerge entirely unscathed. Wilson emphatically agreed with Lloyd George that the occupation must be under civilian control, and Clemenceau undertook to accept arrangements which would satisfy the President.[184] He retained his hopes for covert action in the Rhineland, and regarded civilian control as an obstacle to this which had been forced on him by military indiscretion.[185] But by buying Wilson off in this way, he was able to keep the British isolated over the larger issue of the occupation's length.

The powers of the future Inter-Allied Rhineland High Commission were meanwhile being examined by the Commission for the Left Bank of the Rhine. In it, Loucheur, who represented Clemenceau, clashed with Foch, who tried to protect his and Tirard's independence by demonstrating that the IARHC would be unworkable.[186] The Allied leaders ignored the Marshal's objections, and a convention of 13 June made the High Commission their 'supreme representative' in the occupied territory.[187] By thrusting responsibility for the Dorten incidents on Foch and Mangin Clemenceau had gained means of keeping the French military on a tighter leash in future. But the structure of the IARHC left the Government itself, as opposed to its military subordinates, with opportunities for political penetration in the Rhineland which might yet be great.

Just as in November 1918 doubts persisted almost to the end, but eventually the Germans shrank from the prospect of invasion and the ceremony of signature could proceed. For most of those present in the Hall of Mirrors on 28 June it was an occasion for mixed feelings. After the years of bloodshed and the tense debates in Paris the semblance of peace had returned. The Allied statesmen could seek repose for their bruised nerves, and the rent in the fabric of international life could begin to be repaired. But the post-war years brought neither economic resurgence nor political calm. Instead, France and Germany became the adversaries in a cold war, whose bitterness rivalled that of 1914–18 itself.

The Treaty of Versailles was signed at a moment of maximum international uncertainty. Much of the settlement in the Levant and in Central and South-Eastern Europe had yet to be determined by the peacemakers, in so far as to determine it remained within their power. The outcome of events in Russia was still harder to control, or even to predict. Almost equally unknowable was the new distribution of industrial might in Europe after reconstruction had taken place. Finally, as Clemenceau had expected, the Treaty altered the context in which Franco-German rivalry was played out: but the rivalry itself remained.

Versailles was and probably had to be a dictated Treaty, which enjoyed no legitimacy in the defeated Power's eyes. For this reason, it was as much a beginning as an end: a Treaty, as Clemenceau warned in the ratification debates in Parliament, not of relaxation but of vigilance.[188] Even before the Treaty was signed, the French leaders foresaw that Germany would tenaciously resist its being implemented. In addition, the deeper imbalance in population and industrial capacity between the two countries was likely to reassert itself as the war receded. In consequence, the Government had not ruled out more radical solutions to the German question. After the Dorten affair, it was more cautious in its dealings with the German separatists, but this was from calculation rather than from principle.[189] Clemenceau and Pichon had not abandoned hope of furthering German disunity in the Rhineland and elsewhere, and they quickly resumed covert action.[190] If free to disregard British and American objections, they would undoubtedly have gone much further. But it is unlikely that even a France able to act alone would or could have dismembered Germany at bayonet-point without the aid of much more powerful centrifugal forces than existed in the Weimar Republic of 1919.

Doubts about Germany's good faith were accompanied by continuing friction with the Allies. The epic contest in the Council of Four left an ambiguous balance-sheet. The economic leverage which Britain and America could apply to France had in the end remained unused. Conversely, Clemenceau's own ultimate sanction – the threat of staying in the Rhineland whether his partners so desired or not – appears to have been wielded with effect.[191] Wilson got the League of Nations that he wanted, but he arrived in Paris with only a dim conception of the European settlement and was condemned to fight a series of battles in which Clemenceau held the initiative and American policy followed inconsistent lines. Lloyd George was a more formidable antagonist, although Europe was much less central in British preoccupations than in French. He much reduced the Polish gains from Germany in the east, but lost the struggle against a prolonged occupation of the Rhine. Over reparations and the Saar, Wilson, largely unsupported by Lloyd George, had similarly incomplete success. The settlement with Germany in Europe therefore owed more to French ideas than to those of any other Power. The initial French programme was chipped away at in March and April and again in June, but it was not replaced by a completely different conception. For this reason, the main purpose of the Treaty was to safeguard Germany's neighbours by restricting German independence; removing the causes of tension by applying national self-determination and by promoting economic growth took second place. British and American thinking also hovered between the twin desirables of stabilization and security, but, if only for geographical reasons, the French placed a higher value on the latter than did either maritime Power.

This qualified success over the territorial clauses was offset by two defeats. France would have to overcome its financial crisis and reconstruct its industries from its own resources, supplemented by whatever it could extract from Germany. And the Anglo-American guarantee, which Tardieu and Clemenceau so valued, left many questions unanswered. Would it apply if Germany attacked the Czechoslovaks, Poles, or Belgians, and France came to their defence? And what if Germany passively resisted implementing the disarmament or reparation clauses? Finally, could Lloyd George and Wilson deliver what they had promised? In March 1919 Clemenceau accepted only the hope of a guarantee, not the guarantee itself. When American ratification was denied, the hope was frustrated. The United States began its retreat from European commitments, and Britain was willing to issue a guarantee of its own only on conditions that no French Government in the early 1920s would accept. Clemenceau's successors therefore oscillated, as he had done, between the vision of inter-Allied solidarity and the lure of direct action on the Rhine. None the less, after June 1919 the pattern of Franco-German relations was largely determined by the Treaty of Versailles, and its signature is as good a time as any to halt and to review the evolution of French policy since the outbreak of war. This will be attempted in the next, and concluding, section of this book.

Conclusion

War, Talleyrand is reported to have said, is too serious a business to be left to the Generals. The statesmen of the Third Republic heeded his advice. They had little power over the events that thrust them into conflict with Germany in August 1914. But once the fighting had begun they determined that it must continue to the bitter end, and that the price of victory was worth paying. They reaffirmed this judgement every time that they refused a peace approach or approved a new offensive, in the hope that the next blow would be decisive and redeem the sacrifices thus far made. They submitted by degrees to a holocaust whose full, appalling measure they could know only after victory had been won. None the less, they fought a war which as much as any other war was a furtherance of policy by other means.

During the years when all hinged on the outcome of the fighting this policy remained difficult to define. Indeed, attempting to define it obscures its true nature. French Governments had many war aims, in the sense of objectives that they wished to include in a peace treaty if they were victorious. But few of these were absolute requirements that would never be abandoned short of utter defeat. Governments needed to keep open a maximum of opportunities if the future should prove favourable while being bound by a minimum of commitments if it should not. They retained sets of options rather than of non-negotiable demands, and if these were different and broader sets of options than had existed before the war this was because the likelihood of drastic change in Europe had now so greatly increased. War aims were expressed in a hierarchy of commitment, extending down from parliamentary and inter-Allied declarations through resolutions by the Council of Ministers and confidential *démarches* to other Governments in the coalition, until, at the lowest level, they were voiced merely in the guidelines sent out by Foreign Ministers to French representatives abroad. They came closest to being absolute when, as with Alsace–Lorraine or the restoration of Belgian independence, they were specific and were openly acknowledged. Round other aims a much larger penumbra of uncertainty persisted, and some – such as military security on the Rhine – were alluded to in public only via the code words of 'security' and 'guarantees'. All of this was 'policy', as opposed to Ministers' private aspirations or to internal memoranda by officials, but it was not all of equal weight.

Because French war aims took this form, they showed continuity on one level while on another being in constant flux. They were only one part of French diplomacy as a whole, and were subordinate to objectives which might remain elusive however completely victory was won. In Germany, it appears, war aims altered little between 1914 and the last weeks of the fighting;[1] in France this may have been true of policy-makers' ultimate aspirations, but was not true of their immediate goals. Of these latter, some, such as Alsace–Lorraine, were formulated early and altered little before they were brought forward at Paris in 1919. The aims of destroying German influence on the left bank of the Rhine and of securing France's northern flank in Belgium and Luxemburg, by contrast, were imperfectly defined in the Cambon letter, and even at the Peace Conference were given compromise formulations in which conflicting imperatives struggled to be reconciled. The goal of post-war economic security was embodied in programmes which fluctuated even more, in parallel with changing French assessments of British and American intentions. Finally, the French desire for a counterbalance to Germany in Eastern Europe changed radically in its implications when Tsarist Russia ceased to be the leading candidate for such a part, and was replaced first by Austria–Hungary and then by a hypothetical alliance based on a resurrected Czechoslovakia and Poland.

The line that separated war aims as incorporated into policy from the more constant, if less tangible, desires that lay behind them, was shifting, ill-defined, and could alter in response to circumstances. But what were those underlying desires? In principle, war aims could serve not merely to strengthen the State externally against other States, but also to reinforce the domestic political and social order against its critics.[2] Germany's aims were intended to do both, and in some ways this was true of France as well. The desire of the Ministry of Commerce to

avoid too speedy a return to unregulated international trade after the war was motivated partly by a fear of social unrest. In
addition, France's war effort was financed largely through
borrowing,[3] and in 1919 Parliament's resistance to the extra
taxes needed to pay off the Government's internal and external
debts made more desperate the authorities' search for a method
of shifting the burden on to Germany or the Allies. More
broadly, in Paris as in Berlin the alignment of political opinion
over foreign and internal questions approximately coincided.
Many of the Third Republic's leaders believed that if the war
were lost the existing regime would succumb to social revolution
or, it was sometimes speculated, to a military *coup*.[4]

   Internal and external policy were therefore interlinked. But it
was always the foreign danger which was uppermost in the
French leaders' minds. Although alarmed by Bolshevik 'contagiousness', they were the least willing of the Allies to absolve
the Provisional Government in Petrograd from its obligations
for the purpose of containing the Russian Revolution of 1917,
and the least willing to make concessions to the Weimar authorities in order to damp down the German Revolution two years
later. When forced to choose, they rated the menace of domestic subversion less highly than they did the threat of German
power. Against that power their claims were motivated by the
triad of concerns which have been summarized as 'face, food,
and fear'. French war aims rested on arguments derived from
history and from national self-determination, on arguments from
the exigencies of national security, and on arguments from the
needs of economic stability and growth. No one of these three
purposes – the sentimental, the strategic, and the economic –
could be reduced to either of the others, although all three
overlapped.

   The specific French objectives rested on varying combinations
of these underlying elements, of which the first was often the
most powerful. Alsace–Lorraine was the nearest of the French
territorial desiderata to being an absolute war aim. But this was
less because of the provinces' economic and strategic value than
because of the tradition of irredentist feeling which made the
claim to them acceptable to almost every section of domestic
opinion. Similarly, at the Peace Conference Clemenceau came
nearest to a breach with Wilson not over reparations or the

Rhine but over his desire for sovereignty in the Saar. And, outside Europe, France's material stake in Syria was quite inadequate to explain the intensity of attachment which the territory
aroused.

Such an amalgam of historic precedent with illusions about
the inhabitants' allegiance also influenced French policy towards
the left bank of the Rhine. But here, in contrast to Syria or
even to Alsace–Lorraine, it was the security consideration which
was paramount: that of taking out insurance against a renewed
German attack. In the abstract 'security', too, was an absolute
war aim. But by its nature it remained an intangible goal, whose
contours shifted in interminable official and unofficial debates.
No one component of security, be it a Rhenish buffer State or a
Baltic corridor for Poland, was non-negotiable in the manner of
Alsace–Lorraine. But conversely, if circumstances favoured, the
meaning of the concept could expand indefinitely, and for an
undercurrent of opinion which influenced official policy in 1919
nothing less than the destruction of German unity and the
annexation of the left bank would suffice to meet France's
needs.

French economic aims were in part subsidiary to the strategic
purpose: Germany's recovery must proceed under Allied supervision, and the *Reich*'s pre-war measure of industrial superiority
must never be regained. But France also needed to overcome
the fearsome budgetary and balance-of-payments deficits that
the war had caused. In spite of this, economic aims were less
compelling than Alsace–Lorraine, or even security. They were
the point over which Briand and Painlevé in 1917 were readiest
to compromise, and over which France was least successful in
satisfying its desires at the Peace Conference. In addition,
French economic objectives, even more than French objectives
in other spheres, were liable to be translated into demands not
only upon Germany but also upon France's allies.

Can French desires outside Europe be analysed in the same
way as those within? Even while the war was being fought,
Lenin interpreted continental imperialism and imperialism overseas as aspects of a single phenomenon.[5] French war aims were
certainly imperialist, even in the least contentious sense of tend-
ing to establish political control over territories such as the Saarland and the left bank of the Rhine where such control violated

national self-determination. Men like Paul Tirard brought to
bear in European politics attitudes which were rooted in colonial
experience. There was a sense in which the war aims of 1914–18
were the climax of decades of European expansion into the remainder of the globe. But the balance of motivation on the
mainland differed from that outside. Within Europe, security
against Germany was the strongest motive for French imperialism, and still more for the support France gave to the imperialism of other Powers. The claims of history, of putative cultural
affinities, and of the interests of French commerce and investment also figured, but they mattered much less than in Africa or
the Levant. In colonial questions these proportions were reversed, at the same time as the influence of unofficial lobbyists
was greater.

By what process did French policy emerge? The statesmen who
officially directed it were under pressure from domestic forces
and from the Governments of other nations. Equally, they had
the power to take initiatives and to mould opinions and events
as well as to respond to them. The outcome was a State which
in comparison with its German rival was remarkable for its
autonomy in relation to its citizens, but also for the severity of
the limits placed on it from outside.

It is a truism that French foreign policy was generated within
France. It is less evident that the holders of the relevant executive positions should have had the power to decide that policy.
The Third Republic enjoyed in theory a representative political
system, in which mechanisms for electoral and parliamentary
control of governmental action had been established for a generation. But even in peacetime those mechanisms had been at
their weakest in foreign affairs. And in wartime French democracy was curtailed by the political truce, by the absence of elections, and by the censorship of the press. France also enjoyed a
more solid national consensus than did most belligerents. Its
Socialist Left was smaller and less intransigent than in Germany,
Italy, or Russia; its Right, except briefly over the subject of
passports for the Stockholm Conference, did not challenge Ministerial leadership until 1919. This owed something to the absence of a decline in living standards so catastrophic as that
farther east; something to the war appearing unambiguously de-

fensive in its origin and being fought largely on French soil; something also to the acceptance which the Third Republic had unobtrusively acquired before the war began.

In these circumstances, unorganized French opinion could have influence through two main channels. The first was Parliament; the second the process by which Governments assessed civilian confidence. The wartime Chamber of Deputies had been elected in April-May 1914, at a moment when the Left was gaining ground and the majority in favour of the three-year military service law could only narrowly be preserved. But its influence changed thereafter in accordance with the mood of its constituents, and the unity of August 1914, the exhaustion of 1917, and the intransigence of 1919 all left their mark upon its members. Except during the interlude between Verdun and the rise of Clemenceau, however, the executive was freer from legislative supervision than during the peacetime Third Republic. In 1917 the majority for peace through victory diminished, but the revolt of the Right and Centre against passports being issued for the Stockholm Conference was more formidable than all the criticism from the Socialists. In 1919, correspondingly, Clemenceau struck his bargain over the left bank of the Rhine and obtained its ratification by the Chambers in spite of the vociferousness of Foch's parliamentary support. The National Assembly's power, in principle decisive, was generally held in reserve.

Probably a more effective limit on French statesmen's freedom of manœuvre was their judgement of what was needed to sustain public morale. They were deterred from conversations with the enemy by the belief that such conversations would damage that morale if they became known. A similar concern may have encouraged Clemenceau to put on a show of loyalty to the Fourteen Points in January 1918; and helped persuade him not to reject outright the German armistice request nine months later. But such conflicts between the preferences of the French leaders and their estimate of what unorganized opinion would tolerate were rare. When they did occur, Governments could frequently surmount them with only minor adjustments to their policies. The strikers and mutineers of 1917 challenged the war's effects rather than the principle of fighting, and could be placated by limited concessions. Ribot answered his parliamentary critics by altering the presentation of his aims, but the fine print of his statements remained compatible with the Cambon letter. The currents of Wilsonian sympathy in France ran strong in 1918, but neither in January nor November did the Government give undertakings which it believed would inhibit it at the Peace Conference. And, at the Conference itself, public anxiety about security and reparations did not stop Clemenceau from compromising over both issues. Although Ministers were often preoccupied with public opinion, therefore, they could normally act in harmony with it, and the restrictions which it placed upon them remained hypothetical. It also left them free to determine the content of French war aims and to take the initiative in bringing them forward.

Was this also true of organized opinion: of political parties and of pressure groups? One such group, the colonial party or *parti colonial*, was able to make governmental policy its own with outstanding success.[6] Yet the party was a highly curious organism, whose leaders included strategically located politicians and civil servants as well as newspapermen and professional lobbyists. Ideas circulated freely between its unofficial and official wings, and either might be the source of its *démarches*. It was, however, less a body that put pressure on government from outside than a faction within government that had unofficial means of agitation at its disposal. It was not unique in this, although it was unusually effective. De Margerie, Degrand, and other advocates in the Quai d'Orsay of Eastern European causes were in regular contact with the Czech and Polish nationalists in Paris. Léon Bourgeois in 1919 was simultaneously Clemenceau's chief representative in the Conference's League of Nations Commission and President of the *Association française pour la Société des nations*, the main French internationalist pressure group.[7] Nevertheless, De Margerie, Bourgeois, and Degrand owed their influence to their official status rather than their unofficial connections. And in questions of Western European security the predominance of official as against unofficial influences on policy was even more pronounced.

By 1914 the Paris citizenry had lost much of its old insurrectionary power.[8] The war stimulated the rise of new political and economic formations in French society, but none of them yet possessed the muscle in the streets or in the marketplace which was needed to coerce the State. The one left-wing attempt to alter foreign policy by direct action was the strike of May 1918 in the Loire. It did not succeed. Yet the co-operation in the war effort by the *SFIO* and the *CGT* was little more fruitful. The Socialists failed in 1917 to win governmental sanction for a plebiscite in Alsace–Lorraine or the disavowal of territorial claims on the left bank of the Rhine. The main achievement of their agitation – a French commitment to the League of Nations – was the object of official cynicism from the start.

Elsewhere in the political spectrum, the pattern was more complex. The *Action française* and the *Ligue des patriotes* did not endanger public order during the war, and their more respectable counterparts, the *Comité de la rive gauche du Rhin* and the *Ligue française*, had vague, compromise programmes which did not conflict with the Briand and Clemenceau ministries' confidential thinking. When it came to the test, none could prevent the latter's compromises in 1919. More important were the pro-Government political parties and the representatives of French business. The first crucial decision – to reclaim Alsace–Lorraine – was taken without reference to them. During 1915 and 1916, however, the proliferation of study-groups on the margins of officialdom allowed them to express their views, and these views helped to shape the aims which Briand's Government eventually adopted. Up to a point, the requirements of French capitalism – in so far as it was represented by the *Comité des forges* – and the needs of French military security coincided. But the distinction between the two was understood both by the industrialists who recommended annexations and the politicians who listened to their advice. The claims to Alsace–Lorraine and to the Saar were pursued in spite of the overcapacity that they would cause in the French steel and textile trades. And industrial opinion never again contributed so much to policy as in 1916–17. Two years later this opinion may have helped to shape the demands that Loucheur presented at the Peace Conference for coal deliveries and for reparations in kind. But when the Clemenceau ministry decided its territorial programme it consulted far less widely than had Briand's. At no point did private organizations hold a right of veto over governmental decision.

Among the organs of the State themselves, Parliament was potentially a vehicle through which organized as well as unorganized opinion could assert itself. It proved ineffective in this role. Moreover – and here the contrast with Germany is most glaring – the influence of the military was kept in bounds. The General Staff assisted in the formulation of France's Western European war aims in 1916, and Pétain's opinion was crucial in the Stockholm Conference decision of the following year. In the winter of 1918–19 Foch not only helped to shape the French negotiating programme for the Rhineland and the Saar but also fathered a succession of initiatives on the ground. Yet what followed showed that even against military insubordination that had Presidential and Parliamentary backing a determined Premier could keep control of policy. Like the business community, the military gave specialist advice when war aims were being drawn up; but, again like that community, they did not dictate solutions to the civil power.

Decision therefore rested with Government Ministers and their advisers. Poincaré's influence was considerable, if intermittent, until November 1917, and thereafter evident only rarely. The Council of Ministers, similarly, exercised some collective supervision over Delcassé and Briand; almost none over Pichon and Clemenceau. Within this framework, the exact locus of power varied with the personalities concerned. Clemenceau used the Premiership to oversee his Foreign Minister's activities to a degree that Viviani had been unable to achieve. Briand and Ribot occupied the two posts conjointly. Within the Quai d'Orsay, Delcassé and Ribot took the weightiest decisions themselves; Briand and Pichon left much greater latitude to their officials. Briand relied primarily on Berthelot as *Chef du Cabinet*; Ribot on Jules Cambon as Secretary-General; and Pichon once again on Berthelot, now as acting *Directeur politique*. But when Tardieu set to work in December 1918 the Foreign Ministry lost its say in policy-making at the crucial moment, and was left to handle only secondary negotiations at the Peace Conference. Clémentel and Klotz, correspondingly, had to relinquish the coal-delivery and reparation discussions to Loucheur. Having successfully resisted pressure from outside, the French bureaucracy was deprived of influence by a competing power-centre within the Government itself.

French statesmen, then, compared with their Russian or their German counterparts, were fortunate. The fundamentals of their policy were supported by a majority of parliamentary and public opinion as well as by most of the leading organized interests in French society. The crisis of 1917 was surmounted, and the war was fought to a conclusion. Conversely, French opinion could be satisfied by vague and general public formulations of war aims, and in 1919 the authorities forced through compromises on those aims without being deflected by military insubordination or by parliamentary unrest. The extremes of a February Revolution and of a French Ludendorff were both avoided. Instead, the harshest restrictions on successive Governments were external. Changes in the military balance and in official perceptions of Allied intentions were constantly rebounding on the content and on the manner of presentation of French aims.

The importance of the military balance was twofold. First, there was the map of war. Within weeks of the outbreak of hostilities the Germans overran all the parts of Western Europe that would figure in their aims. In the east, their ambitions grew in parallel with the conquests of their armies. The regions that they occupied continually presented them with administrative decisions of more than provisional significance. The French, by contrast, held no more than a few valleys in Upper Alsace, and were reluctant to negotiate while the balance of acquisitions was so heavily against them. Outside Europe they were likewise handicapped by Britain's crushing local superiority in Africa and the Middle East. Only after November 1918 did the French move in to the areas in Europe that interested them; and they soon attempted to make of the occupation an instrument which would augment their long-term influence.

The military balance had a second, less immediate, effect. As the prospects of success receded and advanced, so different items among the French leaders' objectives became more prominent in their diplomacy. They approved the Cambon letter at a moment when it seemed that victory might be near and France's contribution to that victory the leading one. By the autumn of 1917, both contingencies were very much in doubt, and French diplomacy and strategy grew less ambitious. A year later, however, Clemenceau and Pichon made new commitments to the Belgians and in Eastern Europe as the Allied armies advanced, and once their troops had taken up position on the

Rhine they decided to press for left-bank buffer States under indefinite occupation.

The military variable was therefore one component of the diplomatic one: France's bargaining power in relation to its allies. Aided only by two ramshackle empires and a Balkan kingdom, Germany withstood for four years the massed assaults of the most powerful coalition the world had ever seen. It could, and did, treat the war aims of its partners with contempt. But France, as Clemenceau acknowledged, 'had fought a coalition war; we could not avoid a coalition peace'.[9] Clemenceau's advisers, like Briand's, drew up their programmes in the consciousness not only of Germany's ill-will but also of France's vulnerability; and this constraint upon their freedom was decisive. Reconciliation with the enemy, if possible at all, was deemed a prospect only for the distant future. But ending German unity, if theoretically desirable, was something which even the Clemenceau Ministry felt obliged to leave largely to the Germans themselves. The most likely future was therefore one of indefinite confrontation with a rival of inherently superior strength. It was possible to hope that the artificial alteration of the balance of power caused by the Allied victory could be embodied in the Treaty and prolonged by its strict maintenance. Yet few French statemen felt that this sufficed as an answer to the security problem. Most believed that France must supplement it by taking advantage of the war to forge links with its allies of such strength that any German invasion in the future would automatically embroil the *Reich* in hostilities with a coalition of many times its own power. In this way the diplomatic isolation of the generation after 1870 could never be repeated, and in the war of nerves that was expected to follow victory France would not stand alone.

It remained to combine the second type of security guarantee – a deterrent alliance – with the first: direct limits on German power imposed through the Peace Treaty. During the first half of the war the Tsar remained France's principal ally on land. He was ready to support whatever claims the Paris leaders might bring forward against Germany, although he expected acquiescence in a Russian sphere of influence in Eastern Europe in return. Whatever the misgivings of their colleagues, Delcassé and Briand thought this price worth paying. But after the spring of

1917 Russia's place was taken by the maritime Powers, who were traditionally wary of permanent commitments on the European mainland and had objections of ethics and of *Realpolitik* to French economic and territorial aims. As the war proceeded, the French commercial and financial crisis deepened, and this, as well as the security dilemma, needed British and American co-operation to be resolved. Between the Russian Revolution and 1919, therefore, French Governments were schooled in the politics of weakness: in the uses of a strategy of silence while the war continued, and of local *faits accomplis* combined with ruthless sacrifices of the inessential at the Peace Conference. While preferring multilateral answers to their problems, they tried to keep the unilateral option open. They extended this balancing act into the post-war years, until unilateral action was attempted and abandoned with the occupation of the Ruhr in 1923–5. The ransom of victory in 1918, not defeat in 1870, was France's status as a great and independent Power.

French statesmen in these years made two fundamental choices. They resolved to go on fighting until victory had been won; and to use their influence in favour of a peace whose primary objective would be to limit German independence. The first of these decisions required Ministers and officials to balance the costs of continuing the war against those that would follow a submission to Germany's terms. Neither element in the balance could be known with certainty before the conflict had ended, and the cost of fighting on proved eventually to be so high that it compromised the goals for which it was exacted. 'They will not', wrote one of the French officers who perished at Verdun, 'be able to make us do it again another day: that would be to misconstrue the price of our effort.'[10] France went into the war as a nation of only sons; it lost a higher proportion of its manhood than did any other major combatant, although it was the least able to withstand such a blow. In 1914–18 its accumulated wealth diminished by perhaps a quarter.[11] The Third Republic's financial stability went for good; so too did the foreign investment it had built up in the generation before 1914. Those of the Republic's soldiers who survived the almost unendurable conditions of battle returned to civilian life permanently changed. Not the least of the consequences of the war was the sinister

combination of passivity at the centre with febrile agitation on
the fringes that debased French public life in the regime's declining years.

But the price of submission to the enemy was also high. The
French authorities encouraged their citizens to believe that the
policies of the Berlin Government and those of the German industrial and patriotic pressure groups were as one. The *Ligue
française* began the process by issuing more than two million
copies of a tract which summarized the sweeping demands made
by the German business associations in a memorandum of May
1915. An accompanying commentary by Lavisse took for granted
that the Pan-German League had won control of the *Reich*'s official policy.[12] During the crisis of 1917, Pétain incorporated
these ideas into a message to his troops, Lavisse reasserted them
in an address to a patriotic rally which Poincaré and Ribot's
Ministers officially attended, and Ribot himself reproduced them
in the Chamber.[13] On this interpretation, Germany's intentions
were to annex France's northern coalfield and the remaining
iron ore of Lorraine up to the Meuse, while exacting a ferocious
indemnity which would reduce France to a bankrupt 'tributary'
for years into the future.

This contained an important element of the truth. The German Chancellor, Bethmann-Hollweg, did indeed approximate to
the position of the Pan-Germans and the Ruhr industrialists in
his war-aims programme of 9 September 1914.[14] Once its opening offensive had been checked, however, the Berlin Government hesitated between its maximum ambitions and its need to
split the Allies. For most of the war it considered Russia, and
subsequently Britain, as more likely to defect than was France.
But when, at the climax of the Battle of Verdun, the German
Foreign Ministry spelled out its conditions for a separate peace
with Paris these were still severe. Germany would lose nothing
except for a few frontier districts in Alsace; France, however,
would cede the rest of the iron-ore basin of Lorraine, together
with a protective glacis, and pay a heavy financial penalty. And
if, instead of bringing France into its own diplomatic camp, Germany had to face a continuing Franco-British alignment after
the war, it would impose far more draconian terms.[15]

The choice before the French was bleak. Given the welter of
intelligence that reached them, they could not be sure in private

that the German terms would be so onerous as in public they professed to believe. But on one point there could be no doubt: a separate peace would shatter the alliances that had been so carefully nurtured as the basis of French diplomatic independence in the pre-war years. The new dispensation would be a *rapprochement* with Germany on the most unfavourable of terms, against a background of declining living standards and of political turmoil which the Republic was unlikely to survive. Yet for all the menacing forces which were at work in Imperial Germany, it was not the Third Reich, and the penalties for military failure in 1917 would not have been so harsh as they were a generation later. If defeated, the French State would be shrunken and impoverished, but it was more its external than its internal sovereignty which stood in hazard. The cerebral objective of security took much of its force from the more emotional concerns of French nationhood: a nationhood that for many Frenchmen was still pristine and dated back hardly more than fifty years.[16] That preserving national independence was worth the heaviest of sacrifices was questioned by almost no one in authority at the time. The war was therefore fought to its conclusion as an act of policy: an act whose cost was shocking, but whose alternatives everything in the French leaders' background made to seem even more repellent.

France also paid the price of victory through the damage done to Europe as a whole. It was a price measured in the weakening of the continent against the outside world; in the generation of political hysteria which lay ahead; and in the shock administered to what Keynes described as 'the intensely unusual, unstable, complicated, unreliable, temporary nature of the economic system by which Western Europe has lived for the last half-century'.[17] Could this price have been reduced by a different treaty from the one which was signed at Versailles in June 1919? It is against this question that the great debate at Paris between conceptions of security and of stabilization must be judged.

France had not been alone in fighting for the first of these. 'The general aim of the war' for Bethmann-Hollweg was 'security for the the German *Reich* in west and east for all imaginable time.'[18] But, in the opinion of many Germans, the balance between the Great Powers of Europe, on which the diplomacy of the past two hundred years had centred, was giving way to one between 'World Powers'. In this emerging pattern, only the British Empire, Russia, and the United States had the natural resources, the population, and the industrial capacity for an assured position in the front rank. For this reason, the Berlin Government pursued a comparable concentration of power through the destruction of its European rivals' independence and through arrangements that would guarantee the markets and the raw materials required by German industry both on the continent and beyond.[19]

No French statesman saw affairs so starkly. Consciously, at least, there was no French 'grasp for world power', and the chief objective was rather to frustrate the German one. In the usual, cruel paradox of international politics, however, French independence could be guaranteed only if German independence were curtailed. Like their counterparts in Berlin, the French leaders accepted that the annexation of large, unwilling European populations would be embarrassing, even repugnant. They preferred to reach their goals by less obtrusive means. But they were as deeply committed as the Germans to a policy of encroachments on their enemy's territorial, military, and economic sovereignty: a policy geared to limiting his capacities rather than to trusting his intentions. They also wished to use the settlement as a springboard from which to increase France's absolute, and not merely relative, power. In the obscurity that surrounded them, they followed Machiavelli's exhortation to rely on what they could control, rather than on what they could not. It is true that a less pessimistic tendency had influenced French policy before 1914, and that it survived, in the persons of Briand and Painlevé, even among the wartime leaders. And although French mistrust of Germany ran far deeper than in Britain or America, it was not mistrust of Germany in any shape or form. Rather, it was directed first against the German Empire which was held responsible for the pre-war crises and the invasion of 1914, and subsequently against a Republic in which the old élites retained much of their power and were expected to do all they could to resist the enforcement of the Versailles terms. The French were also, however, less willing than their allies to give any German regime the benefit of the doubt. British thinking about Germany was torn between a great hope – that of a stable and pacific democracy – and a great fear.[20] In France there existed little but the fear.

French policy therefore followed the usual tendency for a defensive inspiration to assume an offensive expression. Its underlying assumption – as Tardieu's memoranda at the Peace Conference made explicit – was that Germany was a delinquent Power, and, in consequence, that only by depriving Germany of most of its external sovereignty could peace be guaranteed. The British and American Delegations at the Conference were influenced by this view, but they also aspired to a settlement which would enable them to extricate themselves from European commitments: an aspiration which for France itself was futile. For this reason, the French conception of security ran up against an alternative conception of stabilization, whose most articulate exponents were the American economic experts and Lloyd George. On this view the purpose of the Treaty was a self-regulating settlement which would remain in being without the continuous exertion of Allied power, as a result of the economic and irredentist roots of tension having been eliminated. In turn, this made the Anglo-Saxon leaders sensitive to the profound changes which had come over European affairs since the eighteenth century, and in particular to the diffusion of national consciousness and to the continent's prodigious economic growth. The implication of the first of these was that territorial readjustments that ignored the wishes of the inhabitants were liable to create a standing source of friction as potent as had been Alsace–Lorraine. The implication of the second was that the political struggles between the European Powers endangered the delicate economic mechanisms on which the stability of all of them depended. In the fifty years before the war the basins of the Rhine and of its tributaries became the industrial heartland of continental Europe. In this narrow zone, criss-crossed on the one hand by flows of commerce and investment and on the other by international boundaries, political co-operation was essential for the regional economy to function. Conversely, the logic of political competition was that all the mines and manufactures of the area should be controlled by one or other side. In the twentieth century this magnified the stakes in the Franco-German rivalry and the disruption caused to the rest of Europe while it was prolonged.

The two conceptions of the settlement clashed most urgently

over the degree of leniency that should be showed to Germany. Both of them contained elements of correct perception: and both were drawn on by the Allies in the more enduring settlement that was constructed after 1945. Is it possible that the best hope for a lasting peace in 1919 lay with the application of the French conception rather than the Anglo-American one?[21] Certainly, in contrast to their Allies, the French wished to divide Germany at the Rhine, and were attracted by a more thoroughgoing fragmentation of the *Reich*. They also wished to delay Germany's economic recovery until the balance of industrial power between the Ruhr and its competitors had come closer to equality. It is less clear that these measures would have had the same effects as they did a quarter of a century later. After 1945 the Franco-German question, like other such historical questions, was less resolved than utterly transformed. This was in part because of the metamorphosis of German society and institutions that took place during the Nazi dictatorship and its aftermath; in part also because of the rise of Soviet Russia. In 1919 the Bolsheviks were an ideological challenge to the Governments of France and Germany; they were not a military threat sufficient to persuade them to resolve their differences. In addition, it is doubtful whether France's domestic political structure would have permitted it to act alone, as Stalin did, in enforcing Germany's division until the distant day when that division was accepted by the Germans themselves. For this reason, inter-Allied solidarity in upholding the treaty limitations on German sovereignty was more important after 1919 than after 1945. But a treaty which came closer to fulfilling France's aspirations than did Versailles would also have made such solidarity in the 1920s even harder to achieve than it was. The return of an Anglo-American commitment to the continent, in the shape of the Dawes Loan of 1924 and the Rhineland Pact of 1925, was essential to the precarious stability that Europe enjoyed during the five years before the onset of the Great Depression. Without such a commitment, neither conciliating Germany nor holding it down were likely to bring French Governments what they desired.

'It will all be useless', murmured Clemenceau, after the news of the Armistice with Germany was broken to a rapturous Paris crowd.[22] It is difficult, when setting the colossal sacrifices of 1914–19 against their meagre results, to escape a feeling of dismay.⌈There is no avoiding risk in foreign policy: it remains the area of the State's activities in which the imponderables are greatest while the penalties for misjudgement are most extreme.⌋ Yet there are moments when the imponderables become so vast that the critical faculties are overwhelmed; when it is barely possible to discern even the criteria by which policy should be assessed. The statesmen of the early twentieth century were hostages to precisely such a climax of uncertainty. The dilemmas that confronted them, however, were more universal in their scope. The tragedies that underlay the foreign policies of the Powers in the First World War were the same as those at other times, both before and since.

Appendix I

Alsace–Lorraine and the Saar

See Map I. The 'frontier of 1871' marked there was in force between France and Germany from 1871 until 1914. It gave Germany possession of what is usually referred to as 'Alsace–Lorraine' but which in fact, although including all of Alsace, took in only the eastern portion of Lorraine. The 'frontier of 1815 and 1919' applied from 1815 to 1870, and has done so again (except during the Nazi occupation) since the Treaty of Versailles. The 'frontier of 1814', which was briefly in force in 1814–15, was revised to France's detriment after Napoleon's Hundred Days. It gave France part of the Saar coalfield, centred on Saarbrücken and Saarlouis, and a small salient north of Alsace, round Landau. The map also shows 'line no. 2', which is discussed in Chapter V, note 75, and Foch's proposed 'strategic frontier' of 1918–19, which appears in Chapters VI and VII. The frontier of 1790, which is not marked, gave France slightly more territory than that of 1814, but was very much more irregular, so that Landau, for example, formed a separate enclave.

The population of Alsace–Lorraine between the frontiers of 1815 and 1871 was 1.874 million in 1910. Since 1871 about 400,000 of the native population had emigrated, and a similar number of Germans had settled in the region. Of the two salients enclosed by the frontier of 1814, the population of that round Saarbrücken and Saarlouis was about 350,000 and of that round Landau about 100,000.

Alsace–Lorraine contained important mineral riches. The potash field of Nönnenbruch, north of Mulhouse, was the biggest one known in the world after that at Staßfurt, in Saxony, although its exploitation had begun only in the decade before 1914. Transferring it to France would break the German monopoly of an important raw material for the chemical industry and of an agricultural fertilizer for which the North American market was particularly lucrative.

In 1913 the Saar coalfield had an output of 17.472 million tonnes, of which only 3.846 million came from the portion south of the frontier of 1815. As Alsace–Lorraine south of this line was consuming 12 million tonnes of coal annually in 1913, the result of regaining the frontier of 1815–70 would be that France's pre-war coal deficit of approximately 23 million tonnes a year would rise to approximately 31 million tonnes. Moreover, the Saar produced very little coking coal, and the acquisition of the iron-and-steel industry of Lorraine was likely to increase the

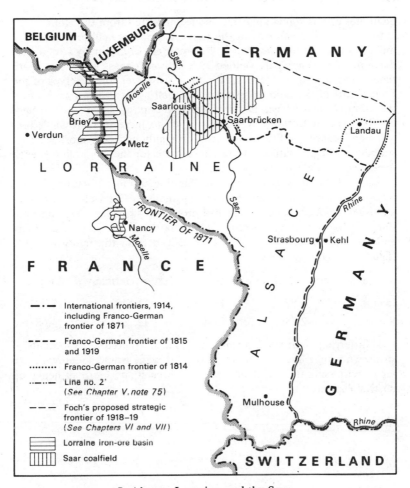

BELGIUM · LUXEMBURG · **G E R M A N Y**

Saar

Moselle

Saarlouis

Briey · **Saarbrücken** · Landau

· Verdun

· Metz

L O R R A I N E

FRONTIER OF 1871

Saar

Rhine

Nancy · Strasbourg ·● Kehl

Moselle

F R A N C E

—·— International frontiers, 1914,
including Franco-German
frontier of 1871

---- Franco-German frontier of 1815
and 1919

········· Franco-German frontier of 1814

··—··— Line no. 2
(*See Chapter V, note 75*)

— — — Foch's proposed strategic
frontier of 1918–19
(*See Chapters VI and VII*)

▨ Lorraine iron-ore basin

▥ Saar coalfield

Mulhouse ·

Rhine

SWITZERLAND

I. Alsace–Lorraine and the Saar
Based on map 'Alsace–Lorraine and the Saar Valley' in C. H. Haskins and R. H. Lord,
Some Problems of the Peace Conference (Cambridge, Mass., 1920), p. 152.

quantities of this commodity that France imported from the Ruhr.

In 1913 the German part of the Lorraine iron-ore field produced 21.1 million tonnes of ore; or about three-quarters of Germany's total production. The French part yielded 19.8 million tonnes, which was more than nine-tenths of France's total output. However, the reserves of the French part of the field were more than half as large again as those of the German, and France had further large deposits of ore in Normandy. The loss of Lorraine was likely much to increase Germany's pre-war dependence on France for iron ore; although not, most wartime studies concluded, sufficiently to compensate for the continuing French dependence on German coking coal.

Alsace–Lorraine was a prosperous farming and manufacturing region with important textiles and engineering industries as well as the iron-and-steel producing area which had grown up since the 1870s on both sides of the frontier in Lorraine. The importance of German Lorraine and the Saar in this respect may be judged from the following table (figures for 1913, millions of tonnes):

	German Lorraine	Saar	Rest of Germany	France
Iron	3.87	1.375	11.516	5.207
Steel	2.286	2.08	12.298	4.687

Transferring German Lorraine to France, therefore, especially if sovereignty over the Saar were altered as well, would in principle go far to redressing the imbalance between French and German heavy industrial capacity.[1]

Appendix II

The Left Bank of the Rhine

In the eighteenth century the political structure of the left bank had been highly fragmented and some of the local States, notably Cologne, had been subsidized by the French Crown in return for providing troops. The whole of the region was overrun by the French Revolutionary armies in the 1790s, and annexed to France by the Treaty of Lunéville in 1801. In 1814–15 a reorganization took place, which was designed to enable the left bank to withstand French expansion in the future. The Rhine Province, in the north, became part of Prussia; the Palatinate, in the south, of Bavaria. Rhenish Hesse, round Mainz, was a province of the German State of Hesse, and the tiny principality of Birkenfeld was part of the Grand Duchy of Oldenburg.[1] The administrative and judicial innovations of the French occupation left their mark on the region until well into the nineteenth century. In addition, the largely Protestant population of the Palatinate resented the Catholic authority of Munich at the same time as the Catholics of the Rhine Province harboured grievances against the Protestant-dominated Governments first of Prussia and subsequently of the German Empire also. In spite of this, even such a body as Ernest Lavisse's *Comité d' études* concluded in 1917 that the left bank had shown no important francophile sentiment for forty years.[2]

In 1910 the Rhine Province had a population of 7.12 million, of whom just over 4 million lived on the left bank. The populations of the Bavarian Palatinate, of Rhenish Hesse, and of Birkenfeld, were respectively 937,000, 382,000, and 50,000. Parts of the industrial complexes centred on Frankfurt and the Ruhr were located on the left bank. In the north these included the textiles of Krefeld and München–Gladbach and the engineering of Cologne; in the south, the great *Badische Anilin* chemical works at Ludwigshafen. There were important lignite deposits between Bonn and Cologne, and three small coalfields round Krefeld, Erkelenz, and Aachen. The French General Staff considered these reserves to be large enough for France to become self-sufficient in energy and in metallurgical coke if it placed the left bank under its control.[3] But this does not seem greatly to have contributed to the Government's interest in the left bank, either in 1916–17 or at the Peace Conference.

Appendix III

Luxemburg

Luxemburg had been conquered by France in 1795, and remained a French possession until the end of the Napoleonic wars. It became a Grand Duchy in 1815, and was linked in personal union with the Kingdom of the Netherlands. After the Belgian Revolution in 1830, however, it was under Belgian rule until 1838–9, at which point the western part of Luxemburg was ceded to Belgium and the eastern part (corresponding to the present territory) resumed its former status. In 1867 the Grand Duchy was demilitarized and placed under a regime of neutrality guaranteed by the Powers, after a crisis caused by the desire of Napoleon III to purchase it from the Dutch. In 1890 the Grand Ducal title passed to a separate branch of the Dutch royal family and the personal union ended. It was this branch which, in the view of the French Government, showed complaisance towards the wartime violation of Luxemburg's neutrality by the Germans.

The Grand Duchy had a population in 1910 of about 260,000. Most of its inhabitants spoke German, although they showed signs of Germanophobia after 1914. Luxemburg was a member of the *Zollverein*, or German customs union, and large sections of its economy were in German ownership. This included its main railway system, the *Guillaume-Luxembourg*, which was transferred from the French *Compagnie des chemins de fer de l'est* to the Prussian Government in 1871. The city of Luxemburg was an important railway focus and a potential source of weakness in a defensive system that followed the French and Belgian borders, although less so in one based on the Rhine.

In the south-western corner of Luxemburg lay the northern tip of the Lorraine iron-ore field. It produced 7.3 million tonnes in 1913, although it was running through its reserves much faster than were the French and German portions of the field. In the same region, round Esch-sur-Alzette, there had grown up a metallurgical industry which in 1913 produced 2.548 million tonnes of iron and 1.631 million tonnes of steel.[1]

II. The Rhine Basin in 1914

Appendix IV

Poland

The historic Kingdom of Poland was partitioned between Russia, Prussia, and Austria in three stages in 1772, 1793, and 1795. The Grand Duchy of Warsaw, created by Napoleon in 1807, regained what had been lost to Prussia in the second and third of these partitions, but not the losses of 1772. After Napoleon's fall Poland was again divided between the three eastern monarchies, and the international boundaries in the region changed little until the First World War (*see Map III*).

In 1914 there were large numbers of Poles under German rule in East and West Prussia, Posen, and Upper Silesia. These four provinces had a combined population of just over seven million; the proportion of Polish extraction, however, in the absence of reliable statistics, is difficult to assess. The Germans of East Prussia were almost separated from the main zone of German inhabitation by a band of Polish settlement which reached the Baltic just west of, although did not include, Danzig and the mouths of the Vistula. The historical and strategic arguments for Polish possession of the port (which Prussia had annexed in 1793) were therefore stronger than the ethnographic ones. The Polish-inhabited regions of Germany were important producers of grain and included the eastern fringes of the coal-mining and manufacturing region of Upper Silesia. Upper Silesia had not, however, formed part of the historic Polish Kingdom, and only one third of its inhabitants voted for union with Poland in the plebiscite held there in 1921.[1]

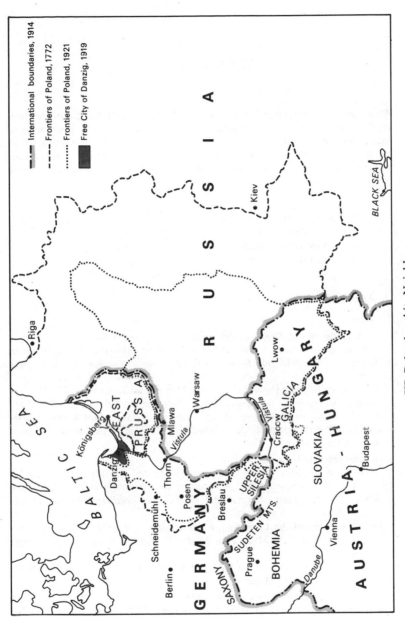

III Poland and its Neighbours

Based on map 'Boundaries of Poland' in the *Statesman's Yearbook*, 1944, p. 1. See also H. C. Darby and H. Fullard (eds.) *The New Cambridge Modern History. Vol. XIV: Atlas* (Cambridge, 1970) pp. 176–9

Bibliography

What follows is not intended as a comprehensive guide to the information available about the subjects considered in this book. Its main purpose is to enable the reader to identify the published and unpublished sources cited in the footnotes to the preceding chapters. Certain other works of relevance, however, have also been included. The Bibliography is divided into five parts:

    I. Archival Sources
    II. Theses and Other Unpublished Writings
    III. Published Primary Material
    IV. Secondary Works: Books
    V. Secondary Works: Articles

I. Archival Sources

A. France

(i) Archives of the *Ministère des affaires étrangères*, Paris:
Volumes in the series: 'A' Paix 1914–20;[1] Guerre 1914–18; Europe 1918–29; Y Internationale 1918–40; *Recueil des actes de la Conférence de la paix* 1919–20.
Volumes of duplicate telegrams to the Hague and London, 1918–19.
Papers of: Robert de Billy; Léon Bourgeois; Jules Cambon; Paul Cambon; Théophile Delcassé; Jean Doulcet; Gaston Doumergue; Jules Jusserand; Pierre Jacquin de Margerie; Maurice Paléologue; Stephen Pichon; André Tardieu.[2]

(ii) *Archives nationales*, Paris:
Records of the Ministry of Commerce (F^{12}) and the Ministry of the Interior (F^7). Also those of the *Association de l'industrie et de l'agriculture française* (27 A.S.) and the *Comité central des houillères de France* (40 A.S.).
Procès-verbaux of the *Commission des affaires extérieures* of the Chamber of Deputies (C 7488–C 7491) and of the *Commission des traités de paix* (C 7773).
Papers of: Paul Deschanel; Charles Mangin; Louis Marin; Paul Painlevé; André Tardieu; Albert Thomas.

(iii) *Service historique de l'armée*, Château de Vincennes, Paris:
Cartons in series: 6.N. (Fonds Clemenceau); 14.N. (Fonds Joffre); 4.N.; and 16.N.

(iv) *Archives du Sénat*, Paris;
Procès-verbaux of the *Commission des affaires étrangères* of the Senate.

(v) *Bibliothèque de documentation internationale et contemporaine*, Nanterre:
Records of the wartime French censorship agency.
Papers of: Louis-Lucien Klotz, Paul Mantoux, Albert Thomas.
(vi) *Bibliothèque de l'Institut de France*, Paris:
Stephen Pichon MSS.
(vii) *Bibliothèque nationale*, Paris:
(a) In the *Cabinet des manuscrits*: Raymond Poincaré MSS (*Notes journalières*, 1914–15).
(b) In the *Département des cartes et plans*: archives of the *Société de géographie*.
(viii) *Institut de l'histoire des relations internationales et contemporaines*, Paris:
Louis Loucheur MSS (on microfilm).
(ix) Archives of the *Ministère des finances* (consulted in Paris):
Records of the Ministry of Finance (F^{30}).
(x) *Archives de la Marine*, Château de Vincennes, Paris:
Records of the Ministry of Marine.
(xi) *Archives départementales du Puy-de-Dôme*, Clermont-Ferrand:
Étienne Clémentel MSS.[3]
(xii) Archives of the *Compagnie de Saint-Gobain-Pont-à-Mousson*, Blois:
Cartons from the series, *Direction générale: Camille Cavallier*.
(xiii) In the possession of M. Louis Cambon:
Papers of Paul Cambon.

B. *Britain*
(i) Public Record Office, Kew:
Volumes in Foreign Office series. FO/368, FO/371, FO/608. Papers of:
Arthur Balfour; Sir Francis Bertie; Sir Edward Grey; Sir Arthur Nicolson
(all in FO/800).
(ii) House of Lords Record Office, London:
David Lloyd George MSS.
(iii) Manuscripts Room of the British Museum, London:
Arthur Balfour MSS.
(iv) India Office Library, London:
Curzon MSS.
(v) On microfilm in the Seeley Library, Cambridge:
British Cabinet Papers.

II. *Theses and Other Unpublished Writings*

Andrew, C. M., and Kanya-Forstner, A. S., 'French Imperial Expansion: the Final Phase, 1914–1924' (to be published in 1981).
Bariéty, J., 'De l'exécution à la négociation: l'évolution des relations franco-allemandes après la première guerre mondiale (11 novembre 1918–10 janvier 1925): forces profondes et actions politiques' (thesis presented to

University of Paris I, 1975). Published as *Les Relations franco-allemandes après la Première Guerre mondiale, 11 novembre 1918–10 janvier 1925: de l'exécution à la négociation* (Paris, 1977).[4]

Godfrey, J. F., 'Bureaucracy, Industry, and Politics in France during the First World War: a Study of Some Interrelationships' (Oxford D. Phil. thesis, 1974).

Jeanneney, J.-N., 'François de Wendel en République: l'argent et le pouvoir, 1914–1940' (thesis presented to University of Paris X, 1975). Published with same title, Paris, 1976.[5]

Kaspi, A., 'La France et le concours américain, février 1917–novembre 1918' (thesis presented to University of Paris I, 1974).

Keiger, J. F. V., 'Raymond Poincaré and French Foreign Policy, 1912–1914' (Cambridge Ph.D. thesis, 1980).

Nouailhat, Y.-H., 'La France et les États-Unis, août 1914-avril 1917' (thesis presented to University of Paris I, 1975). Sinanoglou, I., 'France looks Eastward: Policies and Perspectives in Russia, 1914–1918' (Columbia University Ph.D. thesis, 1974).

III. Published Primary Material

Les carnets de guerre d'Albert Ier, Roi des Belges (R. von Overstraeten, ed., Brussels, 1953).

Annuaire diplomatique et consulaire (Paris, 1914, 1917, and 1921).

Baker, R.S., *Woodrow Wilson and World Settlement* (3 vols., London, 1923).

Barbusse, H., *Le Feu (journal d'une escouade)* (Paris, 1916).

Baruch, B.M., *The Making of the Reparation and Economic Sections of the Treaty* (New York and London, 1920).

Beneš, É., *Souvenirs de guerre et de révolution* (2 vols., Paris, 1928–9).

Benoist, C., *Souvenirs* (3 vols., Paris, 1932–4).

Berger, M., and Allard, P., *Les Secrets de la censure pendant la Guerre* (Paris, 1932).

The Diary of Lord Bertie of Thame, 1914–1918 (Lady Algernon Gordon Lennox, ed., 2 vols., London, 1924).

Blake, R., (ed.), *The Private Papers of Douglas Haig, 1914–1918* (London, 1952).

Bourbon, Prince Sixte de, *L'Offre de paix séparée de l'Autriche (5 décembre 1916–12 octobre 1917)* (Paris, 1920).

Burnett, P.M., *Reparation at the Paris Peace Conference (from the Standpoint of the American Delegation)* (2 vols., New York, 1940).

Cambon, J., 'La Paix (notes inédites, 1919)', *La Revue de Paris*, 1 November 1937, pp. 5–38.

Cambon, P., *Correspondance, 1870–1924* (H. Cambon, ed., 3 vols., Paris, 1940–6).

Clemenceau, G., *Grandeurs et misères d'une victoire* (Paris, 1930).

Clémentel, É., *La France et la politique économique interalliée* (Paris and New Haven, 1931).

Les Conditions de paix et le sentiment national français (? Paris, 1919), *BDIC* O/pièce 2358.F.

Dorten, J.A., *La Tragédie rhénane* (15th edn., Paris, 1945).

Foch, F., *Mémoires pour servir à l'histoire de la guerre de 1914–1918* (2 vols., Paris, 1931)

Foreign Office, *Peace Handbooks* (London, 1920).

(*FRUS*) *Papers Relating to the Foreign Relations of the United States, 1916, 1917, 1918* (10 vols, Washington, 1925–33). *Papers Relating to the Foreign Relations of the' United States. The Lansing Papers, 1914–1920* (2 vols., Washington, 1940). *Papers Relating to the Foreign Relations of the United States. The Paris Peace Conference, 1919* (13 vols., Washington, 1942–7).

Geouffre de Lapradelle, A., (ed.), *La Paix de Versailles. La conférence de la paix et la Société des nations* (*la documentation internationale*) (12 vols., Paris, 1929–36).

House of Commons, *Parliamentary Debates, 1917, 1918*.

Hymans, P., *Mémoires* (F. van Kalken, ed., 2 vols., Bruges, 1958).

Joffre, J.-J. C., *Mémoires, 1910–1917* (2 vols., Paris, 1932).

Journal officiel de la République française. Débats parlementaires: Chambre des députés/Sénat. Compte-rendu in extenso, 1914–1919.

Journal officiel . . . Chambre des députés, 16 May 1925. *Comité secret* of 1 June 1917, pp. 495ff.

——, 2 April 1933. *Comité secret* of 16 October 1917, pp. 545ff.

Journal officiel . . . Sénat, 29 September 1968. *Comité secret* of 6 June 1917, pp. 764ff.

Klotz, L.-L., *De la guerre à la paix* (Paris, 1924).

Lancken Wakenitz, O. Freiherr von der, *Meine dreißig Dienstjahre, 1888–1918* (Berlin, 1931).

Laroche, J., *Au Quai d'Orsay avec Briand et Poincaré, 1913–1926* (Paris, 1957).

Launay, J. de, *Secrets diplomatiques, 1914–1918* (Brussels and Paris, 1963).

Lavisse, E., *Pourquoi nous nous battons* (? Paris, 1917), *BN* 8⁰ L⁵⁷ b. 15654.

Lhopital, General, *Foch, l'armistice, et la paix* (Paris, 1938).

La Ligue française, 1914–1919.

Lloyd George, D., *War Memoirs* (6 vols., London, 1933–6).

Lloyd George, D., *The Truth about the Peace Treaties* (2 vols., London, 1938).

Loucheur, L., *Carnets secrets, 1908–1932* (J. de Launay, ed., Brussels and Paris, 1962).

Malvy, L.-J., *Mon Crime* (Paris, 1921).

Mangin, General, 'Lettres de Rhénanie', *La Revue de Paris*, 1 April 1936, pp. 481ff.

Mantoux, P., *Les Délibérations du Conseil des Quatre (24 mars–28 juin 1919). Notes de l'officier interprète, Paul Mantoux* (2 vols., Paris, 1955).

Miller, D. H., *My Diary at the Conference of Paris* (22 vols, New York, 1924).

Morand, P., *Journal d'un attaché d'ambassade, 1916–1917* (Paris, 1948).

Mordacq, J., *Le Ministère Clemenceau: journal d'un témoin* (4 vols., Paris, 1930–1).

228 Bibliography

Nudant, General, 'A Spa: l'armistice (1918–1919)', *La Revue de France*, 15 March 1925, pp. 270–94, and 1 April 1925, pp. 475–502.

L'Opinion, 10 July 1920, pp. 31–7; 24 July 1920, pp. 87–94; 31 July 1920, pp. 115–21. Three articles on the Armand–Revertera conversations of 1917–18.

Paléologue, M., *La Russie des Tsars pendant la Grande Guerre* (3 vols., Paris, 1921–2).

Poincaré, R., *Au service de la France. Neuf années de souvenirs* (10 vols., Paris, 1926–33).

Poincaré, R., *A la recherche de la paix, 1919* (J. Bariéty and P. Miquel, eds., Paris, 1974).

Ribot, A., *Lettres à un ami: souvenirs de ma vie politique* (Paris, 1924).

Ribot, A., *Journal d'Alexandre Ribot et correspondances inédites, 1914–1922* (A. Ribot, ed., Paris, 1936).

Röhl, J. C. G., (ed.), *From Bismarck to Hitler: the Problem of Continuity in German History* (London, 1970).

Scherer, J., and Grünewald, A., (eds.) *L'Allemagne et les problèmes de la paix pendant la Première Guerre mondiale* (4 vols., Paris, 1966–78).

Scott, J.B., (ed.), *Official Statements of War Aims and Peace Proposals, December 1916–November 1918* (Washington, 1921).

Seymour, C. M., (ed.), *The Intimate Papers of Colonel House*, (4 vols., London, 1926–8).

Stieve, F., *Iswolski und der Weltkrieg* (Berlin, 1924).

Stieve, F., *Im Dunkel der Europäischen Geheimdiplomatie: Iswolskis Kriegspolitik in Paris, 1911–1917* (Berlin, 1926).

Suarez, G., *Briand: sa vie – son œuvre* (6 vols., Paris, 1938–52).

Szeps, B., *My Life and History* (J. Summerfield, transl., London, 1938).

Tardieu, A., La Paix (Paris, 1921).

Tirard, P., *La France sur le Rhin: douze années d'occupation rhénane* (Paris, 1930).

Travaux du Comité d'études (2 vols., Paris, 1918–19).

IV. Secondary Works: Books

Andrew, C. M., *Théophile Delcassé and the Making of the Entente Cordiale: a Reappraisal of French Foreign Policy, 1898–1905* (London and New York, 1968).

Auffray, B., *Pierre de Margerie (1861–1942) et la vie diplomatique de son temps* (Paris, 1976).

Becker, J.-J., *1914: Comment les Français sont entrés dans la guerre* (Paris, 1977).

Bonnefous, G., *La Grande Guerre (1914–1918)* (2nd edn., Paris, 1967) (Vol. II of *Histoire politique de la Troisième République*).

Bonwetsch, B., *Kriegsallianz und Wirtschaftsinteressen: Rußland in den Wirtschaftsplänen ·Englands und Frankreichs, 1914–1917* (Düsseldorf, 1973).

Bréal, A., *Philippe Berthelot* (Paris, 1937).

Chastenet, J., *Jours inquiets et jours sanglants, 1906–1918* (Paris, 1955) (Vol. II of *Histoire de la Troisième République*).

Dahlin, E., *French and German Public Opinion on Declared War Aims, 1914–1918* (Stanford, 1933).

Digeon, C., *La Crise allemande de la pensée française, 1870–1914* (Paris, 1959).

Ducasse, A., Meyer, J., and Perreux, G., *Vie et mort des Français, 1914–1918* (Paris, 1959).

Duroselle, J.-B., *La France et les Français, 1914–1920* (Paris, 1972). *See also* Waites.

Elcock, H., *Portrait of a Decision: the Council of Four and the Treaty of Versailles* (London, 1972).

Field, F., *Three French Writers and the Great War: Studies in the Rise of Communism and Fascism* (Cambridge, 1975).

Fischer, F., *Germany's Aims in the First World War* (English edn., London, 1967).

Floto, I., *Colonel House in Paris: a Study of American Diplomacy at the Paris Peace Conference, 1919* (Aarhus, 1973).

François-Poncet, A., *La Vie et l'œuvre de Robert Pinot* (Paris, 1927).

Gatzke, H., *Germany's Drive to the West: a Study of Germany's Western War Aims during the First World War* (Baltimore, 1950).

Girault, R., *Emprunts russes et investissements français en Russie, 1897–1914: recherches sur l'investissement international* (Paris, 1973).

Gorce, P.-M. de la, *La République et son armée* (Paris, 1963).

Guillen, P., (ed.), *La France et l'Italie pendant la Première Guerre mondiale* (Grenoble, 1976). Particularly chapters by A. Kupferman, 'Les Campagnes défaitistes en France et l'Italie, 1914–1917'; M.-R. Mouton, 'L' Idée d'organisation internationale en France et en Italie pendant la Première Guerre mondiale'; G.-H. Soutou, 'La Politique commerciale et industrielle de la France en Italie pendant la Première Guerre mondiale'.

Hardach, G., *The First World War, 1914–1918* (London, 1977).

Helmreich, J.E., *Belgium and Europe: a Study in Small-power Diplomacy* (The Hague, 1976).

Hölzle, E., *Die Selbstentmachtung Europas: Das Experiment des Friedens vor und im Ersten Weltkrieg* (Frankfurt and Zürich, 1975).

Horne, A., *The Price of Glory: Verdun 1916* (Penguin edn., Harmondsworth, 1978).

Hovi, K., *Cordon sanitaire or barrière de l'est? The Emergence of the New French Eastern European Alliance Policy, 1917–1919* (Turku, 1975).

Hunt, B., and Preston, A., (eds.), *War Aims and Strategic Policy in the Great War* (London, 1977). Chapter by D. Johnson on 'French War Aims and the Crisis of the Third Republic'.

Kaspi, A., *Le Temps des Américains: le concours américain à la France en 1917–1918* (Paris, 1976).

Kehr, E., *Der Primat der Innenpolitik: gesammelte Aufsätze zur preussisch-deutschen Sozialgeschichte im 19. und 20. Jahrhundert* (H.-U. Wehler, ed., Berlin, 1965).

Keynes, J. M., *The Economic Consequences of the Peace* (London, 1920).

King, J. C., *Generals and Politicians: Conflict between France's Command, Parliament, and Government, 1914–1918* (Berkeley and Los Angeles, 1951).

King, J. C., *Foch versus Clemenceau: France and German Dismemberment 1918–1919* (Cambridge, Mass., 1960).

Komarnicki, T., *Rebirth of the Polish Republic: a study in the Diplomatic History of Europe, 1914–1920* (London, 1957).

Kriegel, A., *Aux origines du Communisme français, 1914–1920: contribution à l'histoire du mouvement ouvrier français* (Paris and The Hague, 1964).

Krüger, P., *Deutschland und die Reparationen, 1918–1919: die Genesis des Reparationsproblems in Deutschland zwischen Waffenstillstand und Versailler Friedensschluß* (Stuttgart, 1973).

Lauren, P.G., *Diplomats and Bureaucrats: the First Institutional Responses to Twentieth-Century Diplomacy in France and Germany* (Stanford, 1976).

Lenin, V. I., *Imperialism, the Highest Stage of Capitalism: a Popular Outline* (paperback edition, Peking, 1975).

Maier, C. S., *Recasting Bourgeois Europe: Stabilization in France, Germany, and Italy in the Decade after World War I* (Princeton, 1975).

Mayer, A. J., *Political Origins of the New Diplomacy, 1917–1918* (New Haven, 1959).

Mayer, A. J., *Politics and Diplomacy of Peacemaking: Containment and Counter-Revolution at Versailles, 1918–1919* (London, 1968).

McDougall, W. A., *France's Rhineland Diplomacy, 1914–1924: the Last Bid for a Balance of Power in Europe* (Princeton, 1978).

Mermeix (G. Terrail, pseud.), *Les Négociations secrètes et les quatre armistices* (Paris, 1921).

Mermeix (G. Terrail, pseud.), *Le Combat des Trois: notes et documents sur la conférence de paix* (10th edn., Paris, 1922).

Miquel, P., *Poincaré* (Paris, 1961).

Miquel, P., *La Paix de Versailles et l'opinion publique française* (Paris, 1972).

Nelson, H. I., *Land and Power: British and Allied Policy on Germany's Frontiers, 1916–1919* (London, 1963).

Nelson, K. L., *Victors Divided: America and the Allies in Germany, 1918–1923* (Berkeley, Los Angeles, and London, 1975).

Nicolson, H., *Peacemaking, 1919* (new edn., London, 1937).

Pedroncini, G., *Les Mutineries de 1917* (Paris, 1967).

Pedroncini, G., *Les Négociations secrètes pendant la Première Guerre mondiale* (Paris, 1969).

Pedroncini, G., *Pétain: Général en chef, 1917–1918* (Paris, 1974).

Perman, D., The Shaping of the Czechoslovak State: Diplomatic History of the Boundaries of Czechoslovakia, 1914–1920 (Leiden, 1962).

Pingaud, A., *Histoire diplomatique de la France pendant la Grande Guerre* (3 vols., Paris, 1938–40).

Poidevin, R., *Les Relations économiques et financières entre la France et l'Allemagne de 1898 à 1914* (Paris, 1969).

Poidevin, R., (ed.), *Problèmes de la Rhénanie, 1919–1930* (Metz, 1975). Particularly chapter by H. Köhler, 'Grundlagen und Konzeptionen der Französischen Rhein- und Deutschlandspolitik von der Novemberrevolution bis zum Friedensschluβ von Versailles'.

Poidevin, R., (ed.), *Les Relations franco-belges de 1830 à 1934* (Metz, 1975). Particularly chapters by G.-H. Soutou, 'La Politique économique de la France à l'égard de la Belgique, 1914–1924'; and G. Trausch, 'Les Relations franco-belges à propos de la question luxembourgeoise (1914–1922)'.

Poidevin, R., and Bariéty, J., *Les Relations franco-allemandes, 1815–1975* (Paris, 1977).

Renouvin, P., *The Forms of War Government in France* (New Haven, 1927).

Renouvin, P., *L'Armistice de Rethondes, 11 novembre 1918* (Paris, 1968).

Renouvin, P., *La Crise européene et la Première Guerre mondiale (1904–1918)* (5th edn., Paris, 1969).

Renouvin, P., *Les Crises du XXème siècle: I. De 1914 à 1929* (Paris, 1969) (Vol. VII of *Histoire des relations internationales*).

Rothwell, V. H., *British War Aims and Peace Diplomacy 1914–1918* (Oxford, 1971).

Saatmann, I., *Parlament, Rüstung, und Armee in Frankreich, 1914–1918* (Düsseldorf, 1978).

Schaper, B.W., *Albert Thomas: trente ans de réformisme social* (Paris, ?1960).

Schmidt, M. E., *Alexandre Ribot: Odyssey of a Liberal in the Third Republic* (The Hague, 1974).

Siebert, F., *Aristide Briand, 1862–1932: Staatsmann zwischen Frankreich und Europa* (Zurich and Stuttgart, 1973).

Smith, C. J., *The Russian Struggle for Power, 1914–1917: a Study of Russian Foreign Policy during the First World War* (New York, 1956).

Swart, K., *The Sense of Decadence in Nineteenth-Century France* (The Hague, 1964).

Tabouis, G., *The Life of Jules Cambon* (C. F. Atkinson, transl., London, 1938).

Taylor, A. J. P., and Pares, R. (eds.), *Essays Presented to Sir Lewis Namier* (London, 1956). Chapter by A. J. P. Taylor, 'The War Aims of the Allies in the First World War'.

Taylor, A. J. P., *The Struggle for Mastery in Europe* (paperback edn., Oxford, 1971).

Trachtenberg, M., *Reparation in World Politics: France and European Economic Diplomacy, 1916–1923* (New York, 1980).

Vial-Mazel, G., *Erreurs et oublis de Georges Clemenceau: l'affaire du Rhin* (Paris, 1931).

Waites, N., (ed.), *Troubled Neighbours: Franco-British Relations in the Twentieth Century* (London, 1971). Particularly chapters by J.-B. Duroselle, 'Strategic and Economic Relations during the First World War', and D. R. Watson, 'The Making of the Treaty of Versailles'.

Walworth, A., *America's Moment: 1918. American Diplomacy at the end of World War I* (New York, 1977).

Wandycz, P. S., *France and her Eastern Allies, 1919–1925: French–Czechoslovak–Polish Relations from the Paris Peace Conference to Locarno* (Minneapolis, 1962).

Watson, D. R., *Georges Clemenceau: a Political Biography* (London, 1974).

Weber, E., *Action Française: Royalism and Reaction in Twentieth-Century France* (Stanford, 1962).

Weber, E., *Peasants into Frenchmen: the Modernization of Rural France, 1870–1914* (London, 1977).

Weill-Raynal, É., *Les Réparations allemandes et la France* (3 vols., Paris, . 1947).

Wohl, R., *French Communism in the Making, 1914–1924* (Stanford, 1966).

Wormser, G., *La République de Clemenceau* (Paris, 1961).

Wormser, G., *Le Septennat de Poincaré*, (Paris, 1977).

Wright, G., *Raymond Poincaré and the French Presidency* (Stanford, 1942).

Yates, L. A. R., *The United States and French Security, 1917–1921: a Study in American Diplomatic History* (New York, 1957)..

Zimmermann, L., *Frankreichs Ruhrpolitik von Versailles bis zum Dawesplan* (new edn., Göttingen, 1971).

V. *Secondary Works: Articles*

Andrew, C. M., and Kanya-Forstner, A. S., 'The French Colonial Party and French Colonial War Aims, 1914–1918', *Historical Journal*, XVII, 1 (1974), pp. 79–106.

Carley, M.J., 'The Origins of French Intervention in the Russian Civil War, January-May 1918: a Reappraisal', *Journal of Modern History*, 48, 3 (September 1976), pp. 413–39.

Dutton, D. J., 'The Balkan Campaign and French War Aims in the Great War', *English Historical Review*, XCIV, 370 (January 1979), pp. 97–113.

McCrum, J. R., 'French Rhineland Policy at the Paris Peace Conference, 1919', *Historical Journal*, 21, 3 (1978), pp. 623–48.

McDougall, W.A., 'Political Economy versus National Sovereignty: French Structures for German Economic Integration after Versailles', *Journal of Modern History*, 51 (March 1979), pp. 4–23.

Renouvin, P., 'Le Gouvernement français et les tentatives de paix en 1917', *La Revue des deux mondes*, 15 October 1964, pp. 492–513.

Renouvin, P., 'Les Buts de guerre du gouvernement français, 1914–1918', *Revue historique*, ccxxxv (1966), pp. 1–38.

Renouvin, P., 'Die öffentliche Meinung in Frankreich während des Krieges, 1914–1918', *Vierteljahrshefte für Zeitgeschichte*, 1970, pp. 239–75.

Renouvin, P., 'Les Relations franco-allemandes, 1914–1918', *Revue d'Allemagne* (July-September 1972), pp. 494–504.

Soutou, G., 'Guerre et économie: le premier projet français de nouvel ordre économique mondial', *La Revue universelle des faits et des idées*, 31 (April 1977), pp. 55–67.

Soutou, G., 'La France et les marches de l'est, 1914–1919', *Revue historique*, 528 (October-December, 1978), pp. 341–88.

Trachtenberg, M., '"A New Economic Order": Étienne Clémentel and French Economic Diplomacy during the First World War', *French Historical Studies*, X, 2 (1977), pp. 315–41.

Trachtenberg, M., 'Reparation at the Paris Peace Conference', *Journal of Modern History*, 51 (March 1979), pp. 24–55.

Traversay, G. de, 'La Première tentative de république rhénane', *La Revue de Paris*, 15 November 1928, pp. 404–31; an 1 December 1928, pp. 586–614.

References

PREFACE

1. F. Fischer, *Germany's Aims in the First World War* (London, 1967). (German edition, *Griff nach der Weltmacht*, Düsseldorf, 1961.) V. H. Rothwell, *British War Aims and Peace Diplomacy, 1914–1918* (Oxford, 1971).
2. The starting point was P. Renouvin, 'Les Buts de guerre du gouvernement français, 1914–1918', *Revue historique*, CCXXXV (1966), pp. 1–38. See the subsequent works by J. Bariéty, J.-J. Becker, J.-N. Jeanneney, A. Kaspi, A. Kriegel, K. Hovi, W. A. McDougall, Y.-H. Nouailhat, I. Sinanoglou, and M. Trachtenberg cited in the Bibliography. Mr J. A. Neufeld of the London School of Economics is preparing a Ph.D. thesis on French aims in the earlier part of the war. G.-H. Soutou's penetrating article on 'La France et les marches de l'est, 1914–1918', *Revue historique*, 528 (1978), pp. 341–88, uses similar material to that on which I have worked, but our conclusions have been arrived at independently, and, on some points, differ. M. Soutou's forthcoming thesis on the economic war aims of the Powers will be essential reading for students of the period.
3. Rothwell, p. 1.
4. C. M. Andrew and A. S. Kanya-Forstner, *French Imperial Expansion: the Final Phase* (forthcoming). I should add to the above remarks that I have greatly abridged this study, and Chapters VI and VII in particular, while preparing it for publication. I hope later to return to the subject of the peace settlement.

INTRODUCTION

1. For two examples, see C. M. Andrew, *Théophile Delcassé and the Making of the Entente Cordiale* (London and New York, 1968), p. 19, and P. Miquel, *Poincaré* (Paris, 1961), p. 37.
2. For the problems discussed in this section, see R. Poidevin and J. Bariéty, *Les Relations franco-allemandes, 1815–1975* (Paris, 1977); K. W. Swart, *The Sense of Decadence in Nineteenth-Century France* (The Hague, 1964); C. Digeon, *La Crise allemande de la pensée française, 1870–1914* (Paris, 1959); and R. Poidevin, *Les Relations économiques et financières entre la France et l'Allemagne de 1898 à 1914* (Paris, 1969).
3. In 1910 Germany's population was 65 million; France's 39 million. In 1914 German steel production was 14 million tons; French 3.5 million. Also in 1914, German defence estimates were equivalent to £110.8

million; French to £57.4 million. A. J. P. Taylor, *The Struggle for Mastery in Europe, 1848–1918* (Oxford paperback edition, 1971), pp. xxv, xxviii, xxx.

4. In what follows I have used the important Ph.D. thesis by J. F. V. Keiger, 'Raymond Poincaré and French Foreign Policy, 1912–1914' (Cambridge, 1980).
5. J.-J. Becker, *1914: comment les Français sont entrés dans la guerre* (Paris, 1977), p. 580. I have relied heavily on this exhaustive work.
6. On 23 September 1914 the French Government appointed the Payelle Commission to study German violations of international law. From 1915–19 this body produced twelve volumes of reports, mainly on German actions in the invaded regions. See inventory of its records in *AN*, Série AJ⁴.

CHAPTER I

1. R. Poincaré, *Au service de la France. Neuf années de souvenirs* (10 vols., Paris, 1926–33), v, pp. 15–16.
2. Isvolski to Sazonov, 5 Aug. 1914. F. Stieve (ed.), *Im Dunkel der Europäischen Geheimdiplomatie: Isvolskis Kriegspolitik in Paris, 1911–1917* (Berlin, 1926), p. 245.
3. Below, notes 26 and 27 to this chapter.
4. Jagow (German Foreign Minister) to Romberg (German Minister at Berne), 6 Aug. 1915 and 8 June 1916. A. Scherer and J. Grünewald (eds.), *L'Allemagne et les problèmes de la paix pendant la Première Guerre mondiale* (4 vols., Paris, 1962–78), i, pp. 153, 363.
5. Text in Poincaré, *Service*, v, p. 253.
6. A. Pingaud, *Histoire diplomatique de la France pendant la Grande Guerre* (5 vols., Paris, undated), i, pp. 102–3.
7. Paléologue to Delcassé, 18 Sept. 1914; Delcassé to Paléologue 21 Sept. 1914, *MAE* Paléologue MSS Vol. I. Poincaré, *Service*, v, pp. 314–16.
8. Delcassé circular telegram, 6 Nov. 1914, *MAE* A 'Paix' (1). Viviani to Chevalley, 22 Oct. 1914, ibid. (5). Briand to Bertie, 1 July 1916, *MAE* Paul Cambon MSS Tome V, Vol. 13. Poincaré, *Service*, viii, pp. 279–80.
9. Pingaud, i, pp. 96–7.
10. Jusserand to Delcassé, 8 Sept. 1914; Delcassé to Jusserand, 9 Sept. 1914, *MAE* A 'Paix' (1).
11. Y.-H. Nouailhat, 'La France et les Etats-Unis, août 1914– avril 1917' (Thesis, Paris, 1975), p. 245. C. Seymour (ed.), *The Intimate Papers of Colonel House* (4 vols., London, 1926–8), i, p. 421.
12. Nouailhat, p. 871.
13. Minutes of these conversations (2 and 7 Feb. 1916) in *MAE* Jules Cambon MSS (19). House's account in Seymour, ii, pp. 156–7, 163–4.
14. Nouailhat, p. 648. Seymour, ii, p. 201.
15. F. Bertie, *The Diary of Lord Bertie of Thame, 1914–1918* (ed. Lady

Algernon Gordon Lennox, 2 vols., London, 1924), i, p. 312.
16. Seymour, ii, pp. 273–4.
17. Ibid., p. 276.
18. Briand to Jusserand, 28 May 1916, *MAE* Jusserand MSS (31).
19. Jusserand to Briand, 15 Feb. 1916, ibid. (46).
20. Malvy (Minister of the Interior) to Prefects, 24 Jan. 1915, *AN* F⁷ 13370.
21. For example, reports by the Prefect of Police to Malvy on morale in Paris, Aug.–Nov. 1915, *AN* F⁷ 12936.
22. Instructions to the censorship authorities, 8 Apr. 1915, *BDIC* F. 270 Rés. C.G. 1915/16.
23. Briand in *CAES*, 13 Dec. 1915, *CAES*, 1915, p. 409. Renouvin, 'Buts', p. 8.
24. Message from Poincaré and speech by Viviani, 4 Aug. 1914, *JO* (*Chambre*), 1914, pp. 3110, 3113.
25. Viviani speech, 22 Dec. 1914, ibid., pp. 3124–5. Poincaré, *Service*, v, p. 522.
26. Viviani speech, 18 Feb. 1915, *JO* (*Chambre*), 1915, p. 161. Poincaré, *Service*, vi, pp. 67–71.
27. Poincaré message, 5 Aug. 1915, *JO* (*Chambre*), 1915, p. 1227. Poincaré, *Service*, vii, p. 10.
28. Briand speech, 3 Nov. 1915, *JO* (*Chambre*), 1915, pp. 1681–2, 1690–1.
29. Fischer, *Aims*, Ch. 5. H. Gatzke, *Germany's Drive to the West: a Study of Germany's Western War Aims during the First World War* (Baltimore, 1950), pp. 24ff.
30. See, in general, A. Kriegel, *Aux origines du Communisme français, 1914–1920* (Paris and The Hague, 1964), Pt. I; R. Wohl, *French Communism in the Making, 1914–1924* (Stanford, 1966), Ch. II.
31. G. Bonnefous, *La Grande Guerre, 1914–1918* (*Histoire politique de la Troisième République*, vol. ii), 2nd. edn., Paris, 1967, p. 98.
32. Piou in *CAEC*, 21 Apr. 1915, *AN* C 7488. Marin, 23 Feb. 1916, in sub-commission on France and the Western Front of inquiry set up by the *Société de Géographie*, *SG*, colis 9.
33. Becker, p. 467.
34. Camille Cavallier (Director of the *Pont-à-Mousson* company) to Robert Pinot (Secretary-General of the *Comité des forges*), 17 Mar. 1915, *PAM* 06673.
35. E. Weber, *Action française: Royalism and Reaction in Twentieth-Century France* (Stanford, 1962), pp. 97–8.
36. Police report on the *Ligue des patriotes*, 4 Mar. 1915, *AN* F⁷ 12873. Renouvin, 'Buts', p. 4.
37. See, in general, the *Ligue*'s monthly bulletin, *La Ligue française*, *BN* Jo. 67040 (consulted for 1914–19).
38. De Margerie to Robert de Billy, 3 Aug. 1916, *MAE* Robert de Billy MSS (63). I am indebted to Dr C. M. Andrew for this reference.
39. De Margerie, 'Note', 1 Feb. 1916, *MAE* Jules Cambon MSS (17). Berthelot corroborated this in conversation with the Belgian Minister in

Paris. P. Hymans, *Mémoires* (2 vols., ed. F. van Kalken, Bruges, 1958), i, p. 190.

40. Resolution passed at *SFIO* Congress 25–9 Dec. 1915, AN F⁷ 13072.
41. Poincaré, *Service*, viii, p. 8. Clémentel in *CAES*, 1 July 1916, *CAES*, 1916, pp. 588–9.
42. Poincaré, *Service*, vi, p. 68.
43. On colonial war aims, see C. M. Andrew and A. S. Kanya-Forstner, *Expansion*, and the same authors' 'The French Colonial Party and French Colonial War Aims, 1914–1918', *Historical Journal*, xvii, 1 (1974), pp. 79–106.
44. *GQG*, 'Rapport sur l'organisation des territoires en Alsace', 25 Dec. 1914, *MAE* Guerre (166).
45. Decree of 18 Feb. 1915 founding the *Conférence*, ibid. *Procès-verbaux* in *MAE* Tardieu MSS (43).
46. Folder on the *Groupe lorrain* in *AN* Marin MSS 317.AP.106.
47. The *Comité's* full name was the *Comité d'études économiques et administratives relatives à l'Alsace–Lorraine*. Its president was Jules Siegfried, a Deputy and ex-Minister. See folder in *PAM* 06666. For its role in the preparation of the Alsace–Lorraine clauses at the Peace Conference, note by the *Haut Commissariat de la République* at Strasbourg, 29 Mar. 1919, on 'Clauses à introduire dans le traité de paix intéressant l'Alsace–Lorraine', *MAE* A 'Paix' (N) (256).
48. Meeting of the *Sous-commission des mines*, 2 Apr. 1915, *PAM* 06666.
49. Meetings of the *Commission de direction* of the *Comité des forges*, 18 Mar. and 19 Aug. 1915, *PAM* 06673.
50. e.g. Hearing of Robert Pinot by the *Bureau d'études économiques*, 3 Dec. 1915, *MAE* Série A 'Paix' (178); 'Note du *Comité des forges*', May 1916, *AN* F¹² 7677.
51. Circular from the *ONCE* to French Consulates, etc., 19–20 Aug. 1914, *AN* F¹² 9289. Director of the *ONCE* to Commerce Minister, 19 Dec. 1914, ibid.
52. D. Dutton, 'The Balkan Campaign and French War Aims in the Great War', *English Historical Review*, xciv, no. 370 (Jan. 1979), pp. 107–11.
53. G.-H. Soutou, 'La Politique commerciale et industrielle de la France en Italie pendant la Première Guerre mondiale', in P. Guillen (ed.), *La France et l'Italie pendant la Première Guerre mondiale* (Grenoble, 1976), pp. 319ff.
54. The *Commission d'étude pour favoriser le commerce national avec la Russie* (usually known as the Méline Commission) was set up on 10 Mar. 1915. B. Bonwetsch, *Kriegsallianz und Wirtschaftsinteressen: Rußland in den Wirtschaftsplänen Englands und Frankreichs, 1914–1917* (Düsseldorf, 1973), pp. 115–17. As well as being an ex-Premier, Méline was a leader of the *Fédération républicaine* and honorary President of the *Association de l'industrie et de l'agriculture française*.
55. Painlevé to Poincaré, 9 Nov. 1917, *AN* F¹² 8105.
56. For detailed discussion see Andrew and Kanya-Forstner, *Expansion*, and 'Colonial Party'; C. J. Smith, *The Russian Struggle for*

Power, 1914-1917: a Study of Russian Foreign Policy during the First World War (New York, 1956). The Sykes–Picot Agreement and its Anatolian sequel provided for French rule of the Mediterranean coastal strip in the Lebanon and Cilicia, and of a belt stretching inland as far as Persia, together with exclusive economic rights the prerogative of supplying advisers to a zone under Arab rule to the south and east.

57. Rothwell, pp. 18–21. Grey to Buchanan, 16 Nov. 1914, FO/371/2174.
58. Bertie to Grey, 12 Jan. 1915, FO/371/2506. Delcassé to Paléologue, 7 Mar. 1915, *MAE* A 'Paix' (N) (177). On 6 Apr. 1915 Delcassé instructed Paul Cambon not to raise war aims with the British (*MAE* Delcassé MSS (24)), but this may have been because of his reluctance to delegate to his Ambassador. G.-H. Soutou, 'Marches', p. 345 seems too categorical on this point.
59. See Appendix III, 'Poland', for the background to this question.
60. Paléologue to Delcassé, 13–14 Sept. 1914, *MAE* A 'Paix' (58).
61. Paléologue to Delcassé, 22–3 Nov. 1914, ibid. (1).
62. Isvolski to Sazonov, 30 Sept. 1914. F. Stieve (ed.), *Isvolski und der Weltkrieg* (Berlin, 1924), pp. 267–8.
63. Bertie, *Diary*, i, pp. 120, 143.
64. Delcassé to Paléologue, 10 Oct. 1914, *MAE* A 'Paix' (58). Delcassé reaffirmed to Paléologue on 15 Nov. that his views 'concorded generally' with Sazonov's, ibid.
65. Delcassé to Paul Cambon, 2 Dec. 1914, FO/371/2174.
66. Paléologue to Poincaré, 16 Apr. 1915, *MAE* Paul Cambon MSS Tome V, Vol. 13.
67. Paléologue to Delcassé, 4 and 7 Mar. 1915, *MAE* Paléologue MSS Vol. II. (My emphasis.)
68. Paléologue to Delcassé, 3 Mar. 1915, ibid.
69. Delcassé to Paléologue, 7 Mar. 1915, *MAE* A 'Paix' (N) (177). Russian Embassy Note, 9 Mar. 1915, *MAE* A 'Paix' (59), apparently not answered by Delcassé.
70. Poincaré to Paléologue, 9 Mar. 1915. Delcassé approved the letter in advance. Poincaré, *Service*, vi, pp. 92–5.
71. Bertie, *Diary*, i, p. 143.
72. Paléologue to Poincaré, 16 Apr. 1915, *MAE* Paul Cambon MSS Tome V, Vol. 13.
73. Poincaré, *Service*, vi, pp. 5–6. Delcassé to Paléologue, 6 Jan. 1915. *MAE* Paléologue MSS Vol. II.
74. Von der Lancken (pre-war Counsellor at the German Embassy in Paris) to Lersner, 13 May 1917. Scherer and Grünewald (eds.), ii, p. 196.
75. Paul to Jules Cambon, 7 Dec. 1915. Paul Cambon, *Correspondance* (ed. H. Cambon, 3 vols., Paris 1940–6), iii, pp. 92–3.
76. This was the opinion of George Grahame of the British Embassy: Grahame to Russell, 20 Mar. 1917, FO/800/169.
77. P. Morand, *Journal d'un attaché d'Ambassade, 1916-1917* (Paris, 1948), pp. 10–12.
78. Henri to Paul Cambon, 15 Jan. 1917. Letter in the possession of

M. Louis Cambon.
79. See the fine account in A. Horne, *The Price of Glory: Verdun, 1916* (Paperback edn., Harmondsworth, 1978).
80. For Poincaré and Delcassé, the assurances listed in Hymans to Balfour, 14 Apr. 1919, FO/608/2. For de Margerie, 'Note' of 1 Feb. 1916, *MAE* Jules Cambon MSS (17). For Berthelot, Soutou, 'Marches', p. 353n.
81. Briand to Paul Cambon, 31 Dec. 1915, *MAE* A 'Paix' (N) (189).
82. Pingaud, iii, pp. 253–7. The text was agreed between Briand and Grey.
83. Paléologue to Briand, 8 Mar. 1916, *MAE* Paléologue MSS Vol. III.
84. Briand to Paléologue, undated, LG Papers, D/19/5/7.
85. Pingaud, iii, pp. 268–9.
86. De Margerie, 'Question polonaise', c. 27 Apr. 1916, *AN* Thomas MSS 94 AP. 174.
87. Ibid.
88. Pingaud, iii, 268; T. Komarnicki, *Rebirth of the Polish Republic: a Study in the Diplomatic History of Europe, 1914–1920* (London, 1957), p. 44; Briand to Paléologue 15 Apr. and Paléologue to Briand 18 Apr. 1916, *MAE* Paléologue MSS Vol. III.
89. M. Paléologue, *La Russie des Tsars pendant la Grande Guerre* (3 vols., Paris, 1921–2), ii, pp. 260, 274.
90. Bonwetsch, pp. 161–70.
91. By 1916 French Government expenditure was more than seven times income; and merchandise imports were more than three times the value of merchandise exports. G. Hardach, *The First World War, 1914–1918* (London, 1977), pp. 143, 155.
92. E. Clémentel, *La France et la politique économique interalliée* (Paris and New Haven, 1931), pp. 68–9.
93. Briand in *CAES*, 3 Apr. 1916, *CAES*, 1916, pp. 519–20.
94. In general, see M. Trachtenberg, 'A New Economic Order. Etienne Clémentel and French Economic Diplomacy during the First World War', *French Historical Studies*, X, 2 (1977), pp. 315–41.
95. Briand circular telegram, 21 Dec. 1915, *MAE* Y Internationale (206). Supplementary telegram, 14 Jan. 1916, in F. Pila, 'Projet d'une entente économique générale entre Alliés et la prochaine conférence économique de Paris', 14 Apr. 1916, *MAE* Guerre (1216). Background information in Ministry of Commerce notes, 'Avant la conférence économique: la situation en novembre 1915' and 'La conférence économique de Paris: les négociations', *AN* F^{12} 7988.
96. Dossier of 'Documents sur le contrôle interallié des matières premières', item 1, *AN* F^{12} 7819. Runciman to Clémentel, 12 Feb. and Clémentel to Runciman 27 Feb. 1916, *MAE* Guerre (1216).
97. Text of the agenda: 'Conférence économique inter-alliée: le programme', undated, *MAE* Guerre (1216).
98. *Procès-verbaux* and resolutions of the Conference in *AN* F^{12} 8104.
99. Clémentel, 'Les relations économiques franco-belges', 15 Sept. 1918, *APD* Clémentel MSS XXX.

240 *References to pages 36–41*

CHAPTER II.

1. For example, the congress of the Radical Party in October 1916 voted in favour of the war continuing until 'serious guarantees against a new aggression by German militarism' had been won. Poincaré, *Service*, ix, p. 12.
2. Renouvin, 'Buts', pp. 10–11.
3. Touron in *Comité directeur* of the *AIAF*, 20 Sept. 1916, *AN* 27 A.S. 3, p. 35.
4. Memorandum presented to the Government by the *Fédération des industriels et des commerçants français*, 5 Sept. 1916, *SG* Colis 16bis. *Comité directeur* of the *AIAF*, 17 Jan. 1917, *AN* 27 A.S. 3, pp. 54–8.
5. Folder on the *Comité* in Louis Marin MSS, *AN* 317 A.P. 106. Like other such groups, the *Comité* was small, with only 2,188 members in November 1917. Ibid.
6. Folder on this body in ibid.
7. J.-N. Jeanneney, 'François de Wendel en République: l'argent et le pouvoir, 1914–1940' (Thesis, Paris, 1975), pp. 44–6. G. Suarez, *Briand: sa vie – son oeuvre* (6 vols, Paris, 1938–52), iii, pp. 412–13.
8. Discussion of the *Commission de direction* of the *Comité des forges*, 29 June and 21 Sept. 1916, 15 Mar. 1917, *PAM* 06673. First report of the Peace Treaty Commission (misleadingly dated 19 Aug. 1915) in *PAM* 12119/95. Final version, 21 Jan. 1917, in ibid. 12120/96. The report was mainly the work of Pinot and of de Wendel's brother, Humbert.
9. *GQG*, 'Rapport sur le bassin houiller de Sarrebrück . . .', 16 May 1916. *MAE* Europe 1918–29 Sarre (1).
10. Claudel, 'Note sur les conditions de la paix économique avec l'Allemagne', 31 July 1916, *MAE* A 'Paix' (N) (290).
11. Comert to Berthelot, 10 May 1916, *MAE* A 'Paix' (178). Suarez, iii, pp. 407–12. The reference in Suarez to a 'P . . .' could indicate either Pinot himself or Pralon, a Vice-President of the *Comité des forges*.
12. For Pinot's testimony, Ch. 1, above, note 51. The reader is advised to refer here to Appendix I.
13. 'Note de MM. Schneider et Cie. pour la *Commission de direction* du *Comité des forges*', 24 June 1916, *PAM* 12119/95. cf. C.S. Maier, *Recasting Bourgeois Europe: Stabilization in France, Germany, and Italy in the Decade after World War I* (Princeton, 1975), pp. 71–2.
14. Prince Sixte de Bourbon, *L'Offre de paix séparée de l'Autriche, 5 décembre 1916–12 octobre 1917* (Paris, 1920), p. 75.
15. Ch. I, above, notes 9 and 85.
16. Poincaré, *Service*, viii, pp. 300–1.
17. Paléologue to Briand, 25 July 1916, *MAE* Paléologue MSS vol. III.
18. Briand to Paléologue, 28 July 1916, *MAE* A 'Paix' (9).
19. Bertie to Hardinge, 24 Aug. 1916, FO/800/59.
20. J.-J. C. Joffre, *Mémoires* (2 vols., Paris, 1932), ii, pp. 253, 369.
21. Poincaré, *Service*, viii, p. 323.
22. Rothwell, pp. 39, 40.
23. Paul Cambon to Briand, 10 Sept. 1916, *MAE* Paul Cambon MSS Vol. 7, dossier 23. Cf. Grey to Bertie, 24 Aug. 1916, FO/371/2804.

24. Bertie to Hardinge, 20 Sept. 1916, FO/800/168.
25. 'Mermeix' (G. Terrail, pseud.), *Le Combat des Trois* (10th edn., Paris, 1922), p. 191.
26. Bertie to Grey, 19 Sept. 1916, FO/800/59.
27. Doulcet to William Martin, Oct. 1916, *MAE* Jules Cambon MSS (19). Identified in Soutou, 'Marches', p. 359n.
28. De Fleuriau to Doulcet, 28 Oct. 1916, *MAE* Doulcet MSS (21).
29. Testimony of Ribot to *CAES*, 4 Dec. 1917, recorded in Senator d'Estournelles de Constant, 'Les Traités secrets concernant Constantinople et la rive gauche du Rhin', 15 June 1918, *MAE* A 'Paix' (165). Notes on sessions of the Council of Ministers in *APD* Clémentel MSS XIX.
30. Poincaré, *Service*, ix, pp. 3–4.
31. Undated memorandum of (?) 25 Aug. 1916, and 'Conditions de paix: le statut de l'Allemagne', Oct. 1916, *SHA* 14.N.35; summarized in Joffre, ii, pp. 371–80. Joffre attributes the memoranda to his headquarters staff (*GQG*), but they bear the heading of the Second Bureau of the General Staff (*EMA* 2ème Bureau).
32. 'Projct', 6 Nov. 1916, *MAE* A 'Paix' (60). Manuscript draft by Jules Cambon, 3 Nov. 1916, *MAE* Jules Cambon MSS (19).
33. Paul Cambon to Briand, 22 Nov. 1916, *MAE* A 'Paix' (59); and 13 Dec. 1916, *MAE* Paul Cambon MSS Vol. 7, dossier 23.
34. Paléologue to Briand, 21 Sept. 1916, *MAE* A 'Paix' (10); 31 Oct. and 6 Nov. 1916, *MAE* Paléologue MSS Vol. III.
35. De Fleuriau to Doulcet, 28 Oct. 1916, *MAE* Doulcet MSS (21). According to Mermeix, *Combat*, p. 191, Poincaré desired agreement with Russia before conversations took place with Britain; Poincaré, *Service*, ix, p. 4, suggests Briand's priorities were the reverse.
36. Senator d'Estournelles de Constant, 'Les Traités secrets . . .', 15 June 1918, *MAE* A 'Paix' (165). See also 'Question du Luxembourg', 23 Oct. 1918, *MAE* Tardieu MSS (95).
37. Text of the note in J. B. Scott (ed.), *Official Statements of War Aims and Peace Proposals, December 1916–November 1918* (Washington, 1921), pp. 2–3. For background, Fischer, pp. 296–7.
38. Text in Scott, pp. 12–15.
39. De Margerie, 'Note pour le Ministre', 15 Dec. 1916, *MAE* A 'Paix' (N) (33). The detailed terms the Germans had in mind were known with some accuracy in Briand's *Cabinet du Ministre*. Morand, p. 110.
40. Briand speech, 13 Dec. 1916, *JO* (*Chambre*), 1916, pp. 3638–9. Briand circular telegram, 15 Dec. 1916, *MAE* A 'Paix' (N) (33).
41. De Margerie, 'Paix', 20 Dec. 1916, *MAE* Jules Cambon MSS (19). Nouailhat, p. 792.
42. Ibid. pp. 777ff.
43. Wohl, pp. 80–3.
44. French draft reply to Central Powers, 22 Dec. 1916, FO/371/2805.
45. French draft reply to President Wilson, 23 Dec. 1916, ibid.
46. Briand circular telegram (drafted by Berthelot), 24 Dec. 1916, *MAE* A 'Paix' (N) (34); Briand circular telegram of 26 Dec. 1916, ibid. (35).

47. M.-R. Mouton, 'L'Idée d'organisation internationale en France et en Italie pendant la Première Guerre mondiale'. In Guillen (ed.), pp. 103–4.
48. Morand, p. 17.
49. Briand to de Sillac, 10 Aug. 1916, *MAE* Guerre (511).
50. Conversations of de Sillac with Jules Cambon, de Margerie, and Bourgeois, respectively 8 Feb., 1 Mar., and 14 Feb., 1917, *MAE* Bourgeois MSS (17).
51. Procès-verbaux of the Conference, 26–7 Dec. 1916, in *BDIC*, Dossiers Mantoux F.△.Rés. 156. (Translated) texts of Allied replies to Central Powers and Wilson in Scott, pp. 25–8 and 35–8.
52. Briand to Paul Cambon, 12 Jan. 1917, *MAE* Pichon MSS (4). Published in part in Suarez, iv, pp. 128–30. For the background, 'Question du Luxembourg', 23 Oct. 1918, *MAE* Tardieu MSS (95); A. Ribot, *Lettres à un ami: souvenirs de ma vie politique* (Paris, 1924), pp. 222–3.
53. J.-B. Duroselle, *La France et les Français, 1914–1920* (Paris, 1972), p. 157.
54. On this point I have preferred the testimony of Poincaré to Pichon, 16 Apr. 1918, *BIF* Pichon MSS (MS IV 4398) to that of 'Mermeix', *Combat*, p. 192.
55. Ribot, *Lettres*, p. 223. Also Ribot speech, 2 June 1917, *JO* (*Chambre*) *Comité secret* of 1 June 1917, p. 522.
56. Suarez, iv, p. 130.
57. C. Benoist, *Souvenirs* (3 vols., Paris, 1932–4), iii, pp. 324–9. For the work of the *Comité*, see *Travaux du Comité d'études*: Vol. I, *L'Alsace–Lorraine et la frontière du nord-est* (Paris, 1918) and Vol. II, *Questions européennes* (Paris, 1919), in *BN*, Département des cartes et plans, GeDD 4746 (162, I and II).
58. Mollard to Briand, 12 July 1916, *MAE* Guerre (600).
59. G. Trausch, 'Les Relations franco-belges à propos de la question luxembourgeoise, 1914–1922'; in R. Poidevin (ed.), *Les Relations franco-belges de 1830 à 1934* (Metz, 1975), p. 281.
60. Interview with Clémentel in *La Nation belge*, 14 Feb. 1924, *APD* Clémentel MSS XXX.
61. *Commission de direction* of the *Comité des forges*, 15 June 1916, *PAM* 06673. cf. survey of business attitudes by G.-H. Soutou, 'La Politique économique de la France à l'égard de la Belgique, 1914–1924', in Poidevin (ed.), p. 260.
62. Ibid., p. 259.
63. Paul Cambon to Briand, 27 Dec. 1916, *MAE* A 'Paix' (N) (35); Briand to Paul Cambon, 29 Dec. 1916, ibid.
64. For the General Staff, above, note 31; for Berthelot, Morand, p. 190.
65. Note by Berthelot, 13 Jan. 1917, *MAE* Tardieu MSS (95).
66. Paul Cambon to Briand, 18 Jan. 1917, *MAE* Paul Cambon MSS Vol. 7, dossier 23.
67. Jules Cambon, 'Note en réponse', 22 Jan. 1917, *SHA* 6.N.75.
68. Briand to Paul Cambon, 29 Jan. 1917, *MAE* Tardieu MSS (95).

69. Briand circular telegram, 14 Nov. 1916, *MAE* Guerre (718).
70. Briand and Asquith to Sturmer, 16 Nov. 1916, *MAE* Guerre (719).
71. Viviani to Paléologue, 6 Jan. 1917, *MAE* Guerre (720).
72. De Margerie, 'Répliques russes à l'action austro-allemande', 16 Nov. 1916, *MAE* Guerre (719).
73. De Margerie, 'Note', 24 Apr. 1918, *MAE* A 'Paix' (N) (104).
74. Doumergue in Senate secret session, 6 June 1917. Supplement to *JO* (*Sénat*), 1968, p. 767. cf. Ribot, *Lettres*, p. 220.
75. 'Mermeix', *Combat*, p. 191.
76. Doumergue to Briand, 13 Feb. 1917, *MAE* A 'Paix' (164).
77. D. Lloyd George, *The Truth about the Peace Treaties* (2 vols, London, 1938), i, p. 385.
78. Doumergue to Briand, 1 Feb. 1917, *MAE* A 'Paix' (164).
79. Doumergue to Briand, 4 Feb. 1917, ibid.
80. Paléologue to Briand, 8 Feb. 1917, ibid.
81. Berthelot to Paléologue, 9 Feb. 1917, ibid.
82. Ribot in Senate secret session, 6 June 1917. Supplement to *JO* (*Sénat*), 1968, p. 766.
83. Letters exchanged between Paléologue and Pokrovski, 14 Feb. 1917, *MAE* A 'Paix' (164). Printed in e.g. J. C. G. Röhl (ed.), *From Bismarck to Hitler: the Problem of Continuity in German History* (London, 1970), pp. 78–9.
84. Note presented by Isvolski, 13 Feb. 1917, *MAE* A 'Paix' (164).
85. Berthelot to de Margerie, 14 Feb. 1917, ibid.
86. Poincaré, *Service*, ix, p. 63.
87. Briand to Paléologue, 16 Feb. 1917, *MAE* A 'Paix' (164).
88. 'Note', 15 May 1917, ibid.
89. L. Loucheur, *Carnets secrets, 1908–1932* (J. de Launay ed., Brussels and Paris, 1962), p. 137.
90. Briand to Isvolski, 10 Mar. 1917, *MAE* A 'Paix' (164); Röhl (ed.), pp. 79–80.
91. Thomas to Ribot, 3 May 1917, *MAE* A 'Paix' (164).
92. Statement by Briand, 14 May 1917, ibid.
93. Ribot to Thomas, 20 May 1917, ibid.
94. Note by Jules Cambon on letter communicated by the Belgian Minister in Paris, 4 Oct. 1916, *MAE* A 'Paix' (N) (189).
95. F. Siebert, *Aristide Briand (1862–1932): ein Staatsmann zwischen Frankreich und Europa* (Stuttgart, 1973), p. 177.
96. Scherer and Grünewald (eds.), i, pp. 245–6 (conversation of 30 Dec. 1915).
97. Ibid, i, pp. 594–5, 603; ibid, ii, p. 17.
98. J. Laroche, *Au Quai d'Orsay avec Briand et Poincaré, 1913–1926* (Paris, 1957), p. 38. Suarez, iv, p. 115.
99. É. Beneš, *Souvenirs de guerre et de révolution (1914–1918): la lutte pour l'indépendance des peuples* (2 vols., Paris, 1928–9), i, pp. 261–8.
100. Beau (Ambassador at Berne) to Briand, 27 Dec. 1916; Morier (Military attaché at Berne) to Lyautey (Minister of War), 15 Jan. 1917, *MAE* Guerre (150).

101. Sixte, pp. 17, 28–33, 67–8.
102. Poincaré, *Service*, ix, p. 70. Suarez, iv, pp. 136–7, 145–6.
103. *CAEC:AC* Hearing of Jules Cambon, 7 May 1918. Sixte, pp. 67–8.
     Austria had ceded most of Silesia to Prussia by the Treaty of Dresden
     in 1745.
104. *CAEC:AC* Hearing of Ribot, 30 Apr. 1918.
105. Sixte, p. 86. Emperor Charles to Sixte, 24 Mar. 1917, ibid, p. 97.
     Clarification of the letter in Poincaré to Ribot, 31 Mar. 1917. A.
     Ribot (ed.), *Journal d'Alexandre Ribot et correspondances inédites,
     1914–1922* (Paris, 1936), pp. 62–3.

⟨ CHAPTER III

1. On the mutinies, G. Pedroncini, *Les Mutineries de 1917* (Paris, 1967).
   For the 'crisis of effectives', Painlevé to Vignol (French military
   attaché in the USA), 24 Mar. 1917, *SHA* 16.N.3012; also G. Pedroncini, *Pétain: Général en Chef, 1917–1918* (Paris, 1974), pp. 201–2.
2. Kriegel, p. 158. The French wheat harvest fell from 88 million quintals
   in 1914 to 40 million in 1917. Duroselle, *La France*, p. 217.
3. Monthly 'Bulletins confidentiels résumant la situation morale à l'intérieur', *EMA* 2ème Bureau I; in *SHA* 6.N.147. Also P. Renouvin, 'Die
   öffentliche Meinung in Frankreich während des Krieges, 1914–1918',
   Vierteljahrshefte für Zeitgeschichte (July 1970), pp. 264–5.
4. P. Renouvin, 'Les Relations franco-allemandes, 1914–1918', *Revue
   d'Allemagne* (July–Sept. 1972), pp. 501–3.
5. Loucheur, p. 37. Ribot, *Journal*, p. 95.
6. Ribot speech, 21 Mar. 1917, *JO* (*Chambre*), 1917, pp. 783–4. Poincaré, *Service*, ix, pp. 78–80. Ribot, *Journal*, p. 48.
7. Sixte, pp. 116, 112.
8. Ribot to Thomas, 20 May 1917, *MAE* A 'Paix' (164).
9. For French views of the February Revolution, I. Sinanoglou, 'France
   looks eastward: Policies and Perspectives in Russia, 1914–1918' (Columbia University Thesis, 1974), pp. 93–6.
10. Ribot to Paléologue, 24 Mar. 1917, *MAE* Guerre (648).
11. Paléologue to Ribot, 15 April 1917, *MAE* A 'Paix' (13).
12. Paléologue, iii, p. 306.
13. Ibid., p. 311.
14. Ibid, pp. 313, 317–18.
15. Ibid, pp. 315–16.
16. Ribot to Thomas, 30 Apr. 1917. Ribot, *Lettres*, pp. 234–5.
17. Isvolski to Ribot, 3 May 1917, *MAE* Guerre (651).
18. Poincaré, *Service*, ix, p. 144.
19. Ibid.
20. Ribot speech, 22 May 1917, *JO* (*Chambre*), 1917, pp. 1160–2.
21. Ribot to Doulcet, 24 May 1917, *AN* Thomas MSS 94 A.P. 178.
22. Poincaré, *Service*, ix, p. 132.
23. Kammerer to Paul Cambon, 27 Mar. 1917, *MAE* Guerre (648).

24. Prefects' reports in reply to a Ministry of Interior circular of 10 June 1917, *SHA* 16.N.1538.
25. L.-J. Malvy, *Mon Crime* (Paris, 1921), pp. 76–9.
26. Anglo-French conference in London, 28–9 May 1917. British minutes in CAB/28/2; French in *BDIC* Mantoux MSS F.△.Rés.159.
27. Paul Cambon to de Fleuriau, 2 June 1917, Cambon, *Correspondance*, iii, pp. 171–2. Bertie to Balfour, 2 June 1917, FO/371/2938.
28. Ribot, *Journal*, p. 138.
29. Ibid; and Poincaré, *Service*, ix, p. 149.
30. Ribot speech, 1 June 1917, *JO* (*Chambre*), 1917, pp. 1323–5. Ribot, *Journal*, p. 138. Ribot to Thomas, 2 June 1917, *MAE* Jules Cambon MSS (19).
31. Briand speeches, 2 and 4 June 1917, *JO* (*Chambre*), *Comité secret* of 1 June 1917, pp. 508–15, 531–4.
32. Ribot speeches, 2 and 4 June 1917, ibid., pp. 520–3, 535–7.
33. Printed in Bonnefous, p. 265.
34. Ribot speech, 6 June 1917. Appended to *JO* (*Sénat*), 1968, pp. 764–7.
35. Printed in Bonnefous, pp. 267–8.
36. Ribot, *Lettres*, p. 246.
37. Pingaud, iii, pp. 321–2.
38. Noulens (French Ambassador in Petrograd after 21 July) to Ribot, 26 July 1917, *MAE* A 'Paix' (60).
39. Declaration by Michaelis, 28 July 1917, in *MAE* A 'Paix' (164).
40. Ribot speech, 2 Aug. 1917, *JO* (*Chambre*), 1917, p. 2269.
41. Sevastopoulo to Jules Cambon, 5 July 1917; Ribot to Noulens, 13 Aug. 1917; Noulens to Ribot, 17 Aug. 1917, *MAE* A 'Paix' (164). Tereshchenko later abandoned his opposition to all the secret treaties being published, although this offer was not taken up. Tereshchenko to Sevastapoulo, 24 Sept. 1917, *FRUS* 1917, Supplement II, i, pp. 506–7.
42. Scherer and Grünewald (eds.), ii, pp. 29, 119. Cf. B. Szeps, *My Life and History* (trans. J. Summerfield, London, 1938), pp. 177–92.
43. *EMA* 3ème Bureau A, 'Note sur les conditions du futur traité de paix (frontières belges et françaises)', 12 July 1917, *SHA* 16.N.3265. Published in part in G. Pedroncini, *Les Négociations secrètes pendant la Grande Guerre* (Paris, 1959), pp. 110–11.
44. Herscher, 'Étude sur les conditions d'une paix française', 12 July 1917, *AN* Painlevé MSS 313 A.P.107. On Herscher, see testimony by Commandant Hellbronner in 'Dossier spécial: affaire Bolo', *SHA* 6.N.53.
45. Foch at Abbeville Conference, 8 June 1917, *SHA* 6.N.68.
46. 'Mermeix' (G. Terrail pseud.), *Les Négociations secrètes et les quatre Armistices* (Paris, 1921), pp. 178–9.
47. *EMA* 2ème Bureau I, 'Note', 20 July 1917, *L'Opinion* 10 July 1920, p. 34. (This section is based largely on the selection of documents published in the Parisian weekly, *L'Opinion*, in July 1920).
48. Foch directives, 24 July 1917, ibid., p. 35. Hearing of Painlevé, 30 Apr. 1918, *CAEC:AC*, pp. 55–8.

49. Hearing of Ribot, 30 Apr. 1918, ibid., pp. 37–8.
50. Painlevé to Armand, 4 Aug. 1917, *L'Opinion*, 10 July 1920, p. 37.
51. Armand to Painlevé, 12 Aug. 1917, ibid., 24 July 1920, p. 88.
52. Report by Colonel Goubet (undated), ibid., p. 87.
53. Report by Armand (undated); 'Remarques faites by I.V.', ibid., pp. 90–2.
54. Hearings of Robot and Painlevé, 30 Apr. 1918, *CAEC:AC*, pp. 38, 72.
55. Hearings of Ribot and Painlevé, ibid., pp. 38, 63.
56. Briand to Jusserand, 8 Mar. 1917, *MAE* Jusserand MSS (31).
57. Morand, p. 195.
58. Henri Cambon to Paul Cambon, 10 Feb. 1917. Letter in the possession of M. Louis Cambon.
59. Bertie, ii, p. 119 (8 Apr. 1917).
60. A. Kaspi, *Le Temps des Américains: le concours américain à la France en 1917–1918* (Paris, 1976), pp. 16–24, 37–45. Pedroncini, *Pétain*, pp. 147–9.
61. Decree of 15 Apr. 1917, *SHA* 6.N.141.
62. Viviani to Ribot, received 3 May 1917, *MAE* Guerre (511).
63. Ribot speech, 22 May 1917, *JO* (*Chambre*), 1917, p. 1162. Also 2 June 1917, *JO* (*Chambre*), *Comité secret* of 1 June 1917, p. 522.
64. For example, Jules Cambon. Sixte, p. 110. De Margerie, however, may have been more favourable to encouraging revolution in Germany. De Margerie, 'Note: ouvertures de paix', 19 Dec. 1916, *MAE* A 'Paix' (N) (33).
65. Sharp to Ribot, 6 Aug. 1917, *MAE* Jules Cambon MSS (19).
66. Ribot to Jusserand, 2 July 1917, *MAE* Jusserand MSS (31 bis).
67. Jusserand to Ribot, 7 Aug. 1917, ibid. (47).
68. Ribot to Jusserand, 18 July 1917; Jusserand to Ribot, 4 Aug. 1917, *MAE* Jules Cambon MSS (19).
69. Ribot speech, 21 Mar. 1917, *JO* (*Chambre*), 1917, p. 790. However, Wilson's own thinking at the time was similar.
70. Thomas had suggested that approaching Wilson would help in this. Poincaré, *Service*, ix, p. 203.
71. Decree of 22 July 1917, *MAE* Jules Cambon MSS (19).
72. Poincaré, *Service*, ix, p. 177.
73. Balfour to Bertie, 5 July 1917, FO/371/2937.
74. Blumenthal to Jules Cambon, 3 Aug. 1917, *MAE* Jules Cambon MSS (21). A. Kaspi, 'La France et le concours américain, février 1917–novembre 1918' (Thesis, Paris, 1974), pp. 450–7.
75. Jusserand to Ribot, 12 July 1917, *MAE* Jusserand MSS (47).
76. Poincaré, *Service*, ix, p. 208.
77. Jules Cambon, 'Note en réponse', 22 Jan. 1917, *SHA* 6.N.75. For Paul Cambon, Balfour to Bertie, 2 July 1917, FO/371/2937.
78. Morand, p. 307.
79. War Cabinet, 3 Apr. and 20 Aug. 1917, CAB/23/2 and CAB/23/3.
80. Balfour to Bertie, 2 July 1917, FO/371/2937. Paul Cambon to Ribot, 10 July 1917, *MAE* Pichon MSS (4).
81. Text of the note, dated 1 Aug. 1917 and forwarded to the Allies on

16 Aug., in Scott, pp. 129–31.

82. Henri to Paul Cambon, 17 July 1917. Letter in possession of M. Louis Cambon.
83. Beau to Ribot, 30 July 1917, *MAE* A 'Paix' (13). French Embassy in London to the Foreign Office, 2 Aug. 1917, FO/371/3077.
84. Renouvin, 'Meinung', p. 261.
85. Poincaré, *Service*, ix, p. 251. Paul Cambon to Foreign Office, 17 Aug. 1917, FO/371/3083. Ribot to Jusserand, 17 Aug. 1917, *MAE* Jusserand MSS (32).
86. Ribot to Jusserand, 30 Sept. 1917, ibid.
87. Docket note by 'C.H.S.' on conversation with de Fleuriau, 22 Aug. 1917, FO/371/3083.
88. Barrère to Ribot, undated. Ribot, *Journal*, p. 186.
89. Ribot to de Fleuriau, 25 Aug. 1917. Ibid., p. 188. Balfour to de Salis, 26 Aug. 1917, FO/371/3083.
90. Ribot to Jusserand, 17 Aug. 1917, *MAE* Jusserand MSS (32).
91. Wilson to the Pope, 17 Aug. 1917. Scott, pp. 133–5.
92. Undated communiqué, *MAE* A 'Paix' (17).
93. Note from British Embassy in Paris, 1 Sept. 1917; Ribot to British Embassy, 5 Sept. 1917, both ibid.
94. Jusserand to Ribot, 11 Sept. 1917, *MAE* Jusserand MSS (14).
95. Andrew and Kanya-Forstner, *Expansion*, Chapter V.
96. Clémentel, 'Les relations économiques franco-belges', 15 Sept. 1918, *APD* Clémentel MSS XXX.
97. Circular dispatch by Ribot, 9 June 1917, *MAE* Tardieu MSS (95); Hymans, i, pp. 190–3.
98. Hymans to Balfour, 'Declarations of Statesmen in Favour of the Union of Luxemburg to Belgium', 14 Apr. 1919, FO/608/2.
99. Ribot to Jusserand, 30 Sept. 1917, *MAE* Jusserand MSS (32)
100. Jusserand to Ribot, 3, 11, and 21 Oct. 1917, ibid. (48).
101. Bertie to Lloyd George, 24 Sept. 1917, FO/800/169.
102. Untitled, undated, typescript by Painlevé, *AN* Painlevé MSS 313 A.P. 107.
103. Lloyd George, 11 Oct. 1917. Scott, p. 161. Poincaré, *Service*, ix, p. 315.
104. Note by (?) Joffre, 23 May 1916. Pedroncini, *Pétain*, p. 112n. The following section is based on Pedroncini's work.
105. *GQG* 3ème Bureau, 'Étude sur la directive du 15 août', 17 Sept. 1917, *SHA* 16.N.1712. Pedroncini, *Pétain*, pp. 133–4.
106. *GQG* 3ème Bureau, 'Directive en vue des opérations en Haute Alsace', 27 Nov. 1917, *SHA* 16.N.1690. Pedroncini, *Pétain*, p. 123.
107. Ibid.
108. Jusserand to Ribot, 30 Aug. 1917, *MAE* Jusserand MSS (14).
109. Statement by Clémentel at the Foreign Office, 16 Aug. 1917; Clémentel to Stanley, 23 Aug. 1917, *AN* F^{12} 7819. (Dossier of 'Documents sur le contrôle interallié des matières premières').
110. Text in Bertie to Balfour, 6 Sept. 1917, FO/371/2934. cf. Poincaré, *Service*, ix, p. 269.

111. Note by Clémentel's *Cabinet du Ministre*, 5 Oct. 1917, *AN* F^{12} 7819.
112. Clémentel to Wilson, 6 Oct. 1917, ibid.
113. Memorandum by Stanley, 16 Oct. 1917, ibid.
114. Ribot to Velten, 23 March 1917, *MAE* Guerre (722).
115. Komarnicki, pp. 152–64.
116. Ribot to Paléologue, 1 Apr. 1917; Franco-British-Italian declaration, 14 Apr. 1917, *MAE* Guerre (722).
117. Ribot in *CAES*, 11 July 1917, *CAES*, 1917, p. 976.
118. Komarnicki, pp. 168–9. Ribot to Jusserand, 12 July 1917, *MAE* Jusserand MSS (31 bis).
119. Komarnicki, pp. 177–8. Note by Degrand, 16 Oct. 1917, *MAE* Guerre (727).
120. Ribot to Dmowski and Piltz, 20 Sept. 1917, MAE Tardieu MSS (72).
121. Ribot to Barrère and Jusserand, 20 Oct. 1917, *MAE* Guerre (727).
122. De Margerie to de Fleuriau, 28 Sept. 1917, ibid. (726).
123. Barthou to Jusserand, 30 Oct. 1917, *MAE* Jusserand MSS (33).
124. Painlevé to Barthou, 5 Nov. 1917, *MAE* Guerre (728).
125. Reports by EMA 2ème Bureau I, 7 and 14 Nov. 1917, ibid.
126. Painlevé to Barthou, 13 Nov. 1917, ibid.
127. *EMA* 2ème Bureau I, 'Bulletin confidentiel résumant la situation morale à l'intérieur', 15 Dec. 1917, *SHA* 6.N.147.
128. Thomas, 'Relation des événements qui se sont succédés du 2 au 12 septembre 1917', 12 Sept. 1917. *AN* Thomas MSS 94 A.P. 356.
129. Poincaré, *Service*, ix, pp. 291, 365.
130. Painlevé and Ribot speeches, 18 and 19 Sept. 1917, *JO* (*Chambre*), 1917, pp. 2322, 2359.
131. Painlevé speech, 18 Sept. 1917, ibid., p. 2322.
132. Poincaré, *Service*, ix, pp. 291, 305.
133. O. Freiherr von der Lancken Wakenitz, *Meine dreißig Dienstjahre, 1888–1918* (Berlin, 1931), p. 258.
134. Scherer and Grünewald (eds.), ii, p. 161.
135. Briand in *CAES*, 14 Nov. 1917, *CAES*, 1917, p. 1108. Suarez, iv, pp. 239–40.
136. Poincaré, *Service*, ix, p. 167. Ribot in *CAES*, 14 Nov. 1917, *CAES*, 1917, pp. 1167–8.
137. Suarez, iv, pp. 241–2. Scherer and Grünewald (eds.), ii, pp. 257–8.
138. Suarez, iv, pp. 258–61.
140. Painlevé to Poincaré, 18 Sept. 1917, Poincaré, *Service*, ix, pp. 289–90.
141. Suarez, iv, p. 268. Poincaré, *Service*, ix, pp. 284–6 gives the opposite impression. Suarez was a tendentious writer, but in his account of the affair he cites many of Briand's contemporary jottings; Poincaré, however, edited and retouched his notes while composing his memoirs fifteen years later. A comparison of his 'Notes journalières' in *BN Cabinet des manuscrits* with his memoirs for 1914–15 (the notes for 1916–18 have not survived) shows that Poincaré was capable of suppressing and distorting evidence.
142. Suarez, iv, pp. 270, 271.

143. Scherer and Grünewald (eds.), ii, pp. 348, 387–90, 442. The Germans attached much more importance to a simultaneous feeler to the British.

144. Briand to Ribot, 20 Sept., 1917, Suarez, iv, pp. 272–4.

145. Ribot to Paul Cambon and Barrère, 20 Sept. 1917, quoted by Ribot in Chamber, 16 Oct. 1917, *JO* (*Chambre*), *Comité secret* of 16 Oct. 1917, pp. 547–8.

146. Paul Cambon and Barrère to Ribot, 21 Sept. 1917. Ribot, *Journal*, pp. 212–14. Jusserand to Ribot, 26 Sept. 1917, *MAE* Jusserand MSS (48).

147. D. Lloyd George, *War Memoirs* (6 vols, London, 1933–6), iv, pp. 2100–1.

148. Poincaré, *Service*, ix, p. 299. Ribot, *Journal*, pp. 216–17.

149. D. Lloyd George, *War Memoirs*, iv, pp. 2100–1.

150. Suarez, iv, p. 289. Scherer and Grünewald (eds.), iii, pp. 293ff.

151. Scott, p. 159.

152. Ribot speech, 12 Oct. 1917, *JO* (*Chambre*) 1917, pp. 2695–7.

153. *JO* (*Chambre*), *Comité secret* of 16 Oct. 1917, passim.

154. Poincaré, *Service*, ix, pp. 320, 329.

155. Barthou speech, 25 Oct. 1917, *JO* (*Chambre*), 1917, pp. 2782, 2781. Some content was given to these ideas in an anonymous Quai d'Orsay 'Note préliminaire sur la réorganisation de l'Allemagne', 27 Oct. 1917, *BDIC* Dossiers Klotz, Fol. 223 Rés. Dossier 18. In contrast to the Cambon letter, this did not envisage separating the left bank of the Rhine from Germany. Instead, Germany should be forbidden to recruit troops on or fortify the left bank, whose railways would be under Allied control. Germany would be divided into three economic zones, with the left bank and the Austrian Germans receiving the most generous tariff concessions and raw-material deliveries from the Allies, and Prussia the least generous. The memorandum also hoped for a post-war defensive alliance between France and Britain and an economic association which would include the United States. Perhaps for this reason it sought means of weakening Germany which would not overtly violate national self-determination. Instead, it shared in the tendency of the time to overestimate the influence given to the Allies by their economic leverage.

156. Note by Jules Cambon, 12 Mar. 1917, MAE Guerre (575); Ribot to Barrère, 8 Apr. 1917, ibid. (576); Barrère to Ribot, 9 Apr. 1917, ibid.; note by (?) Laroche, 29 June 1917, ibid. (577).

157. For example, *EMA* 2ème Bureau A, 'Mémorandum des questions à traiter à la Conférence des États-majors Alliés', 4 July 1917, *SHA* 6.N.68; and *EMA* 2ème Bureau A, 'Note sur l'attitude qu'il convient à prendre à l'égard de la Russie', 11 Oct. 1917, *SHA* 6.N.232. Both of these considered sympathetically the idea of a separate peace concluded at Russia's expense. When questioned by Ribot on 15 Sept. 1917, Briand was silent about Russia. Ribot in *CAES*, 14 Nov. 1917, *CAES*, 1917, p. 1169.

CHAPTER IV

1. Clemenceau in *CAEC*, 19 Dec. 1917, *AN* C 7490. Meeting of the *Comité de guerre*, 12 Dec. 1917, *SHA* 3.N.2.
2. Paul Cambon in conversation recorded by Lord Robert Cecil, 28 Oct. 1918, FO/371/3445.
3. Clemenceau speech, 20 Nov. 1917, *JO* (*Chambre*), 1917, p. 2973.
4. G. Wormser, *La République de Clemenceau* (Paris, 1961), p. 341.
5. Diary of Derby (British Ambassador from April 1918), 16 Aug. 1918, BL Balfour MSS Add. 49743. J. Mordacq, *Le Ministère Clemenceau; journal d'un témoin* (4 vols., Paris, 1930–1), iii, p. 118n.
6. Bertie to Balfour, 6 Dec. 1917, FO/800/201. Mordacq, iii, p. 76.
7. B. Auffray, *Pierre de Margerie (1861–1942) et la vie diplomatique de son temps* (Paris, 1976), p. 347. Laroche, pp. 51–2.
8. This impression is given by the Ministry of Finance archives and by L.-L. Klotz, *De la guerre à la paix: souvenirs et documents* (Paris, 1924).
9. Clemenceau speech, 8 Mar. 1918, *JO* (*Chambre*), 1918, p. 856.
10. In general, see Renouvin, 'Meinung', pp. 266–9; Kriegel, pp. 193–233; D. R. Watson, *Georges Clemenceau: a Political Biography* (London, 1974), pp. 283–90.
11. Pichon to Noulens, 23 Nov. 1917, *MAE* A 'Paix' (60).
12. Seymour, iii, p. 292.
13. Clemenceau speech, 20 Nov. 1917, *JO* (*Chambre*), 1917, p. 2972.
14. Dmowski to Pichon, 13 Nov. 1917; de Margerie, 'La Question de la Pologne', 26 Nov. 1917, *MAE* Guerre (728).
15. Pichon in *CAES*, 10 Dec. 1917, *CAES*, 1917, p. 1242.
16. Ibid., p. 1243. Minutes of conversations at the Quai d'Orsay, 1 and 3 Dec. 1917, FO/371/3438.
17. Seymour, iii, pp. 297–8, 290.
18. Pichon in *CAES*, 7 Dec. 1917, pp. 17–18, *AN* C 7490
19. Scott, pp. 193–202, esp. pp. 195, 197. Wilson suggested that if the autocracy survived 'it might be impossible . . . to admit Germany to the free economic intercourse which must inevitably spring out of the other partnerships of a real peace'.
20. Clemenceau to House, 6 Dec. 1917, *AN* F¹² 7819.
21. The most important part of this machinery was the Allied Maritime Transport Council, whose permanent executive committee apportioned shipping space. Import programmes for each class of commodity were prepared by 'programme committees' or 'executives', and American credits were extended through the Inter-Allied Council on War Purchases and Finance.
22. Kaspi, 'Concours', ii, p. 548n.
23. Lord Robert Cecil to Lloyd George, 27 Dec. 1917, LG Papers F/6/5/11.
24. Mordacq, i, pp. 105ff.
25. Pichon speech, 27 Dec. 1917, *JO* (*Chambre*), 1917, pp. 3626–31.
26. Sinanoglou, p. 260.

27. *EMA* 2ème Bureau I, 'Résumé de deux rapports sur "La Paix allemande" et "Les Grèves allemandes"', 10 Mar. 1918, *SHA* 6.N.115. Clemenceau in *CAEC*, 19 Dec. 1917, *AN* C 7490.

28. Pichon to Paul Cambon, Jusserand, and Barrère, 2 Jan. 1918; Pichon to Jusserand, 7 Jan. 1918, *MAE* A 'Paix' (82).

29. Clemenceau to Lloyd George, 3 Jan. 1918, LG Papers F/50/2/2. Poincaré, *Service*, x, pp. 2–3.

30. Paul Cambon to (?) de Fleuriau, 5 Jan. 1918. Cambon, *Correspondance*, iii, p. 205.

30. Rothwell, p. 149. The final wording ran: 'We mean to stand by the French Democracy to the death in the demand they make for the reconsideration of the great wrong of 1871, when, without any regard to the wishes of the population, two French provinces were torn from the side of France and incorporated in the German Empire'. Scott, p. 229.

32. Clemenceau to Lloyd George, 6 Jan. 1918. Ibid., p. 233.

33. Seymour, iii, p. 338. According to the Eighth Point, 'All French territory should be freed and the invaded portions restored, and the wrong done to France by Prussia in 1871 in the matter of Alsace–Lorraine . . . should be righted in order that peace may once more be made secure in the interest of all'. Scott, p. 238.

34. *EMA* 2ème Bureau I, 'L'État de l'opinion en France d'après le contrôle de la correspondance du 15 janvier au 15 février 1918', *SHA* 6.N.147.

35. Mordacq, i, pp. 123–4.

36. Pichon speech, 11 Jan. 1918, *JO* (*Chambre*), 1918, pp. 39–44.

37. Scott, p. 244.

38. Pichon to Jusserand, 11 Jan. 1918, *MAE* Jusserand MSS (34). Jusserand to Pichon, 18 Jan. 1918, ibid. (17). Tardieu to Clemenceau and Pichon, 24 Jan. 1918, *MAE* Guerre (165).

39. The Supreme War Council was created by the Rapallo Conference in November 1917. It comprised: (i) monthly meetings of the civilian leaders of Britain, France, and Italy, with an American observer; (ii) a permanent committee of military and naval representatives at Versailles.

40. Draft by Pichon, 27 Jan. 1918; revision by Clemenceau, 28 Jan. 1918, *MAE* Pichon MSS (4).

41. Seymour, iii, pp. 370–1. Pichon in *CAEC*, 8 Feb. 1918, *AN* C 7490.

42. Kaspi, 'Concours', ii, p. 810n.

43. Jusserand to Pichon, 20 Feb. 1918, *SHA* 6.N.138. The Third Principle was that 'every territorial settlement involved in this war must be made in the interest and for the benefit of the population concerned, and not as a part of any mere adjustment or compromise of claims amongst rival States'. Scott, pp. 269–70.

44. Wilson to Lansing, 16 Feb. 1918. *FRUS. The Lansing Papers* (2 vols, Washington, 1940), ii, p. 95.

45. Poincaré, *Service*, x, pp. 57–8; Pichon to Jusserand, received 23 Feb. and 5 Mar. 1918, *MAE* Jusserand MSS (35); Jusserand to Pichon, 4 Mar. 1918, *SHA* 6.N.138.

252   References to pages 104–108

46. Clemenceau speech, 8 Mar. 1918, *JO* (*Chambre*), 1918, pp. 855–8.
47. Scott, p. 312.
48. Balfour speech, 19 Dec. 1917. 100 H.C. DEB.5s. column 2017. Balfour speech, 16 May 1918. 106 H.C. DEB.5s. column 579.
49. M. J. Carley, 'The Origins of French Intervention in the Russian Civil War, January–May 1918: a Reappraisal', *Journal of Modern History*, 48, 3 (1976), pp. 413–39.
50. For Lloyd George, Rothwell, pp. 190–1, 195–6. For the General Staff, *EMA* 3ème Bureau A, 'Mémorandum pour la conférence interalliée du 29 novembre 1917', undated, *SHA* 6.N.69. For the similar views of Paléologue, P.-M. de la Gorce, *La République et son armée* (Paris, 1963), p. 190.
51. Jusserand to Pichon, 25 July 1918, *SHA* 6.N.53; Pichon to Jusserand, 27 July 1918, *MAE* A 'Paix' (63).
52. Wormser, *Clemenceau*, p. 261. Szeps, p. 190.
53. *L'Opinion*, 31 July 1920, p. 116. The Government also grudgingly approved the Smuts–Mensdorff meeting between British and Austrian representatives. Seymour, iii, pp. 282–3. Pichon to Paul Cambon and Barrère, 8 Dec. 1917, *MAE* Guerre (729).
54. Armand–Revertera conversations, 1 and 23 Feb. 1918, *L'Opinion*, 31 July 1920, pp. 116–120.
55. Seymour, iii, pp. 383–4, 393–5. Pedroncini, *Négociations*, p. 85. Pichon to Jusserand, 27 Feb. 1918, *MAE* Jusserand MSS (35).
56. Scott, pp. 298–322.
57. Clemenceau in *CAES*, 19 Apr. 1918, *CAES*, 1918, pp. 1504, 1506/10. Also hearings of Clemenceau and Pichon, 3 and 7 May 1918, by *CAEC:AC*, pp. 57–8 and 48 respectively.
58. K. Hovi, *Cordon sanitaire or barrière de l'est? The Emergence of the New French Eastern European Alliance Policy, 1917–1919* (Turku, 1975), p. 75.
59. Pichon to Paul Cambon, Jusserand, and Barrère, 7 Mar. 1918, *MAE* Guerre (732).
60. Proposals by Dmowski, Degrand, and de Margerie, 5 Mar. 1918, ibid.
61. Pichon to Barrère, 19 Mar. 1918, ibid.
62. Background discussion in D. Perman, *The Shaping of the Czechoslovak State: Diplomatic History of the Boundaries of Czechoslovakia, 1914–1920* (Leiden, 1962), Ch. II.
63. Beneš, ii, pp. 127, 216, 220. Anglo-French Conference at 10 Downing Street, 28 May 1918, *CAB*/28/3.
64. Lansing to Page, 29 May 1918. *FRUS, 1918*. Supplement I, i, p. 809.
65. Declaration at Versailles, 3 June 1918, *SHA* 16.N.3267.
66. Pichon to Beneš, 29 June 1918. Beneš, ii, pp. 231–2.
67. Pichon to Barrère, 6 June 1918, *MAE* Europe 1918–29 Pologne (63).
68. Pichon to Barrère, 10 June 1918, *MAE* Guerre (732).
69. Clémentel speech, 7 Feb. 1918, *JO* (*Sénat*), 1918, pp. 70–3. After this debate the Senate passed a resolution favouring the 'centralization' of the Allies' resources of raw materials. Ibid., p. 73.
70. The argument was presented to Clemenceau by Commandant Fran-

çois-Marsal, of his *Cabinet du Ministre*, in a note entitled 'Deux moyens de pression sur l'Allemagne', 29 Jan. 1918, *SHA* 4.N.71. See François-Marsal to General Bélin, 16 Apr. 1918, ibid.

71. De Fleuriau to Pichon, 6 Mar. 1918, *MAE* Guerre (1218).
72. Clémentel to Pichon, 30 Mar. 1918, ibid. (1222).
73. Tardieu to Clémentel, 25 and 27 Jan. 1918, *AN* F^{12} 8044.
74. Pichon and Clémentel to Tardieu, 16 Apr. 1918, *AN* F^{12} 7819.
75. Tardieu to Clémentel and Pichon, 13 May 1918, *MAE* Guerre (1219); Pichon and Clémentel to Tardieu, 19 May 1918, *AN* F^{12} 7819.
76. Balfour to Paul Cambon, 16 May 1918, *MAE* Guerre (1219); Derby to Pichon, 28 May 1918, *AN* F^{12} 7819.
77. Proceedings and conclusions of the Commission in *AN* F^{12} 8106.
78. Paul Cambon to Balfour, 1 July 1918, FO/371/3439.
79. Poincaré, *Service*, x, p. 245.
80. Seymour, iv, p. 38.
81. Mordacq, iii, p. 8.
82. American oil deliveries to France in 1918 were ten times the 1913 level; cereal deliveries thirty times the 1913 level. The effectives of the American Expeditionary Force rose from 284,000 on 30 Mar. to 1,872,000 on 2 Nov. 1918. Kaspi, *Temps*, pp. 238, 267.
83. Watson, p. 308.
84. Poincaré, *Service*, x, p. 335.
85. Clemenceau speech, 5 Sept. 1918, *JO* (*Chambre*), 1918, p. 2316.
86. Derby to Balfour, 18 Sept. 1918, FO/371/3212.
87. Mordacq, ii, p. 257.
88. Pichon to Defrance (Le Havre), 18 Sept. 1918, *MAE* A 'Paix' (N) (190). Pichon in *CAES*, 23 Sept. 1918, pp. 1597–1601.
89. Clémentel, 'Les Relations économiques franco-belges', 15 Sept. 1918, *APD* Clémentel MSS XXX.
90. Pichon to Jusserand, 30 Sept. 1918, *MAE* Jusserand MSS (38).
91. Conversations in Paris, 23–5 Oct. 1918, Hymans, i, pp. 199–210.
92. Perman, p. 47n. Pichon to Jusserand, 2 Oct. 1918, *MAE* Jusserand MSS (39).
93. Dutasta (Berne) to Pichon, 26 Aug. 1918, *MAE* Europe 1918–29 Pologne (65). This reported a German offer of the 1772 frontier for Poland against Russia.
94. Klobukowski, 'La Question de la Pologne', 23 Aug. 1918, ibid. (64).
95. Degrand, 'Note pour le Ministre', 4 Sept. 1918, ibid. (65).
96. Pichon in *CAEC*, 14 July 1918, *AN* C 7491.
97. Clemenceau to Zamoyski, 5 Sept. 1918, *MAE* Europe 1918–29 Pologne (65).
98. Clémentel to Clemenceau, 5 Sept. 1918; Pichon to Clémentel, c. 18 Sept. 1918, *MAE* Y Internationale (211).
99. Hauser, 'Esquisse d'une politique économique de l'Europe occidentale', (?) July 1918, *AN* F^{12} 8106.
100. Clémentel to Clemenceau, 19 Sept. 1918, *AN* F^{12} 8104. Printed in Clémentel pp. 337–48. Preliminary Hauser memorandum, 'Principales questions d'ordre économique . . .', undated, *AN* F^{12} 8106.

101. 'Réunion chez M. le Président du Conseil . . .', *AN* F^{12} 8104.
102. Seymour, iv, pp. 65–6.
103. Scott, pp. 399–405.
104. Ibid, pp. 386–9.
105. Clemenceau speech, 17 Sep. 1918, *JO* (*Sénat*), 1918, p. 604. This became the official French reply: Pichon to Swiss Minister in Paris, 19 Sept. 1918, *MAE* A 'Paix' (N) (39).
106. Jusserand to Pichon, 18 Sept. 1918, *SHA* 6.N.138.

CHAPTER V

1. P. Renouvin, *L'Armistice de Rethondes: 11 novembre 1918* (Paris, 1968), pp. 144–5.
2. Clemenceau to Pichon, 23 Oct. 1918, *MAE* Europe 1918–29 Russie (208).
3. Renouvin, 'Meinung', pp. 269–71.
4. M. Berger and P. Allard, *Les Secrets de la censure pendant la Guerre* (Paris, 1932), pp. 369–72.
5. Renouvin, *L'Armistice*, pp. 123–4, 130–1, 134–5.
6. Derby to Balfour, 11, 13, and 17 Oct. 1918, BL Balfour MSS Add.49744. Also, *EMA* 2ème Bureau A, 'L' Etat de l'opinion en France d'après le contrôle de la correspondance du 15 octobre au 15 novembre 1918', *SHA* 6.N.147.
7. A. Bréal, *Phillipe Berthelot* (Paris, 1937), p. 185.
8. Mordacq, iii, p. 191.
9. Clemenceau, 6 Oct. 1918. I have used the minutes taken by Paul Mantoux, in *BDIC* Mantoux MSS F.△.Rés. 163/2.
10. Clemenceau, 7 Oct. 1918, ibid., 163/3. For the first version of the Prime Ministers' text; 'Premières bases d'un project d'armistice', 6 Oct. 1918, *SHA* 6.N.69. Printed in *FRUS, Lansing Papers*, ii, p. 290.
11. Barrère to Pichon, 6 Oct. 1918, *MAE* A 'Paix' (45); Paul Cambon to Pichon, 6 Oct. 1918, *MAE* Paul Cambon MSS Vol. 7, dossier 23; Jusserand to Pichon, 8 Oct. 1918, *SHA* 6.N.138.
12. Poincaré to Clemenceau, 8 Oct. 1918. Printed in G. Wormser, *Le Septennat de Poincaré* (Paris, 1977), pp. 146–8. Poincaré, *Service*, x, p. 379.
13. Foch, 'Note sur les conditions d'un armistice avec l'Allemagne'. Printed in F. Foch, *Mémoires pour servir à l'histoire de la Guerre* (2 vols., Paris, 1931), ii, pp. 270–2.
14. 'Avis collectif', 8 Oct. 1918. Printed in *FRUS, Lansing Papers*, ii, pp. 291–2.
15. Clemenceau, 8 Oct. 1918, and Foch, 9 Oct. 1918, *BDIC* Mantoux MSS F.△.Rés. 165/5–6.
16. De Billy to Tardieu, 9 Oct. 1918, *MAE* Série A 'Paix' (45). See discussion in A. Walworth, *America's Moment: 1918. American Diplomacy at the end of World War I* (New York, 1977), p. 19. Renouvin, *L'Armistice*, p. 121.

17. Clemenceau, 9 Oct. 1918, *BDIC* Mantoux MSS F. △.Rés. 163/6. Text of Wilson's reply in Scott, pp. 418–19.
18. Pichon to Jusserand, 11 Oct. 1918, *MAE* A 'Paix' (45).
19. Jusserand to Pichon, 9 Oct. 1918, ibid.
20. Jusserand to Pichon, 10 Oct. 1918, ibid.
21. Pichon to Paul Cambon, 16 Oct. 1918, ibid. Text of Wilson's note of 14 Oct. in Scott, pp. 421–3.
22. Pichon speech, 15 Oct. 1918, *JO* (*Sénat*), 1918, p. 707.
23. Pichon to Paul Cambon, 14 Oct. 1918, *MAE* A 'Paix' (45).
24. Andrew and Kanya-Forstner, *Expansion*, Chapter VI.
25. Hymans, i, p. 201.
26. Pedroncini, *Pétain*, pp. 422–9.
27. Foch to Clemenceau, 16 Oct. 1918. Printed in Foch, ii, pp. 276–8.
28. Pichon to Clemenceau, 21 Oct. 1918; Clemenceau to Foch, 23 Oct. 1918. Printed in Commandant Lhopital, *Foch, l'Armistice et la Paix* (Paris, 1938), pp. 33–9.
29. Military attaché at Copenhagen to Clemenceau, 7 Oct. 1918, *MAE* A 'Paix' (45). German Foreign Ministry to German Embassy in Madrid, 26 Oct. 1918, *SHA* 6.N.70.
30. Dutasta to Pichon, 15 Oct. 1918, ibid.
31. Dutasta to Pichon, 14 Oct. 1918, ibid. Carton 6.N.70 contains the intelligence reports forwarded to Clemenceau during this period.
32. Foch to Clemenceau, 18 Oct. 1918, ibid. Derby to Balfour, 18 Oct. 1918, BL Balfour MSS Add. 49744.
33. Text of Wilson's note in Scott, pp. 428–9. For French reactions, see Perman, pp. 57–8; Derby to Balfour, 20 Oct. 1918, BL Balfour MSS Add. 49744; Note by Robert de Caix, 25 Oct. 1918, *MAE* A 'Paix' (N) (110).
34. Pichon to Jusserand, 24 Oct. 1918, *MAE* Jusserand MSS (40).
35. Derby to Balfour, 24 Oct. 1918, FO/371/3445.
36. Scott, pp. 434–6.
37. Pichon to Jusserand, Paul Cambon, and Barrère, 24 Oct. 1918, *MAE* A 'Paix' (46).
38. R. Blake (ed.), *The Private Papers of Douglas Haig, 1914–1918* (London, 1952), p. 336. Foch, ii, pp. 280–2.
39. Foch to Clemenceau, 26 Oct. 1918. Printed in Lhopital, pp. 60–6. See Mordacq, ii, p. 295.
40. Prussia had gained Schleswig–Holstein from Denmark in 1864–6. Northern Schleswig was still Danish-speaking in 1918.
41. De Caix, 'Sur l'armistice en ce qui concerne l'Allemagne', and 'Note sur les demandes d'armistice', *c.* 20 Oct. 1918, *MAE* A 'Paix' (N) (279).
42. L. Zimmermann, *Frankreichs Ruhrpolitik von Versailles bis zum Dawesplan* (New edn., Göttingen, 1971), pp. 15–17.
43. Pichon, 'Notes pour les clauses militaires de l'armistice allemand', undated, *SHA* 6.N.73.
44. These proposals, entitled 'Conditions de l'Armistice avec l'Alle-

magne', appear as Annexe 'B' to the procès-verbal of the Paris Conference of 29 Oct.–4 Nov. 1918, *SHA* 6.N.64.

45. Report by Franklin-Bouillon to *CAEC*, 31 Oct. 1918, *AN* C 7491.
46. Mordacq, ii, pp. 295–7.
47. The French Government also objected to the third of the Fourteen Points, concerning 'the removal . . . of all economic barriers, and . . . the establishment of an equality of trade conditions . . .', in so far as it could understand what this meant. Pichon to Paul Cambon, 20 Oct. 1918, *MAE* Y Internationale (212).
48. The British feared that to accept the principle of 'absolute freedom of navigation upon the seas, . . . alike in peace and in war' would compromise their right of blockade.
49. Conversation at the Quai d'Orsay, 29 Oct. 1918, *BDIC* Mantoux MSS F.△.Rés. 164/1.
50. Mordacq, ii, p. 297. Memorandum by Pichon, 30 Oct. 1918, *MAE* Pichon MSS (6).
51. *FRUS, 1918*, Supplement I, i, p. 425.
52. Ibid., pp. 425–6.
53. In the 'Lansing Note' of 5 Nov. 1918. Scott, pp. 456–7.
54. Seymour, iv, p. 122.
55. *FRUS, 1918*, Supplement I, i, p. 426. Seymour, iv, p. 123.
56. Mordacq, ii, pp. 297–8.
57. Perman, pp. 64, 65n. I.Floto, *Colonel House in Paris: a Study of American Diplomacy at the Paris Peace Conference*, 1919 (Aarhus, 1973) pp. 53–5.
58. Article XII of the Armistice (which is printed in Renouvin, *L'Armistice*, pp. 415–22). Discussion of this article on 1 and 2 Nov. 1918 is printed in J. de Launay, *Secrets diplomatiques, 1914–1918* (Brussels and Paris, 1963), pp. 118, 121, 130, 133.
59. Discussion of 2 Nov. 1918, ibid., pp. 132–3.
60. Article XVI gave the Allies free access to the territories evacuated by Germany in the east, for the purposes of famine relief and maintaining order.
61. De Launay, *Secrets*, p. 129. Article XIX of the Armistice eventually opened: 'With the reservation that any future claims and demands of the Allies and the United States of America remain unaffected, the following financial conditions are required: reparation for damage done. . . .'
62. Derby to Balfour, 18 Oct. 1918, BL Balfour MSS Add.49744.
63. Berger and Allard, *Censure*, p. 378.
64. Seymour, iv, p. 121.
65. Renouvin, *L'Armistice*, pp. 239–52. Radiotelegram from Foch, 11 Nov. 1918, *SHA* 6.N.70.
66. Clemenceau to Lloyd George, 9 and 10 Nov. 1918, LG Papers F/50/3/46–7.
67. Pichon to Clemenceau, 21 Oct. 1918; Pichon circular telegram 22 Nov. 1918, *MAE* Europe 1918–29 Allemagne (403).
68. Mordacq, ii, pp. 345–6.

69. Paul Cambon, *Correspondance*, iii, p. 286.
70. He wrote on 21 July 1917, 'When the war is over we can force them [i.e. Britain and France] to our way of thinking because by that time they will, among other things, be financially in our hands'. A. J. Mayer, *Political Origins of the New Diplomacy, 1917–1918* (New Haven, 1958), p. 332.
71. Reports by *EMA* 2ème Bureau on 'L'État de l'opinion en France d'après le contrôle de la correspondance', 15 Sept. and 15 Oct. 1918, *SHA* 6.N.147. Prefects' reports, Oct. 1918, in *SHA* 16.N.1538.
72. Sir Eyre Crowe, 'President Wilson's Fourteen Points', 16 Oct. 1918, FO/371/3444. Minute by Lord Robert Cecil, 28 Oct. 1918, FO/371/3445.
73. Kaspi, *Temps*, p. 239.
74. The evidence is only indirect; but for Foch, see Renouvin, *L'Armistice*, pp. 263–4; and for Clemenceau, Chapter IV, above, notes 83 and 84.
75. That the French interpreted the Armistice in this light is also shown by the revival of their claim to the 1814 frontier for Alsace–Lorraine. On 7 Oct. 1918 Clemenceau told Poincaré he would claim this at the Peace Conference (Poincaré, *Service*, x, p. 378). On 26 Oct., however, Mordacq, Foch, and Clemenceau agreed that the claim should be incorporated in the Armistice itself (Mordacq, ii, p. 294).

    Clemenceau did not raise the subject at the second Paris Conference, and the Americans would have opposed him if he had. The Cobb–Lippmann memorandum described the claim as a 'clear violation' of the Fourteen Points. Instead, on a map prepared by Foch and annexed to the Armistice convention, 'line no. 2', which marked the northern border of Alsace–Lorraine, was drawn so as to include in the provinces two German districts lying north of the frontier of 1870. An important part of the Saar basin was thereby brought, with Alsace–Lorraine, into a zone of direct French rule in which the former German administration was rapidly dismantled. The British and Americans apparently overlooked this action, despite the 'political motives' which Foch admitted lay behind it. Foch to Clemenceau, 7 Jan. 1919, *AN* F^{12} 8041. (*See Map I.*)

CHAPTER VI

1. H. Nicolson, *Peacemaking, 1919* (London, 1937 edn.). p. 192.
2. Andrew and Kanya-Forstner, *Expansion*, Chapter VII.
3. A. J. Mayer, *Politics and Diplomacy of Peacemaking: Containment and Counter-Revolution at Versailles, 1918–1919* (London, 1968), pp. 294–301.
4. Perman, pp. 73–7.
5. Ibid., p. 84.
6. Laroche, 'L'Allemagne de demain et les Allemands d'Autriche', 25 Oct. 1918, *MAE* Pichon MSS (5); and 'La Physionomie de l'Allemagne de demain . . .', 6 Nov. 1918, *MAE* A 'Paix' (N) (110).

7. Clemenceau to Lloyd George, undated but 10 Nov. 1918, LG Papers F/50/3/47.
8. Pichon to Jusserand, 19 Nov. 1918, *MAE* Jusserand MSS (42).
9. Derby to Balfour, 20 and 27 Nov. 1918, BL Balfour MSS Add.49744.
10. Pichon circular telegram, 23 Mar. 1919, *MAE* Europe 1918–29 Autriche (3).
11. Degrand to Piltz, 14 Nov. 1918, ibid. Pologne (67). For background, see Komarnicki, Chapter V, and P. S. Wandycz, *France and her East-.ern Allies 1919–1925: French-Czechoslovak–Polish Relations from the Paris Peace Conference to Locarno* (Minneapolis, 1962), Chapter I.
12. Pichon to Paderewski, 26 Jan. 1919, *MAE* Europe 1918–29 Pologne (130).
13. Pichon to Paul Cambon, 14 Dec. 1918, ibid. Danzig (1) and Pologne (67).
14. Foch to Clemenceau, 9 Jan. 1919, *SHA* 6.N.53. Supreme War Council, 12 Jan. 1919, *Papers Relating to the Foreign Relations of the United States, 1919. The Paris Peace Conference* (13 vols., Washington, 1942–7), iii, pp. 471–2.
15. Council of Ten (the Peace Conference's main decision-making body in January–March 1919) 22 Jan. 1919, ibid., pp. 670–4, 684–6.
16. Convention prolonging the Armistice, 16 Feb. 1919, ibid., ii, pp. 15–16.
17. Soutou, 'La Politique économique de la France à l'égard de la Belgique, 1914–1924', in Poidevin (ed.), *Relations franco-belges*, pp. 261–3.
18. Balfour, 'Memorandum of Conversation with Monsieur Hymans', 6 Feb. 1919, FO/608/2.
19. Pichon to Allizé, 13 and 23 Dec. 1918, *MAE* duplicate telegrams to the Hague, 1918 (5).
20. Foch, 'Note', 22 Dec. 1918, *SHA* 6.N.70.
21. Hymans, i, p. 347.
22. G. W. T. Omond to Headlam-Morley, 3 Jan. 1919, FO/608/121.
23. Pichon in *CAEC*, 24 Dec. 1918, *AN* C 7491. 'Rapport du Général Roques sur sa mission d'enquête à Luxembourg', 8 Feb. 1919, p. 7, *SHA* 6.N.198.
24. Ibid., pp. 32–3.
25. Ibid., p. 30.
26. Foch to Clemenceau, 9 Feb. 1919; Clemenceau to Foch, 10 Feb. 1919; *SHA* 6.N.198.
27. Pichon circular telegram, 27 Jan. 1919, *MAE* Europe 1918–29 Luxembourg (12).
28. R. Poincaré, *A la recherche de la paix, 1919* (J. Bariéty and P. Miquel eds., Paris, 1974), pp. 42, 57.
29. Jeanneney to Foch, 24 Nov. 1918, *AN* F^{12} 8041. (For 'line no. 2', see note 75 to Chapter V, above.)
30. Ibid.
31. Foch to Clemenceau, 10 Dec. 1918, *AN* F^{12} 8041.
32. For the occupation arrangements, see K. L. Nelson, *Victors Divided:*

America and the Allies in Germany, 1918–1923 (Los Angeles, 1975), pp. 26–41; and J. Bariéty, 'De l'exécution à la négociation: l'évolution des relations franco-allemandes après la Première Guerre mondiale . . .', (Thesis, Paris, 1975), pp. 43–6, 51.

33. An assumption made explicit in 'Les Frontières de l'Alsace–Lorraine et le statut de la rive gauche du Rhin', 1 Nov. 1918 (unsigned, but in Laroche's hand), *MAE* A 'Paix' (N) (289).

34. Pétain to Foch, 30 Dec. 1918; Foch to Clemenceau, 3 Jan. 1919, *MAE* Tardieu MSS (44).

35. Pichon to Clemenceau, 9 Jan. 1919; Clemenceau to Foch, 11 Jan. 1919. Bariéty, pp. 51–3.

36. Ibid., p. 53. Waterlow to Leslie, 10 Apr. 1919, FO/608/222.

37. Tirard, 'Rapport sur l'occupation de la rive gauche du Rhin au point de vue politique et économique', 31 Jan. 1919; Foch to Clemenceau, 8 Feb. 1919; Pichon to Jeanneney, 11 Mar. 1919. Bariéty, pp. 55–9.

38. For the background, see H. Köhler, 'Grundlagen und konzeptionen der Französischen Rhein- und Deutschlandpolitik von der Novemberrevolution bis zum Friedensschluβ von Versailles' in R. Poidevin (ed.), *Problèmes de la Rhénanie, 1919–1930* (Metz, 1975), pp. 59–87. Also *GQG* 2ème Bureau, 'Compte-rendu mensuel sur l'état d'esprit des régions occupées et de l'Alsace–Lorraine', 25 May 1919, *SHA* 6.N.285.

39. Pichon to Paul Cambon, undated but (?) 7 Dec. 1918, *MAE* duplicate telegrams to London, 1918 (35).

40. Clemenceau to Pichon, 8 Mar. 1919. Hovi, p. 186. Clemenceau in Council of Ten, 12 Feb. 1919, *FRUS, PPC*, iii, p. 975; 8 Mar. 1919, ibid., iv, pp. 281–2.

41. In general, see Mayer, *Peacemaking*, Chapter IX.

42. Pichon circular telegram, 27 Nov. 1918, *MAE* duplicate telegrams to the Hague, 1918 (5).

43. 'Note sommaire remise par M. Tardieu sur le contrôle et le règlement des matières premières à fournir à l'Allemagne', 24 Jan. 1919, *MAE* Série Y Internationale (213).

44. Pichon to House, 23 Dec. 1918, *FRUS, PPC*, ii, pp. 684–5. Clemenceau in Council of Ten, 7 Feb. 1919, ibid., iii, p. 904; and 8 Mar. 1919, ibid., iv, pp. 281–2.

45. Pichon to Jusserand, 1 Dec. 1918, *MAE* Jusserand MSS (42). There was, however, disagreement in the Government. Poincaré, *Recherche*, p. 41.

46. Haguenin to (?) Pichon, 10 Mar. 1919, *MAE* Europe 1918–29 Allemagne (6).

47. Haguenin to Pichon, 16 Mar. 1919, ibid. (352). Pichon had just promised such preferential supplies to the Bavarian politician, Dr Mühlon, if he should come to power. Pichon to Clinchant, 26 Feb. 1919, ibid.

48. Supreme Economic Council, 27 Mar. 1919, FO/608/126. Pichon in *CTP*, 28 July 1919, pp. 2–3.

49. Poincaré, *Recherche*, p. 375.

50. In addition to the Franco-Italian colonial disputes, Italy in December

1918 requested the cession of the Roya valley, part of metropolitan France. 'Note sur le canton de Breil', 20 Jan. 1919, *MAE* A 'Paix' (N) (259).

51. Mordacq, iii, p. 6..
52. Clemenceau to Lloyd George, 15 Nov. 1918, *FRUS, PPC*, 1, pp. 131–2.
53. 'Examen des conditions de paix', with covering letter from Hardinge to Balfour, 26 Nov. 1918, FO/371/3446. 'Préliminaires de paix – propositions du Ministre des Finances', 18 Nov. 1918, *MAE* Tardieu MSS (3). 'Note du Maréchal Foch', 21 Nov. 1918, ibid. (43).
54. Mordacq, iii, p. 6.
55. Minutes of conference at 10 Downing Street, 2 Dec. 1918 (11 am.), *SHA* 6.N.72.
56. 'Conversation entre M. Lloyd George et le Maréchal Foch', 1 Dec. 1918, *SHA* 6.N.73. Also Lloyd George, *Truth*, i, pp. 132–6. Foch had already argued the point in a 'Note' of 27 Dec. 1918. Printed in Mermeix, *Combat*, pp. 205–10.
57. Andrew and Kanya-Forstner, 'Colonial Party', p. 104.
58. Notably in Lloyd George's conversation with Foch, 1 Dec. 1918, cited in Note 56 above.
59. Derby to Balfour, 14 Dec. 1918, LG Papers F/52/2/52.
60. Clemenceau to Lloyd George, 15 Nov. 1918, *FRUS, PPC*, i, pp. 131–2.
61. H.I. Nelson, *Land and Power: British and Allied Policy on Germany's Frontiers, 1916–1919* (London, 1963), p. 134.
62. Pichon to Jusserand, Paul Cambon, and Barrère, 27 Nov. 1918, *MAE* Pichon MSS (6). Jusserand to Lansing, 29 Nov. 1918, *FRUS, PPC*, i, pp. 365ff. By 'demilitarization' in French documents of this kind was meant denying the left bank to a German, but not Allied, military presence.
63. Laroche, p. 63. Nicolson, p. 103.
64. Paul Cambon, 'Correspondance échangée entre l'Ambassade de France à Londres et le Département à propos de la procédure des négociations de paix', 4 Apr. 1919, *MAE* Paul Cambon MSS Tome VI, vol. 14. Also Cambon, *Correspondance*, iii, p. 291.
65. 'L'Opinion française et le Président Wilson', 26 Nov. 1918, *SHA* 6.N.137. Unsigned, but 'Note pour le Président du Conseil' is written on it in Tardieu's hand. Clemenceau wrote 'absurd' against the idea that Britain and France were reaching a prior agreement. Tardieu's sympathy for Wilson is recorded in Poincaré, *Service*, x, p. 435.
66. Ibid., p. 451. Derby to Balfour, 20 Dec. 1918, LG Papers F/52/2/54.
67. Tardieu note, 5 Jan. 1919, *MAE* Tardieu MSS (3). Printed in A. Tardieu, *La Paix* (Paris, 1921), pp. 97–101.
68. Council of Ten, 12 and 13 Jan. 1919, *FRUS, PPC*, iii, 492, 536.
69. Walworth, p. 155. Mayer, p. 187.
70. Clemenceau speech, 29 Dec. 1918, *JO* (*Chambre*), 1918, pp. 3732–3.
71. J. M. Keynes, *The Economic Consequences of the Peace* (London, 1920), pp. 229–30.
72. Curzon to Derby, 21 Feb. 1919, FO/608/124.

73. Derby to Lloyd George, 13 Mar. 1919, LG Papers F/52/3/10.
74. Clemenceau press interview, 10 Feb. 1919. P. Miquel, *La Paix de Versailles et l'opinion publique française* (Paris, 1972), p. 195.
75. Pichon to Paul Cambon, 13 and 14 Nov. 1918, *MAE* duplicate telegrams to London, 1918 (26). J. Monnet, 'Note pour M. Clémentel no. 2', Nov. 1918, *AN* F^{12} 7796.
76. Clémentel to Reading, 12 Dec. 1918, *AN* F^{12} 7798.
77. Reading to Clémentel, 31 Dec. 1918, *AN* F^{12} 7819.
78. Tardieu to House, 24 Dec. 1918, *FRUS, PPC*, i, pp. 379–80.
79. The whole of the following section relies heavily on Miquel, *Versailles*, passim.
80. Pichon in *CAEC*, 24 Dec. 1918, *AN* C 7491. For the *CAEC*'s programme (2 Dec. 1918), Miquel, *Versailles*, p. 295. The *CAEC* desired: full reparation for damage, and the repayment of war costs by Germany; that France should gain the 1814 frontier and the whole of the Saar basin; and 'guarantees', including notably demilitarization, on the left bank of the Rhine. Buffer States were not mentioned.
81. Andrew and Kanya-Forstner, *Expansion*, Chapter VII.
82. *La Ligue française*, issues for January–February and March 1919. For Barrés, Miquel, *Versailles*, pp. 305–8.
83. Ibid., pp. 327–31. Report on the Congress in *Les Conditions de la paix et le sentiment national français*, *BDIC* O pièce 2358.F. The Congress passed resolutions for the 1814 frontier; for an Allied military protectorate on the left bank; for the occupation of the Ruhr until the German indemnity had been paid in full; and for a refusal to recognize the German federal Government.
84. *Comité directeur* of the *AIAF*, 18 Dec. 1918, *AN* 27.A.S.3. Statements at this meeting suggest that members of the *AIAF* had discussed reparations and German coal deliveries with the Government.
85. Note by the *Comité central des houillères de France*, Dec. 1918, *MAE* A 'Paix' (N) (290).
86. *Comité des forges*, 'Note sur le statut futur de la Sarre', undated, *MAE* Tardieu MSS (51). *Commission de direction* of the *Comité*, 1918–19, *PAM* 7246. The meeting of 9 Nov. 1918 suggests the *Comité* was consulted over German coal deliveries.
87. Derby to Curzon, 10 Feb. 1919, IOL Curzon MSS Eur.F.112/96. Miquel, *Versailles*, p. 506.
88. Jeanneney, p. 155.
89. Loucheur to Pichon, 14 June 1919, *MAE* Europe 1918–29 Sarre (1). This letter argued that it was more important to win the goodwill of the population of the Saar than to protect French iron-and-steel producers against competition from the region.
90. *EMA* 2ème Bureau I, 'Bulletin confidentiel résumant la situation morale à l'intérieur', 15 Mar. and 15 Apr. 1919, *SHA* 6.N.147.
91. Miquel, *Versailles*, pp. 19–36.
92. Ibid., pp. 543–8.
93. Poincaré, *Service*, x, p. 458; *Recherche*, pp. 85, 160, 207, 236, 253, 294.

94. eg. Pichon to Clémentel, 15 Nov. 1918, *AN* F¹² 8105.
95. 'Préliminaires de paix – propositions du Ministère des Finances', 27 Dec. 1918, *MAE* Tardieu MSS (3). Ministry of Commerce, 'Avant-projet des clauses économiques des préliminaires de paix', 31 Dec. 1918, *AN* F¹² 8104.
96. Andrew and Kanya-Forstner, *Expansion*, Chapter VII.
97. Reports from portions of the Ministry are in *SHA* 16.N.3271.
98. Above, note 53.
99. Tardieu note of 5 Jan. 1919, above, note 67.
100. 'Préliminaires de paix – propositions du Ministre des Finances', 18 Nov. and 27 Dec. 1918, *MAE* Tardieu MSS (3). The Government had not yet reached an estimate of the damage in the invaded areas. Pichon to House, 5 Dec. 1918, *FRUS, PPC*, ii, p. 583.
101. Clémentel to Clemenceau, 31 Dec. 1918, *AN* F¹² 8104.
102. Ministry of Commerce, 'Avant-projet des clauses économiques des préliminaires de paix', 31 Dec. 1918, ibid.
103. Hauser, 'Note sur le mémoire de M. Sayous relatif aux moyens de paiement de l'Allemagne', 28 Dec. 1918, *AN* F¹² 7895.
104. 'Note relative à l'Autriche allemande', unsigned, 17 Mar. 1919, *SHA* 6.N.75. For Tardieu's probable authorship, Poincaré, *Recherche*, p. 258.
105. Laroche, pp. 58–9. Benoist, iii, pp. 331–2, suggests Tardieu's consultation of the *Comité* was cursory. But there is no doubt of its influence on the memoranda he presented to the Peace Conference, particularly those on the Saarland.
106. 'Pologne', meeting of 29 Jan. 1919, *MAE* Europe 1918–29 Pologne (68).
107. 'Une méthode d'action en Pologne', unsigned, 20 Dec. 1918, *BDIC* Dossiers Klotz Fol. 223 Rés.14. H. I. Nelson, pp. 117–19.
108. 'Les Frontières de la Tchécoslovaquie', undated meeting, *MAE* Tardieu MSS (77).
109. 'Les Frontières de la Belgique', meeting of 17 Feb. 1919, ibid. (95).
110. Undated 'Notes sur l'Alsace', with correction in Berthelot's hand, *MAE* A 'Paix' (N) (289); 'Les Frontières de l'Alsace–Lorraine et le statut de la rive gauche du Rhin', 1 Nov. 1918, unsigned but in Laroche's hand, ibid.
111. See discussion in section 3 of this Chapter, above.
112. Tardieu, 'Exposé de la question de la Sarre et des solutions possibles', 25 Jan. 1919, *MAE* Tardieu MSS (51).
113. 'Note du Maréchal Foch', 21 Nov. 1918, ibid. (43). Aubert, 'Note sur l'Alsace (présentation de la question aux Américains)', 22 Dec. 1918, with covering letter, *MAE* A 'Paix' (67).
114. Meeting of 6 Feb. 1919, recorded in two undated memoranda by Tardieu, both entitled 'Sarre', in *MAE* Tardieu MSS (51) and (52). cf. Poincaré, *Recherche*, p. 105.
115. 'Note du Maréchal Foch', 10 Jan. 1919. Printed in Mermeix, *Combat*, pp. 210–19. According to Soutou, 'Marches', p. 384, the note was drafted by Tardieu himself.

116. Tardieu, p. 164.
117. Tardieu, 'Le Rôle international du Rhin', 'Le Statut des pays rhénans de la rive gauche', and 'Le Rôle militaire de la rive gauche du Rhin dans les agressions allemandes', undated, FO/608/142. Also *MAE* Tardieu MSS (49), where dated as 20 Jan. 1919.
118. Tardieu, 'Note sommaire', ibid. Dated in same carton as 19–23 Feb. 1919.
119. Tardieu, 'Mémoire du gouvernement français sur la fixation au Rhin de la frontière occidentale de l'Allemagne et l'occupation interalliée des ponts du fleuve', 25 Feb. 1919. Printed in Tardieu, pp. 165–84.
120. 'Le Statut des pays rhénans de la rive gauche', 20 Jan. 1919, *MAE* Tardieu MSS (49).
121. 'Le Rôle international du Rhin', 20 Jan. 1919, ibid.
122. Maps accompanying the 'Note sommaire', 19–23 Feb. 1919, ibid.
123. Tardieu, pp. 174, 176.
124. Conversation of Tardieu with Philip Kerr and Dr Mezes, 11 Mar. 1919, LG Papers F/89/2/40.
125. Copy of the memorandum, with Clemenceau's alterations, in *MAE* Tardieu MSS (45).
126. Poincaré, *Recherche*, p. 182.
127. '. . . the other western States, with whom . . . they may desire one day freely to reunite themselves'. 'Note du Maréchal Foch', 10 Jan. 1919, FO/608/142. The phrase is omitted in Mermeix, *Combat*, p. 217.
128. Poincaré, *Recherche*, p. 183. The wording of Tardieu, p. 184, suggests this amendment was rejected. However, the amendments appears in at least one version of the note as it was forwarded to the Allies. Floto, p. 127. Poincaré suggested the left bank should not be annexed *'against the will of the population'*: this would leave it possible for economic inducements to have an effect.
129. Ribot, *Journal*, p. 259. (16 Feb. 1919).
130. Conference at 10 Downing Street, 2 Dec. 1918, 11 am., *SHA* 6.N.72.
131. Pichon to Jeanneney, 24 Dec. 1918, *MAE* A 'Paix' (N) (64).
132. R. S. Baker, *Woodrow Wilson and World Settlement* (3 vols, London, 1923), ii, p. 21.
133. Andrew and Kanya-Forstner, *Expansion*, Chapter VII.

CHAPTER VII

1. M. Trachtenberg, *Reparation in World Politics: France and European Economic Diplomacy, 1916–1923* (New York, 1980), pp. 40–1.
2. Poincaré, *Recherche*, p. 436.
3. Both Berthelot and de Margerie had aspired to the position. Auffray, pp. 348–55.
4. See 'Conditions de paix', undated, outlining allocation of work at the Conference, *MAE* Tardieu MSS (45).
5. Laroche to Allizé, undated but May 1919, *MAE* Europe 1918–29 Autriche (3). Berthelot to Barrère, 14 June 1919, *MAE* Barrère MSS I.
6. Poincaré, *Recherche, passim.*

7. For example, the contribution of the Public Works Minister, Claveille, to the section of the Treaty dealing with inland waterways.
8. Poincaré, *Recherche*, pp. 412–13.
9. Jules Cambon, 'La Paix (notes inédites, 1919)', *Revue de Paris*, 1 Nov. 1937, p. 7.
10. Poincaré, *Recherche*, pp. 112, 179–80.
11. Watson, pp. 374–6. Mayer, *Peacemaking*, pp. 428–35.
12. Andrew and Kanya-Forstner, *Expansion*, Chapter VIII.
13. Miller to House, 3 Dec. 1918, *FRUS, PPC*, i, p. 335. Seymour, iv, pp. 280–1.
14. Bourgeois, 11 Feb. 1919. A. Geouffre de Lapradelle (ed.), *La Paix de Versailles. La Conférence de la Paix et la Société des Nations (la documentation internationale)* (12 vols., Paris, 1929–36), i, p. 169. Bourgeois amendment of 13 Feb. 1919, FO/608/240.1614/1/1.3536.
15. Miquel, *Versailles*, pp. 196–213.
16. Clémentel and Loucheur, 'Note à Monsieur le Président du Conseil au sujet des problèmes économiques qui se posent au cours des préliminaires de paix', 20 Jan. 1919 (with covering letter by Clémentel), *AN* F¹² 8039.
17. Trachtenberg, *Reparation*, pp. 35–7.
18. 'Memorandum Concerning a General Scheme of Financial Settlement', 21 Jan. 1919, by (?) Philippe Masson; 'Conversation avec M. Hughes', 22 Jan. 1919 *MAE* Tardieu MSS (24).
19. De Billy to Tardieu, 10 Mar. 1919, ibid. Klotz, p. 126.
20. Klotz, pp. 128–9. 'Projet d'une "Section financière de la Ligue des Nations"', 4 Feb. 1919, ibid., p. 198.
21. Tardieu, pp. 175–8.
22. Kerr to Lloyd George, 11 Feb. 1919, LG Papers F/89/2/7. cf. Poincaré, *Recherche*, p. 104; Miquel, p. 200.
23. Tardieu, 'Sarre', undated, *MAE* Tardieu MSS (51). 'Pièce no. 2', 6 Feb. 1919, ibid.
24. 'Categories of Damage for which Reparation may be Demanded', 20 Feb. 1919. P. M. Burnett, *Reparation at the Paris Conference (from the Standpoint of the American Delegation)* (2 vols., New York, 1940), ii, pp. 395–8.
25. B. M. Baruch, *The Making of the Reparation and Economic Sections of the Treaty* (London and New York, 1920), pp. 51–3. Burnett, i, p. 47; ii, pp. 383, 487.
26. Trachtenberg, *Reparation*, pp. 57–9. Loucheur considered that a capital levy would be the only way in which very large sums could be extracted from Germany. Burnett, ii, p. 632. (24 Feb. 1919).
27. Note by Tardieu to the *Commission des traités de paix* (henceforward *CTP*), 25 July 1919, p. 82 of report to *CTP* by Louis Barthou, FO/608/125. Clemenceau in *CTP*, 29 July 1919, p. 108, *AN* C 7773.
28. Foch, 'Note', 18 Feb. 1919, *SHA* 6.N.53. Conversation of Foch with the (British) General du Cane, 18 Feb. 1919, LG Papers F/89/2/24. Foch in Council of Ten, 24 and 25 Feb. 1919, *FRUS, PPC*, iv, pp. 107, 121–3.

29. Poincaré, *Recherche*, pp. 157, 160. Seymour, iv, pp. 345–6.
30. cf. Chapter VI, notes 117, 118, 119.
31. Seymour, iv, p. 357. 'An Independent Republic on the West Bank of the Rhine: Summary of Conversation with Monsieur Tardieu' (undated), FO/608/142. 'Conversation avec le Colonel House', 2 Mar. 1919, *MAE* Tardieu MSS (51). Guest to Clive, 13 Feb. 1919, FO/608/136.
32. Lloyd George, *Truth*, i, p. 286.
33. Seymour, iv, p. 368.
34. Kerr, 'Notes of discussion with M. Tardieu and Dr Mezes', 13 Feb. 1919, LG Papers F/89/2/40. Tardieu, 'Conversation du 11 mars' and 'Deuxième conversation (12 mars)', *MAE* Tardieu MSS (45).
35. Loucheur, p. 71. Poincaré, *Recherche*, p. 245. Andrew and Kanya-Forstner, *Expansion*, Chapter VIII.
36. When it was reported in February that Klotz might have to introduce a capital levy in order to redress the Government's finances Parliament and the press reacted so vehemently that the idea was abandoned. Miquel, *Versailles*, pp. 437–53.
37. Poincaré, *Recherche*, p. 275.
38. Loucheur, p. 71. Klotz was not kept informed of Loucheur's negotiations. Poincaré, *Recherche*, p. 279.
39. Burnett, i, pp. 25–8.
40. Ibid., p. 50. Cunliffe to Lloyd George, 2 Mar. 1919, LG Papers F/89/2/37.
41. Burnett, i, pp. 689–91.
42. Ibid., p. 670.
43. Poincaré, *Recherche*, p. 245.
44. Clemenceau was also concerned that the German Army should be able to resist domestic insurgency: a rare example of his giving weight to this. Clemenceau in *CTP*, 11 July 1919, pp. 72–6. *AN* C 7773.
45. Supreme War Council, 3 and 6 Mar. 1919, *FRUS, PPC*, iv, pp. 183–4, 217, 230ff.
46. Lloyd George, *Truth*, i, p. 587.
47. General Nudant, 'A Spa: l'Armistice '(1918–1919)', *La Revue de France*, 15 Mar. 1925, p. 288. Clemenceau in *CTP*, 17 July 1919, p. 107. *AN* C 7773.
48. Lloyd George, *Truth*, i, p. 285.
49. The French archives shed little extra light on these questions. For a full discussion, Nelson, *Land and Power*, pp. 145–97, 282–320.
50. Jules Cambon chaired the Commission; Le Rond and Laroche were the other French representatives. Procès-verbaux in *MAE Recueil des actes de la Conférence de la Paix* (henceforth *MAE Recueil*) (49) and (50).
51. The French representation was as for the Polish Commission. *MAE Recueil* (48).
52. Laroche report, 8 Mar. 1919. D. H. Miller, *My Diary at the Conference of Paris* (22 vols., New York, 1924), x, pp. 94–6, 99ff. Pichon to Brugère, 13 Mar. 1919, *MAE* A 'Paix' (141). Marling to Curzon, 20

May 1919, FO/608/138.

53. Tardieu and Laroche were the French representatives. Procès-verbaux in Miller, x, pp. 3ff.

54. Nelson, *Land and Power*, p. 221.

55. Loucheur, pp. 71–2.

56. Tardieu, 'Note sur la conversation du 14 mars', 15 Mar. 1919, *MAE* Tardieu MSS (51).

57. 'Note sur la suggestion présentée le 14 mars 1919', 17 Mar. 1919, FO/608/142 and Tardieu, pp. 197–200.

58. 'Proposal: Stipulations to be Embodied in the Treaty', 28 Mar. 1919, *SHA* 6.N.73. The French made an uncompromising reply on 4 April: 'Amendements français à la proposition Wilson', *MAE* Tardieu MSS (45).

59. 'Some Considerations for the Peace Conference before they Finally Draft their Terms', 25 Mar. 1919. Printed in part in Lloyd George, *Truth*, pp. 404–16.

60. Clemenceau, 27 Mar. 1919. P. Mantoux, *Les Délibérations du Conseil des Quatre (24 mars – 28 juin 1919)* (2 vols., Paris, 1955), i, pp. 43–4.

61. 'Observations sur la note de M. Lloyd George . . .', 28 Mar. 1919, *MAE* Tardieu MSS (51); Tardieu, pp. 129–32.

62. 'Conditions d'évacuation de la rive gauche du Rhin', anonymous, 4 Apr. 1919, *MAE* Tardieu MSS (49). Mordacq, iii, p. 214.

63. Wilson, 'Memorandum on the Amendments Proposed by France to the Agreement Suggested by President Wilson regarding the Rhine Frontier', 12 Apr. 1919, *SHA* 6.N.73. Nelson, *Victors*, p. 86.

64. 'Mémorandum en réponse à la note du Président Wilson en date du 12 avril', 15 Apr. 1919, *MAE* Tardieu MSS (50). Seymour, iv, p. 422.

65. Poincaré, *Recherche*, p. 337.

66. 'Textes adoptés le 20 avril par le Président Wilson et M. Clemenceau', *MAE* Tardieu MSS (49).

67. Mantoux, i, pp. 318–19.

68. 'Articles relatifs à la garantie de l'exécution du traité', 24 and 30 Apr. 1919, *MAE* Tardieu MSS (49). Treaty of Versailles, Article 429. (The Treaty is printed in *FRUS, PPC*, xiii, pp. 57ff.)

69. Tardieu, pp. 233–6.

70. Poincaré, *Recherche*, p. 362. This conversation with Poincaré on 22 April may have moved Clemenceau to safeguard himself.

71. Loucheur, p. 72. Clemenceau in *CAES*, 25 Aug. 1919, *CAES*, 1919, pp. 1952–4. On this occasion Clemenceau singled out the development of aviation as among the circumstances likely to reduce the Rhine frontier's value.

72. Burnett, i, pp. 55–6.

73. Ibid., pp. 61–2.

74. Clemenceau in Council of Four, 26 Mar. 1919; Klotz, 28 Mar. 1919. Mantoux, i, pp. 29, 58–9

75. Burnett, i, pp. 784, 796. Mantoux, i, pp. 153–6, 160–1.

76. Burnett, i, p. 75.

77. Council of Four, 7 Apr. 1919. Mantoux, i, p. 171.
78. Poncaré, *Recherche*, pp. 313–14, 316, 318.
79. Remarks of Touron, President of the AIAF, to its *Comité directeur*, 18 Dec. 1918. Touron conveyed his ideas to Loucheur. *AN* 27 A.S.3, pp. 139–41.
80. French memorandum: 'Control and Guarantees', 12 Mar. 1919. Burnett, ii, pp. 775–8. Also, 'Dispositions à imposer à l'Allemagne: clauses financières', 28 Mar. 1919. Klotz, pp. 215ff. 'Note sur la suggestion présentée le 14 mars 1919', 17 Mar. 1919. Tardieu, pp. 197–200.
81. Loucheur, p. 72. Poincaré, *Recherche*, pp. 285, 320.
82. Ibid., pp. 348, 419.
83. 'Articles relatifs à la garantie d'exécution du traité', 20 Apr. 1919, *MAE* Tardieu MSS (49).
84. Bariéty, p. 83.
85. Clemenceau in the Council of Four, 28 Mar. 1919. Mantoux, i, pp. 69–71.
86. 'Note sommaire sur la frontière de 1814 et le bassin de la Sarre', 27 Mar. 1919, *MAE* Tardieu MSS (52).
87. Council of Four, 28 Mar. 1919. Mantoux, i, pp. 67, 73. Lloyd George did, however, consent in principle to the 1814 frontier in the Fontainebleau Memorandum, only to withdraw this on 2 April. Lloyd George, *Truth*, i, pp. 414, 422.
88. Tardieu, 'Note sur la conversation du 14 mars', 15 Mar. 1919, *MAE* Tardieu MSS. (51). Poincaré, *Recherche*, p. 310.
89. Nelson, *Land and Power*, pp. 256–7.
90. 'Note sur la question de la Sarre', 29 Mar. 1919. Tardieu, pp. 294–6.
91. Proposals 'A', 'B', and 'C' submitted to Tardieu by Headlam-Morley on 31 Mar. 1919, *MAE* Tardieu MSS (51).
92. Tardieu, 'Pièce no. 6', 29 Mar. 1919, ibid. 'Proposition Wilson', 31 Mar. 1919, *MAE* Tardieu MSS (52).
93. Note by Headlam-Morley, 5 Apr. 1919, FO/608/141.
94. 'Report: the Saar Basin', 5 Apr. 1919, ibid.
95. 'Note du Président Wilson sur la Sarre', 8 Apr. 1919, *MAE* Tardieu MSS (51).
96. 'Réponse à la note du Président Wilson du 8 avril', 9 Apr. 1919, ibid.
97. Council of Four, 9 Apr. 1919. Mantoux, i, pp. 203–7.
98. Report of this Committee, with note by Headlam-Morley, 6 May 1919, FO/608/125. Minute by Hurst, 4 Apr. 1919, ibid. Tardieu, pp. 268–76.
99. Treaty of Versailles, Articles 116, 433. The first of these clauses was proposed by Clemenceau on 2 May. Mantoux, i, pp. 461–3.
100. Watson, p. 376. Mayer, *Peacemaking*, pp. 481, 483, 823–5.
101. Lloyd George, *Truth*, i, pp. 407–8; Tardieu, p. 130.
102. Watson, p. 376. Mayer, *Peacemaking*, pp. 724–5.
103. Council of Ten, 19 Mar. 1919, *FRUS, PPC*, iv, pp. 416–18.
104. Lloyd George, *Truth*, i, p. 413.
105. Council of Four, 27 Mar. 1919. Mantoux, i, pp. 43–4.

106. Council of Four, 1 and 3 Apr. 1919. Ibid., pp. 111–13, 125–6.
107. Polish National Committee, 'Le Problème de Danzig et de Koenigsberg', 3 Mar. 1919, FO/608/141. Quai d'Orsay memorandum, 'Le Territoire de la Pologne', 1 Mar. 1919, *MAE* Europe 1918–29 Pologne (68). These writers envisaged that the whole of East Prussia, after a transitional period as a nominally independent Republic, might be absorbed into Poland. Clemenceau himself advocated such an East Prussian Republic on 7 Mar. 1919. Lloyd George, *Truth*, i, p. 288.
108. Procès-verbal in *SHA* 6.N.74.
109. Council of Four, 4 Apr. 1919. Mantoux, i, p. 149. Perman, Chapter VII.
110. 'Note relative à l'Autriche allemande', 17 Mar. 1919, *SHA* 6.N.75.
111. Indépendance de l'Autriche allemande', 20 Apr. 1919, *MAE* Tardieu MSS (49).
112. Council of Four, 2 May 1919. Mantoux, i, pp. 461–2.
113. Council of Four, 14 June 1919. Mantoux, ii, p. 424.
114. Leygues in *CTP*, 1 Aug. 1919, pp. 100–3, *AN* C 7773.
115. King Albert of Belgium in the Council of Four, 4 Apr. 1919. Mantoux, i, p. 145.
116. Council of Four, 16 Apr. 1919. Mantoux, i, pp. 261–3.
117. Trausch, in Poidevin (ed.), *Relations franco-belges*, p. 288.
118. Balfour note, 8 Mar. 1919, FO/608/121.
119. Council of Ten, 11 Feb. 1919, *FRUS, PPC*, iii, p. 967.
120. Clemenceau in Council of Four, 4 and 15 Apr. 1919. Mantoux, i, pp. 147, 246.
121. Clemenceau in Council of Four, 28 May, 1919. Mantoux, ii, p. 249.
122. Foch to Clemenceau, 21 Feb. 1919, *MAE* A 'Paix' (N) (239). Schaefer to Crowe, 3 Apr. 1919, FO/608/121.
123. Pichon to de Margerie, 5 May 1919, *MAE* Europe 1918–29 Luxembourg (32).
124. 'Avant-projet' presented to the Conference's Economic Commission, undated (but mid-March 1919), *APD* Clémentel MSS XXXI.
125. Ibid. (Article 7). Tardieu, 'Note sommaire . . . sur le contrôle et le règlement des matières premières à fournir à l'Allemagne', 24 Jan. 1919, *MAE* Y Internationale (213).
126. Council of Four, 25 Apr. 1919. Mantoux, i, pp. 368–72. Clémentel in *CAES*, 14 Aug. 1919, *CAES*, 1919, pp. 1929, 1934–5.
127. Bariéty, p. 166.
128. This was explicitly stated as one object of reparations in a note by one of Klotz's Finance Ministry advisers, L. Petit, 'Comment prévoir l'indemnité de guerre pour empêcher l'Allemagne de faire faillite', 9 Nov. 1918, *AN* AJ[5] 47.
129. Loucheur in Second Sub-Committee of the CRD, 18 Feb. 1919; Clémentel in ibid., 31 Mar. 1919. Burnett, ii, pp. 598–9, 724.
130. Loucheur in Second Sub-Committee of the CRD, 18 Feb. 1919. Geouffre de Lapradelle, ii, pp. 708–15.
131. Bariéty, pp. 187, 189, 191. Jeanneney, p. 155. To be precise, some rep-

resentatives of French industry were consulted about their coal needs in the winter of 1918, but not subsequently. Chapter VI above, notes 84 –9.

132. The following section owes much to Miquel, *Versailles*, pp. 363–86 and to J. R. McCrum, 'French Rhineland Policy at the Paris Peace Conference, 1919', *The Historical Journal*, 21, 3 (1978), pp. 623–48.
133. Miquel, *Versailles*, pp. 351–2. Foch to Clemenceau, 6 Apr. 1919, *SHA* 6.N.114.
134. Clemenceau to Foch, 9 Apr. 1919, ibid.
135. Foch to Clemenceau, 15 Apr. 1919, ibid.
136. Poincaré, *Recherche*, p. 335.
137. Foch to Clemenceau, 17 Apr. 1919, *SHA* 6.N.114. Mordacq, iii, pp. 229–30.
138. Miquel, *Versailles*, p. 371.
139. (17 Apr. 1919). Ibid., pp. 371–3, 377.
140. Pichon in *CAES*, 18 Apr. 1919, *CAES*, 1919, p. 1792.
141. Mordacq, iii, p. 245.
142. Poincaré, *Recherche*, pp. 298, 412–13, 416.
143. Poincaré to Clemenceau, 28 Apr. 1919. Lloyd George, *Truth*, i, pp. 427ff.
144. Cf. note 84, above.
145. For one of many examples, Clemenceau in *CTP*, 29 July 1919, p. 111. *AN* C 7773.
146. P. Krüger, *Deutschland und die Reparationen, 1918–1919: die Genesis des Reparationsproblems in Deutschland zwischen Waffenstillstand und Versailler Friedenschluß* (Stuttgart, 1973), pp. 131–2.
147. Ibid., pp. 134–6.
148. Reports by Haguenin, 29 Apr. and 3 May 1919, *MAE* Europe 1918–29 Allemagne (8) and (9) respectively.
149. Haguenin report, 22 Apr. 1919, *MAE* Europe 1918–29 Allemagne (8).
150. Haguenin report, 29 Apr. 1919, ibid.
151. Krüger, p. 177. Massigli reports, 12 and 15 May 1919, *MAE* Europe 1918–29 Sarre (1).
152. Krüger, p. 179.
153. Jules Cambon note, 2 May 1919. Mermeix, *Combat*, pp. 168–71.
154. Pichon in *CTP*, 28 July 1919, p. 2. *AN* C 7773.
155. Jules Cambon note, 5 May 1919, *MAE* Pichon MSS (8).
156. 'Entrevue entre le Général Desticker et le Docteur Helm (*sic*), Député bavarois, à Luxembourg, le 19 mai 1919', *SHA* 6.N.72. Council of Four, 12 Apr. 1919. Mantoux, i, pp. 232–3.
157. Mangin, 'Compte-rendu', 9 June 1919, *MAE* Europe 1918–29 Allemagne (346). See also 'Compte-rendu II' (unsigned, c. 11 June 1919), *AN* Mangin MSS 149 A.P. 21.
158. Nelson, *Victors Divided*, pp. 97–103.
159. G. de Traversay, 'La Première tentative de République rhénane' (2 parts, *La Revue de Paris*, 15 Nov. 1928, pp. 404–31 and 1 Dec. 1928, pp. 586–614), Part II, pp. 588–9.

270   *References to pages 191–196*

160. Mangin to Fayolle, May 1919, *AN* Mangin MSS 149 A.P. 21.
161. Clemenceau to Mangin, 31 May 1919, *SHA* 6.N.73.
162. Wilson to Clemenceau, 23 May 1919. G. Clemenceau, *Grandeurs et misères d'une victoire* (Paris, 1930), pp. 180–1.
163. Mantoux, ii, pp. 253–5. P. Tirard, *La France sur le Rhin: douze années d'occupation rhénane* (Paris, 1930), pp. 103–4.
164. McCrum, p. 644. Ribot, *Journal*, p. 273. J. A. Dorten, *La Tragédie rhénane* (Paris, 1945 edn.), pp. 71, 76.
165. C. Mangin, 'Lettres de Rhénanie', *Revue de Paris*, 1 Apr. 1936, p. 502.
166. Tirard to Pichon, 9 June 1919, *MAE* Europe 1918–29 Rive gauche du Rhin (1).
167. Poincaré, *Recherche*, p. 449.
168. Ibid.
169. Clemenceau to Mangin, 31 May 1919, *SHA* 6.N.73.
170. Foch to Allied Commanders, 29 May 1919, ibid. My emphasis.
171. Dorten, pp. 76–8. Mangin appears not to have received Clemenceau's letter of 31 May before this incident. Mangin, p. 524.
172. Poincaré to Clemenceau, 1 June 1919. Clemenceau, pp. 188–9.
173. Mordacq, iii, p. 298. McCrum, p. 646.
174. Council of Four, 2 June 1919. Mantoux, ii, pp. 265–73.
175. Council of Four, 3 June 1919. Ibid., ii, pp. 277–83.
176. Minutes of Commission on the Eastern Frontiers of Germany, 6–9 June 1919, FO/608/126. Le Rond represented France.
177. Council of Four, 11 June 1919. Mantoux, ii, p. 380.
178. Council of Four, 10 June 1919, ibid., p. 360.
179. Burnett, ii, pp. 110, 124–5.
180. Clemenceau, 2 and 10 June. Mantoux, ii, pp. 270, 364. Loucheur, 3 and 7 June 1919, ibid., pp. 284, 338. Tardieu to House, 10 June 1919. Seymour, iv, p. 493.
181. Council of Four, 9 and 10 June 1919. Mantoux, ii, pp. 356–7, 362–4.
182. Clemenceau, 13 June. Ibid., pp. 408–9.
183. Printed in Burnett, ii, pp. 202–3 (where dated 16 June).
184. Clemenceau, 10 and 11 June 1919. Mantoux, ii, pp. 367, 394.
185. Clemenceau in *CTP*, 17 July 1919, p. 113. *AN* C 7773.
186. Procès-verbaux (31 May – 9 June 1919) in *AN* AJ⁹ 2891. Foch notes of 5 and 9 June 1919 in *SHA* 6.N.73.
187. 'Convention Regarding the Military Occupation of the Territories of the Rhine', *FRUS, PPC*, xiii, pp. 762–9.
188. Watson, p. 361.
189. Berthelot to Seydoux, 10 June 1919, *MAE* Europe 1918–29 Rive gauche du Rhin (1). Clemenceau to Foch and Mangin, 30 June 1919, *MAE* Europe 1918–29 Allemagne (348). Clemenceau in *CAES*, 25 Aug. 1919, *CAES*, 1919, pp. 1969–71. Clemenceau in *CTP*, 11 July 1919, pp. 78–100, *AN* C 7773.
190. W. A. McDougall, *France's Rhineland Diplomacy, 1914–1924: the Last Bid for a Balance of Power in Europe* (Princeton, 1978), pp. 89–92.
191. Clemenceau in *CAES*, 25 Aug. 1919, *CAES*, 1919, p. 1950.

CONCLUSION

1. Fischer, *Aims*, p. 106. Professor Fischer's evidence, however, casts doubt on this generalization's applicability to Germany's aims in Eastern, as opposed to Western, Europe.
2. Cf. the distinction drawn in E. Kehr, *Der Primat der Innenpolitik: gesammelte Aufsätze zur preussisch-deutschen Sozialgeschichte im 19.und 20. Jahrhundert* (H.-U. Wehler, ed., Berlin, 1965), pp. 87–8.
3. Only fifteen per cent of France's war expenditure was covered by taxation. Hardach, pp. 162–3.
4. cf. views of Poincaré, in Poincaré, *Service*, v, p. 221; Millerand (the French War Minister in 1914–15), in *Les Carnets de guerre d'Albert Ier, Roi des Belges* (R. von Overstraeten, ed., Brussels, 1953), p. 79. In October 1914 there were fears of a military *coup* even if France were victorious. Bertie, i, p. 48.
5. V. I. Lenin, *Imperialism, the Highest Stage of Capitalism: a Popular Outline* (first published, 1917; I have used paperback edition, Peking, 1975).
6. C. M. Andrew and A. S. Kanya-Forstner, 'Colonial Party', *passim*.
7. M.-R. Mouton, 'L'Idée d'organisation internationale', in Guillen (ed.), p. 115.
8. The fear of it, however, survived. Poincaré, *Service*, v, p. 221.
9. Clemenceau, p. 168.
10. Horne, p. 326.
11. J. Chastenet, *Jours inquiets et jours sanglants, 1906–1918* (Paris, 1955), p. 344.
12. Special issue of *La Ligue française: 'La Paix que les Allemands voulaient faire'* (undated, but Oct.–Nov. 1915), *PAM* 12120/96. For the German memorandum, Fischer, *Aims*, pp. 167–8.
13. Pétain, 'Pourquoi nous nous battons', 27 June 1917, FO/800/201, p. 73. Lavisse speech at the Sorbonne, 7 Mar. 1917, in tract, 'Pourquoi nous nous battons', *BN* 8° L 57 b. 15654. Ribot speech, 2 Aug. 1917, *JO (Chambre)*, 1917, pp. 2268–9.
14. Fischer, *Aims*, pp. 103–5.
15. Jagow to Romberg, 8 June 1916. Scherer and Grünewald (eds.), i, pp. 363–4.
16. E. Weber, *Peasants into Frenchmen: the Modernization of Rural France, 1870–1914* (London, 1977), Chapter 7.
17. Keynes, p. 1.
18. Fischer, *Aims*, p. 103.
19. Ibid., p. xxii. Fischer originally entitled his book *Griff nach der Weltmacht* ('Grasp for World Power').
20. Rothwell, p. 283.
21. This is argued in W. A. McDougall, 'Political Economy versus National Sovereignty: French Structures for German Economic Integration after Versailles', *Journal of Modern History*, 51 (March 1979), pp. 4–23.
22. Wormser, *Clemenceau*, p. 341.

APPENDIX I

1. The material in this appendix is taken from: Foreign Office 'Peace Handbook' no. 28, *Alsace–Lorraine* (London, 1920); 'Peace Handbook' no. 29, *Lorraine and Saar Minefields* (London, 1920); Tardieu, 'Mémoire du gouvernement français sur la frontière septentrionale de l'Alsace–Lorraine', 8 Mar. 1919, *MAE* Tardieu MSS (43); and Pralon, 'Rapport sur l'industrie minière et sidérurgique de la Lorraine', 1 June 1918, ibid.

APPENDIX II

1. *See Map II.* In preparing this appendix I have used, besides the *Encyclopaedia Britannica*, Foreign Office 'Peace Handbooks' nos. 32 and 33, *Bavarian Palatinate* and *Rhenish Prussia and Birkenfeld* (London, 1920).

2. Report to the *Comité d'études* by Ernest Denis on 'L'Opinion publique dans les pays rhénans après 1815', 2 July 1917. *Travaux du Comité d'études* (2 vols., Paris, 1918–19), i, pp. 395ff.

3. *EMA* 2ème Bureau I: section technique, 'Le Problème du charbon en France après la guerre dans ses rapports avec le traité de paix', 30 Dec. 1918, *MAE* A 'Paix' (220).

APPENDIX III

1. The data in this appendix came from the *Encyclopaedia Britannica*; from Foreign Office 'Peace Handbooks' nos. 27 and 29, *Luxemburg and Limburg* and *Lorraine and Saar Minefields* (London, 1920); and from Pralon, 'Rapport sur l'industrie minière et sidérurgique de la Lorraine', 1 June 1918, *MAE* Tardieu MSS (43).

APPENDIX IV

1. Germany's coal production in 1913 was approximately 190 million tons. Of this, some 44 million came from Upper Silesia, as against 114 million from the Ruhr. For a more detailed representation of the evolution of Poland's frontiers than is given in Map III, see H. C. Darby and H. Fullard (eds.), *The New Cambridge Modern History. Vol. XIV: Atlas* (Cambridge, 1970), pp. 176–9.

BIBLIOGRAPHY

1. I consulted the series A 'Paix' 1914–20 on two occasions, in 1977 and 1980. By the latter date the series had been recatalogued. In this book references in the form *MAE* A 'Paix' (N) (110) correspond to entries in the new catalogue; those in the form *MAE* A 'Paix' (45) to entries in the old one.

2. I consulted Tardieu Papers in the *Ministère des Affaires étrangères* from the 1946 and 1965 depositions. All references in the text are to cartons in the 1946 group.
3. Catalogue numbers for cartons from the Clémentel MSS are provisional.
4. References to 'Bariéty' in the text are to the thesis rather than the book.
5. References to 'Jeanneney' in the text are to the thesis rather than the book.

Index